CARROLL QUIGLEY
LIFE, LECTURES & COLLECTED WRITINGS

DISCOVERY PUBLISHER

Book Cover, Art Design, Concept and Editing:
Copyright 2015 © Discovery Publisher
Book Content: Copyright © Carroll Quigley, where not otherwise cited

Author: Carroll Quigley, where not otherwise cited
Editor in Chief: Adriano Lucca
Transcription: Léo Hercouet

DISCOVERY PUBLISHER

616 Corporate Way
Valley Cottage, New York, 10989
www.discoverypublisher.com
books@discoverypublisher.com
facebook.com/DiscoveryPublisher
twitter.com/DiscoveryPB

New York • Tokyo • Paris • Hong Kong

TABLE OF CONTENTS

INTRODUCTION — 2
Carroll Quigley An Introduction — 4

LIFE — 14
LIFE — 15
The Improbable Dr. Quigley — 17
"Quigley... making Birchers bark" — 21
The Professor Who Knew too Much — 24
Quigley: Another Side of a Reflective Man — 32
The Evolution of Civilizations — 35
The Evolution of Civilizations: a Review — 40
Carroll Quigley: Some Aspects of His Last Twelve Years — 43
Recent Off-Campus Activities of Professor Carroll Quigley — 48
Carroll Quigley Endowed Chair Brochure — 51

LECTURES — 54
The Holistic, Morphological & Cognitive Qualities of Carroll Quigley's Historiography — 55
  Selected Bibliography — 72
  References — 72
Comparative National Cultures — 75
  Introduction — 75
  Comparative National Cultures — 76
  Comparative National Cultures Part I — 77
  Comparative National Cultures Part II — 88
  General Discussion — 95
Changing Cognitive Systems as a Unifying Technique in American Studies — 100

Round Table Review: The Naked Capitalist	105
The Naked Capitalist	105
The Cult of Conspiracy	107
Quigley's Response	117
Skousen's Reply	119
Midgley's Rejoinder	123
Dissent: Do We Need It?	126
The Mythology of American Democracy	143
That Anglo-Saxon Heritage	145
The Constitution and the Powers	146
The Stages of Political Growth	148
Threats to Democracy	151
Remedies	154
Discussion	155
Public Authority and the State in the Western Tradition: A Thousand Years of Growth, A.D. 976-1976	160
The Oscar Iden Lectures	160
Part I: "The State of Communities", A.D. 976-1576	161
Part II: "The State of Estates", A.D. 1576-1776	175
Part III: "The State of Individuals", A.D. 1776-1976	192

COLLECTED WRITINGS   212

Dr. Quigley explains how Nazi Germany seized a stronger Czechoslovakia Faculty Corner	213
Politics	218
Father Walsh as I Knew Him	221
Constantine McGuire: Man of Mystery	232
Better Training for Foreign Service Officers	241
Quigley Probes Possibilities for Foreign Service Curriculum Reform	242
Wartime Efforts	243
Revised Curriculum	244
Crucial Problems	246
Is Georgetown University Committing "Suicide"?	248
Conant-Dodds Influence	250
The Christian West	252
Catholic Scholarship	253
A Difference of Goals	255
Trahison des Clercs	256
Obsolete Academic Disciplines	259

Today's Problems	259
On the Borders	260
Self-Education	261
Needed: A Revolution in Thinking	263
The Partisan Side of Quigley	270
Mexican National Character and Circum-Mediterranean Personality Structure	272
References Cited	276

THE '74 INTERVIEW — 280

1974 Interview with Rudy Maxa of the Washington Post	281

PROFESSOR QUIGLEY'S QUOTES — 314

Quotes from Quigley's Work	315
The Evolution of Civilizations (1961) (Second Edition 1979)	315
Tragedy and Hope: A History of the World in Our Time (1966)	319
Oscar Iden Lecture Series, Lecture 3: "The State of Individuals" (1976)	320

PHOTO GALLERY — 328

Boston Latin School, 1929	329
Harvard, 1933	330
Year 1943	331
SFS yearbook, 1948	332
Year 1950	333
Year 1950	334
Year 1951	335
Year 1951	336
Year 1956	337
Year 1956	338
Year 1961	340
Carroll Quigley & wife Lillian, History, Year 1962	342
Year 1963	343
Year 1963	344

Year 1966	345
Year 1966	348
Year 1967	350
Year 1969	352
Year 1970	353
Year 1970	355
Year 1971	358
Year 1973	360
Year 1973	361
Year 1976	363
Year 1976	364

INTRODUCTION

CARROLL QUIGLEY
AN INTRODUCTION

Carroll Quigley was born in Boston and attended Harvard University, where he studied history and earned B.A., M.A., and Ph.D. degrees. He taught at Princeton University, at Harvard, and then at the School of Foreign Service at Georgetown University from 1941 to 1976. After teaching at Princeton and Harvard, Quigley came to Georgetown University in 1941 and became an on-line resource for Washington. He lectured at the Industrial College of the Armed Forces, the Brookings Institution, the Stare Department's Foreign Service Institute and consulted with the Smithsonian and the Senate Select Committee on Aeronautical and Space Sciences.

In addition to his academic work, Quigley served as a consultant to the U.S. Department of Defense, the U.S. Navy, the Smithsonian Institution, and the House Select Committee on Astronautics and Space Exploration in the 1950s. He was also a book reviewer for *The Washington Star*, and a contributor and editorial board member of *Current History*. Quigley said of himself that he was a conservative defending the liberal tradition of the West. He was an early and fierce critic of the Vietnam War, and he opposed the activities of the military-industrial complex.

To those duties and to his teachings, he brought his holist philosophy: the belief that knowledge cannot be divided into parts, that the world can be viewed only as an interlocking, complex system. This philosophy complemented his life: he had reveled in the traditions and contrasts of his neighborhood, eschewed fame in favor of keeping his emotional and social development on track, and applied himself to science and economics as well as history. His passion to consider the "big picture" never cooled.

Quigley had no small regret that some of the best minds of his generation insisted on treating the world in a 19th Century fashion by tinkering with its problems as a mechanic looks at an engine: spreading the separate parts on the floor and considering each one to find the malfunction. "This reductionist way of thinking," Quigley maintained, "had gotten Western civilization into all kinds of trouble."

In an age characterized by violence, extraordinary personal alienation, and the disintegration of family, church, and community, Quigley chose a life dedicated to rationality. He wanted an explanation that in its very categorization would give meaning to a history which was a record of constant change. Therefore the analysis had to include but not be limited to categories of subject areas of human activity — military, political, economic, social, religious, and intellectual. It had to describe change in categories expressed sequentially in time — mixture, gestation, expansion, conflict, universal empire, decay, and invasion. It was a most ambitious effort to make history rationally understandable.

On such views, in 1961 Quigley published the book *The Evolution of Civilizations*. It was derived from a course he taught on world history at Georgetown University. One of Quigley's closest friends was Harry J. Hogan. In the foreword to *The Evolution of Civilizations* he wrote:

> *The Evolution of Civilizations* expresses two dimensions of its author, Quigley, like for most extraordinary historian, philosopher, and teacher. In the first place, its scope is wide-ranging, covering the whole of man's activities throughout time. Second, it is analytic, not merely descriptive. It attempts a categorization of man's activities in sequential fashion so as to provide a causal explanation of the stages of civilization.
> Quigley coupled enormous capacity for work with a peculiarly "scientific" approach.

He believed that it should be possible to examine the data and draw conclusions. As a boy at the Boston Latin School, his academic interests were mathematics, physics, and chemistry. Yet during his senior year he was also associate editor of the *Register*, the oldest high school paper in the country. His articles were singled out for national awards by a national committee headed by George Gallup.

In 1966, Macmillan Company published *Tragedy and Hope*, a work of exceptional scholarship depicting the history of the world between 1895 and 1965 as seen through the eyes of Quigley. *Tragedy and Hope* was a commanding work, 20 years in the writing, that added to Quigley's considerable national reputation as a historian.

Tragedy and Hope reflected Quigley's feeling that "Western civilization is going down the drain." That was the tragedy. When the book came out in 1966, Quigley honestly thought the whole show could he salvaged; that was his hope.

During his research, Quigley had noticed that many prominent Englishmen and outstanding British scholars were members of an honorary society:

> [...] The powers of financial capitalism had another far-reaching aim, nothing less than to create a world system of financial control in private hands able to dominate the political system of each country and the economy of the world as a whole, this system was to be controlled in a feudalist fashion by the central banks of the world acting in concert by secret agreements arrived at in frequent private meetings and conferences. The apex of the system was to be the Bank for International Settlements in Basle, Switzerland, a private bank owned and controlled by the world's central banks which were themselves private corporations....
>
> It must not be felt that these heads of the world's chief central banks were themselves substantive powers in world finance. They were not. Rather, they were the technicians and agents of the dominant investment bankers of their own countries, who had raised them up and were perfectly capable of throwing them down. The substantive financial powers of the world were in the hands of these investment bankers (also called 'international' or 'merchant' bankers) who remained largely behind the scenes in their own unincorporated private banks. These

formed a system of international cooperation and national dominance which was more private, more powerful, and more secret than that of their agents in the central banks; this dominance of investment bankers was based on their control over the flows of credit and investment funds in their own countries and throughout the world. They could dominate the financial and industrial systems of their own countries by their influence over the flow of current funds through bank loans, the discount rate, and the re-discounting of commercial debts; they could dominate governments by their own control over current government loans and the play of the international exchanges. Almost all of this power was exercised by the personal influence and prestige of men who had demonstrated their ability in the past to bring off successful financial coups, to keep their word, to remain cool in a crisis, and to share their winning opportunities with their associates.

At the time, Quigley had no way of knowing he had just written his own ticket to a curious kind of fame. He was about to become a reluctant hero to Americans who believe the world is neatly controlled by a clique of international bankers and their cronies. Quigley learned of the country's great appetite for believing a grand conspiracy causes everything from big wars to bad weather.

Tragedy and Hope is not all juicy conspiratorial material. Most of it is straight diplomatic, political, and economic history. All of it is brilliant. His insights on such otherwise ignored (and crucially important) topics as Japanese military history and its relation to family dynasties is fascinating. But it did not gain its notoriety or its sales because of these non-conspiratorial insights.

Quigley never claimed he was a conspiracy theorist; on the contrary:

> You can't believe what people think. Some believe it is all a Jewish conspiracy, that is part of the Protocols of the Elders of Zion which we now know were perpetuated by the Czarist Russian police force in 1904. And that this conspiracy is the same thing as the Illuminati, a secret society founded in 1776 in Bavaria. And that the Illuminati are a branch of the Masons. There are some people who say the Society of Cincinnati, of which George Washington was a member during the American Revolution, was a branch of the Illuminati and that's why the Masons built their monument in Alexandria to George Washington, since he was

a Mason and head of the Illuminati before he helped start the Society of Cincinnati.

I generally think that any conspiracy theory of history is nonsense for the simple reason that most conspiracies that we know about seem to me to be conspiracies of losers, people who have been defeated on the historical platforms of public happenings. Now, there is not the slightest doubt that the international bankers have tried to make banking into a mystery. But we are dealing with two different things. I don't think that is a conspiracy; because something is a secret does not mean it is a conspiracy.

In essence, the message of *Tragedy and Hope* is that the last century was a tragedy that could have been avoided. Quigley believed that the tragedy would not have happened if we had given diligent heed of warnings. In other words, unless we carefully study his book and learn the untold history of the twentieth century and avoid allowing these same people, their heirs and associates — the rulers of various financial, corporate and governmental systems around the world — to ruin the twenty-first century, his work and the work of countless others will have been in vain.

Tragedy and Hope received mixed, though generally favorable, reviews. *Opined the Library Journal*: "Mr. Quigley ... has written a very remarkable book: very long, very detailed, very critical, very daring and very good... His coverage of the world is amazingly encyclopedic and well-balanced." *Saturday Review* was less flattering: "For those who approve of this way of writing history, his rambling volume may have a certain excellence." *The New York Times*: "The book provides a business-like narrative in which an incredible amount of information is compressed — and in some cases presented — with drama and distinction."

After it sold 8,800 copies, and for reasons not clear to Quigley (but he did not attribute it to any conspiracy), Macmillan stopped publishing *Tragedy and Hope* and subsequently destroyed the plates:

> The original edition published by Macmillan in 1966 sold about 8,800 copies and sales were picking up in 1968 when they "ran out of stock," as they told me. But in 1974, when I went after them with a lawyer, they told me that they had destroyed the plates in 1968. They lied to me for six years, telling me that they would reprint when they got 2,000 orders,

which could never happen because they told anyone who asked that it was out of print and would not be reprinted. They denied this until I sent them Xerox copies of such replies to libraries, at which they told me it was a clerk's error. In other words they lied to me but prevented me from regaining the publication rights by doing so (on out-of-print, rights revert to holder of copyright, but on out-of-stock, they do not.) Powerful influences in this country want me, or at least my work, suppressed.

[...] Macmillan never got in touch with me offering the plates. I learned in March of this year [1971] that they destroyed the plates, of *Tragedy and Hope*. I learned in the summer, 1971, because my wife got mad and called Macmillan on the phone, every week, while I was in England, and finally got from them a letter in which they said the plates had been destroyed. They said 'inadvertently destroyed.'

That, there's something funny. They lied and lied and lied and lied to me. On everything. And I have letters to prove that.

***Tragedy and Hope* was never republished.**

In the last 12 years of his life, from 1965 to 1977, Quigley taught, observed the American scene, and reflected on his basic values in life. He was simultaneously pessimistic and radically optimistic. Teaching was the core of Quigley's professional life and neither his craving to write nor his discouragement with student reaction of the early seventies diminished his commitment to the classroom:

> For years I have told my students that I have been trying to train executives rather than clerks. The distinction between the two is parallel to the distinction previously made between understanding and knowledge. It is a mighty low executive who cannot hire several people with command of more knowledge than he has himself. And he can always buy reference works or electronic devices with better memories for facts than any subordinate. The chief quality of an executive is that he has understanding. He should be able to make decisions that make it possible to utilize the knowledge of other persons. Such executive capacity can be taught, but it cannot be taught by an educational program that emphasizes knowledge and only knowledge. Knowledge must be assumed as given, and if it is not sufficient the candidate must be eliminated. But the vital thing is understanding. This requires possession of techniques that, fortunately, can be taught.

[...] I am sure that you will enjoy teaching increasingly, as I do. It is the one way we can do a little good in the world. The task is so important, the challenge so great, and the possibilities for improvement and for variation as infinite that it is the most demanding and most difficult of human activities. Even a virtuoso violinist can be made to order easier than a good teacher.

[...] It will be obvious to you that I have enjoyed my work, although at the end of my career I have no conviction that I did any good. Fortunately, I had a marvelous father and a marvelous mother, and we were taught you don't have to win, but you have to give it all you've got. Then it won't matter.

Unlike his underlying faith in the efficacy of teaching, Quigley found little basis for optimism about the future of American society. A journal asked him in 1975 to write an upbeat article on the country's prospects:

I told the editor that would be difficult, but I would try. I wrote it and they refused to publish it because it was not optimistic enough...

In 1976, Quigley wrote congratulating Carmen Brissette-Grayson's husband for his decision to give up any idea of leaving state politics for the federal arena. Quigley concluded:

It is futile, because it is all so corrupt and the honest ones are so incompetent. I should not say this, as students said it to me for years and I argued with them.

It was more than the institutionalization of the American political system which concerned him:

We are living in a very dangerous age in which insatiably greedy men are prepared to sacrifice anybody's health and tranquility to satisfy their own insatiable greed for money and power.

He feared that these values had virtually destroyed the roots of the Western outlook and had made the creation of a satisfying life in contemporary America a hazardous undertaking:

I am aghast at what selfishness, and the drive for power have done to our society... I worry as I find the world so increasingly horrible that I do not see how anything as wonderful as your life can escape.

Less than six months before Quigley passed away, he advised:

> The best thing you can do is to keep some enclaves of satisfying decent life.

Much of the joy of teaching left Quigley in his last years. He complained bitterly that his 1970s college students were woefully under-educated and ill-prepared for college level work and that too many of them had their minds elsewhere, fixated more on bringing about a social revolution than on achieving an education.

Helen Veit, the person closest to Quigley during the last ten years of his life, wrote in reply to a student who had so strongly opposed Quigley's "tough grading standards":

> [...] Impatient he may have been; arrogant he was not. His emphatic manner derived from his experience of teaching large classes and the need for catching and retaining their attention. But he never believed that he had "answers"; what he taught was methods of approaching problems. He often stressed how little we know about the important things of life, especially human relationships. What he sought above all was to help people to become mature, by realizing their potentials and understanding that material things, however necessary, should never be ends themselves, while what is important is seeking the truth in cooperation with others, with the knowledge that one will never find it.
> Nor was he ever cynical, much as he deplored inefficiency and ignorance. His beliefs and principles were of the highest order; his greatest joy came from finding people who could meet his standards, and from whom he could learn.
> Quigley's impatience came from his deep awareness that a man who wants to do so much can never have enough time. He was a man in a hurry — events have proved him right.

Yet pessimism about American society did not weaken a radical optimism rooted in his essential values: nature, people, and God:

The need for others is present on all levels; the physical, emotional, and intellectual. Indeed, every relationship has in it all three aspects. The desire to help others experience these things and to grow as a result of such experiences is called love. Such love is the real motivating force of the universe and is, in its ultimate nature, a manifestation of the love of God. Because while God is pure Reason and man's ultimate goal is Reason, it cannot be reached directly and must always be approached step by step, not alone but in companionship with others, and thus through love. Thus love of others, ultimately love of God, are the steps by which man develops reason and slowly approaches pure Reason.

Adriano Lucchese
Discovery Publisher
August 1, 2015

LIFE

- Some things are important, but most things are only necessary.

- Necessary things are only important when you do not have them and are generally ignored when they are amply supplied. These include oxygen, food, drink, shelter, and all physical needs.

- Important things are important all the time whether you have them or not, whether you realize it or not.

- People who regard necessary things as important are unhappy and frustrated even when they get them and even if they are quite unaware that the important things exist.

- Important things are those which can be made ends in themselves, worth seeking and worth having. Necessary things, since they are not important for their own sakes, should never made ends in themselves, but must be permitted only to be means to important ends. Thus, material wealth, power, popularity, and prestige should never be ends but only means to ends, because however necessary they may be they are never important.

- THE ONLY THING WHICH IS IMPORTANT IS TRUTH—that is the total structure of reality. The meaning of anything arises from its relationship to that total structure. The reason that material things are not important is because of the subordinate position they hold in that total structure.

- From this point of view, important things may exist on any level of reality. For example, physical health, exercise, and coordination are important on the physical level, but are not as important as things on higher levels, even though they can be made ends in themselves.

- On the higher levels are such things as feelings and intellectual awareness.

- The important things are those concerned with the realization of the potentialities of an individual because such realization brings the individual in closer contact with the total structure of reality—that is, with TRUTH.

- Each individual is so inadequate that there are only a few things he can do to help realize his potentialities. Among these few are will—the desire to do this and the determination to do it.

- Because of the inadequacy of the individual—that is, his basic need for other persons and his inability to direct his efforts unless he has recognition of his relationships with the rest of reality, the individual can achieve nothing by seeking to obtain things for himself, because this makes him the center of the universe, which he is not. Thus, selfishness achieves nothing.

- Thus the chief immediate aim in life of each individual must be to help others realize their potentialities. This is what Kant meant when he said that others must never be treated as means to be used, but always as ends in themselves. It is basic in human experience that those things a person seeks for himself directly are never obtained. They are only obtained indirectly as a by-product of an effort to obtain them for others. Thus the man who seeks only wealth for himself never feels rich, as the man who seeks power never feels secure, and the man who seeks pleasure never feels satisfied. But the man who seeks important things for others often feels rich, secure, and satisfied.

- The need for others is present on all levels, the physical, emotional, and intellectual. Indeed, every relationship has in it all three aspects. The desire to help others experience these things and to grow as a result of such experiences is called love. Such love is the real motivating force of the universe and is, in its ultimate nature, a manifestation of the love of God. Because while God is pure Reason and man's ultimate goal is Reason, it can not be reached directly and must always be approached step by step, not alone but in companionship with others, and thus through love. Thus love of others, ultimately love of God, are the steps by which man develops reason and slowly approaches pure Reason.

Carroll Quigley, August 1967

THE IMPROBABLE DR. QUIGLEY

Austin hyde
COURIER, Vol. X, No. 2, October 1961, pp. 12-13

A close friend of Dr. Carroll Quigley defines the fact in the legend about one of the most outstanding of the Georgetown faculty.

Images of people who are at all controversial are in most cases dreams based on few or no facts at all. Our minds delight in dwelling on the fantastic. It really does not matter how we feel about the individual, whether it is admiration or dislike, the dreaming tendency is there nevertheless. To a great extent, such is the situation of Dr. Carroll Quigley. Being the extremely intense person that he is, particularly in his approach to life, many stories and wishful dreams have developed around his person. This, then, is an attempt to set the record straight.

Dr. Quigley was born in Boston in 1910. He attended the Boston Latin School from 1924 to 1929. His scholastic record there was one of an honor student who was dedicated to his work. For example, in his Senior year he took seven courses. This meant that he had no study periods, had to cut his military drill, and do his homework during his lunch time. The extra course was a science; thus he was at once taking physics and chemistry. His best subject had been mathematics, in which on several occasions he received a score of one hundred on the monthly reports sent home. During his senior year he was Associate Editor of the Register, the high school paper which is the oldest in the country. For three of his articles Carroll Quigley was awarded highest individual honors in the country by a committee of the Quill and Scroll headed by George Gallup (of the U.S. opinion polls) which had examined the writings of over fifty thousand high school journalists.

As a result of this contest and his extremely high scores on the English Achievement Examination, he received credit for most of the required English courses that he was to take later at Harvard. This proved to be very important, as it enabled him to spend more time on the courses of his direct interest.

Bio-Chemistry was to be his major. In his freshman year he took, among other things, experimental physics and calculus. In the latter he turned in a perfect final examination, for which he received an "A+". But there was a problem, since he also was required to take something in the social sciences.

He chose a history course called "Europe Since the Fall of Rome" (receiving a "C" as a final grade) which was given by a professor who opened for him a new horizon in history. In his sophomore year he changed his major to history and then somehow managed to spend more time on political science (a total of thirty hours) than in any other field. When asked why he did this, he said that he was interested in the development of ideas.

In his junior year he took three courses, one a graduate course in History of Political Theory with Professor Charles Howard McIlwain. This he took by special permission, the only junior to have done so. In his senior year there were only two courses, but as an Honor Student he was obliged to write a thesis; his concerned "The Influence of the Romantic Movement on Political Theory." In 1933 he was graduated by Harvard University *magna cum laude* and as the top history student of his class. As a result of his fine record he was awarded the Dillaway Fellowship.

He got his master's degree in one year and at the end of the second year of graduate work he stood for his oral examination for a Ph.D. His areas of study were, to say the least, varied. Included among them were Russian History, Constitutional History of England, and the History of France (1461 to 1815). The Chairman of the examining board, Professor McIlwain, a trustee of Princeton, was most impressed with the examination, especially with Mr. Quigley's ability to answer his opening question with a long quotation in Latin from the writings of Robert Grosseteste, Bishop of Lincoln in the 13th Century. As a result of his proficiency, Dr. Quigley was given a job at Princeton, where he taught for two years.

At the end of the two years Harvard granted Carroll Quigley a travelling fellowship to go to Europe to write as a doctoral dissertation a study of the Napoleonic public administration of the Kingdom of Italy (1805 to 1814). He took with him his nineteen year old bride, Lillian Fox Quigley. In Paris they lived for five months with a French viscount and his wife, their daughter and son-in-law, the count of Brabant. Because of these connections most of their associations in France were with monarchists and nobles, a strange experience during the first "Popular Front Government." In January, 1938, they went to Milan where they stayed several months while he examined the manuscripts in the rich archives. The finished thesis, bound in three large volumes (by an Italian who embossed the author's name in gold on the cover as "Qiugley"), was delivered to Harvard by messenger. The Ph.D. was awarded in absentia in June 1938. The diploma, which Dr. Quigley picked up that September, has yet to be unrolled!

While returning from Europe on the *Île de France*, he received a telegram from Harvard University offering him a job. He accepted the offer and thus tutored honor students in Ancient and Medieval History. While at Harvard he took advantage of its vast and extremely rich collection on Italian history (among the best in the country) to continue his study on the subject.

In 1941, the late Father Walsh invited Dr. Quigley to come to Georgetown to lecture on history. Dr. Quigley accepted because he felt he needed experience in lecturing, as all of his work thus far had been in the preceptorial work at Princeton (directing round tables of seven students) and tutoring honor students at Harvard, with but an occasional lecture.

He certainly has obtained all the experience he wanted at Georgetown!

"Development of Civilization" was his first course, and he is now delivering it for the twenty-first year. It was first worked out in 1934 as the first version of his recently published book, *The Evolution of Civilizations*. The second version of the book was produced in 1942 in a suite of rooms at Princeton (this was to be his last summer off from teaching in eighteen years). The third and last revision of the book was written in the space of about five weeks in the fall of 1958.

In the spring of 1943 the School of Foreign Service dedicated itself in full to the war effort. In one week under the personal direction of Fr. Walsh the Foreign Area and Language Program was established as a part of the Army Specialized Training Program. In the fall of 1943, Professor Quigley had close to 700 students in one class, held in Gaston Hall. In this course Dr. Quigley lectured five hours a week continually for nine months on the "History of Europe in the Twentieth Century"—without finishing what he wanted to say on the subject. Most of the students for this course were college graduates and fifty-five had Ph.D.'s.

Early in the war the School recognized that its graduates had difficulty getting commissions in the Navy because of their poor background in mathematics. So Dr. Quigley gave an elective course in college algebra to Foreign Service students, most of whom have had little inclination in that direction.

At the end of the war, when the School of Foreign Service enrollment felt the tidal wave of veterans, the student body was over 2,200. In the fall of 1947 Dr. Quigley had 1,307 students, including two sections of about 400 each (at present in his four courses he has a total of 400).

In this period he taught courses on the Fascist state, Public Administration, Government Regulation of Industry, and United States History (which he taught from 1942, when almost everyone in the department was called for duty in the army, until February of 1946, when Dr. Jules Davids joined the faculty of Georgetown).

Dr. Quigley is a consultant in American History for the Smithsonian

Institution. His chief work there has been to draw a detailed plan for layout of the new Museum of History and Technology now under construction. He has been consultant on numerous occasions to the Industrial College of the Armed Forces at Fort McNair, his work being particularly connected with questions of curriculum reform. For the last twelve years Dr. Quigley has annually lectured to the Industrial College (usually on the History of Czarist Russia).

In addition, he was consultant to the Select House Committee on Astronautics and Space Exploration, which set up the present space agency. It was in connection with this work that Professor Quigley made his first flight in an airplane—Washington to San Francisco—to inspect the Ames Laboratory at Moffett Field.

Professor Quigley's versatility may be judged from the fact that during the last week of October 1961, he had planned to lecture to a government agency on Russian History, lecture at another local University on African History, testify before the Senate Anti-Trust and Monopoly Committee on American business practices, and spend five days in Boston as an invited delegate to the UNESCO Conference on Africa.

Dr. Quigley, in a unique way, bears out Henry Adams' observation that, "A teacher affects eternity; he can never tell where his influence stops." There are no means available to measure the intellectual impact and the far-reaching effects of his influence on the minds of his students. For this reason it is impossible to give Dr. Quigley recognition commensurate with his value to thousands of Georgetown students since his arrival here from Harvard in the Fall of 1941.

"QUIGLEY... MAKING BIRCHERS BARK"

An article by Wes Christenson in Georgetown Today,
Volume 4, Number 4 (March 1972), pp 12-13.

Georgetown Professor Carroll Quigley, doing some writing on his West Virginia farm, picked up the ringing telephone and answered it. The man on the other end of the line said he was from Dallas and wanted to ask the Georgetown historian "a few questions."

He did. For 40 minutes. When Dr. Quigley begged to be allowed to get back to his books, the caller said: "Just one more question, Professor. Why is Governor Nelson Rockefeller a Communist?"

Dr. Quigley has been plagued by hundreds of letters and telephone calls from the American political spectrum's far right since he wrote his well-known *Tragedy and Hope: A History of the World in Our Time* in 1966.

The John Birch Society, the Liberty Lobby, the Phyllis Schafly Report and the telephone outlet known as "Let Freedom Ring" are among the groups which have been titillated by the book but strangely have denounced the author.

The far right-wingers claim that Dr. Quigley's 1,348-page book, which sold some 8,000 copies and is now indefinitely out of stock, reveals the existence of a conspiracy by international capitalists on Wall Street and in London to take over the world and turn it over to the Communists. What's more, Dr. Quigley is an "insider" in the scheme, they charge.

The Georgetown historian says that's nonsense, that he never wrote as much, and that he is not, as the right-wingers charge, a member of this group of super rich and elite "pro-Communist insiders."

One right-wing author, in particular, has been giving Dr. Quigley a hard time. He is W. Cleon Skousen, a teacher of religion at Brigham Young University in Provo, Utah, whose background, Dr, Quigley said, includes 16 years with the FBI, four years as Salt Lake City's police chief and 10 years as editorial director of the magazine *Law And Order*.

Professor Skousen, who wrote *The Naked Communist* in 1961, has followed it up with *The Naked Capitalist: A Review and Commentary on Dr. Carroll Quigley's Book, Tragedy and Hope*, a 121-page treatise which has 30 pages of direct quotations from Dr. Quigley's book.

Meanwhile, the Utah professor has sold more than 55,000 copies of his book, and the Washington office of Liberty Lobby estimates it sells 25 copies a day now at $2 each. What's more, Dr. Quigley is less than happy with Professor Skousen's "lifting" 30 pages of his quotations without permission and, Dr. Quigley thinks, in violation of copyright laws.

"Skousen's book is full of misrepresentations and factual errors," Professor Quigley said. "He claims that I have written of a conspiracy of the super-rich who are pro-Communist and wish to take over the world and that I'm a member of this group. But I never called it a conspiracy and don't regard it as such. "I'm not an 'insider' of these rich persons," Dr. Quigley continued, "although Skousen thinks so. I happen to know some of them and liked them, although I disagreed with some of the things they did before 1940."

Skousen also claims, Dr. Quigley believes, the influential group of Wall Street financiers still exists and controls the country. "I never said that," Dr. Quigley said flatly. "In fact, they never were in a position to 'control' it, merely to influence political events."

The influential Wall Street group of which he wrote about 25 pages in *Tragedy and Hope* ceased to exist about 1940, Dr. Quigley claims. He also faults Skousen for saying that *Tragedy and Hope*'s intention was, in Dr. Quigley's words, "to reveal anything, least of all a purely hypothetical controversy. My only desire was to present a balanced picture of the 70 years from 1895-1965. The book is based on more than 25 years of research."

Meanwhile, *Tragedy and Hope* is becoming a rare commodity following the publicity from right-wing groups. Copies often aren't returned to libraries around the country, although some right-wingers claim that left-wing librarians are removing it to "suppress" Dr Quigley's "revelations."

Some rightists are claiming that Macmillan, *Tragedy and Hope*'s publishers, won't reprint it because Macmillan allegedly has had second thoughts and now wants to hush up Dr. Quigley's "findings."

Second-hand copies are being sold in bookstores now at $20 and up, with waiting lists of 12 to 20 persons seeking copies. Classified advertisements seeking the book are not uncommon in varied periodicals.

Dr. Quigley says *Tragedy and Hope*, priced at $12.95 five years ago, never could be sold for that price today because "it was underpriced then. It cost less than a penny a page, when most hard-backed books now sell for at least two cents a page. I doubt if a reprinted version could be priced at $20 or more."

The Georgetown historian, who has been taking the whole thing in a combination of stride and amusement, is nevertheless irked because the controversy takes up so much of his time.

School of Foreign Service alumni regularly write, wanting to know more. (Dr.

Quigley's "Development of Civilization" course was named their favorite in a recent survey of SFS alumni of 1955-69.) People from all over the U.S. send in clippings about him from right-wing publications.

Ironically, the parts of *Tragedy and Hope* from which Professor Skousen quotes most freely are in the second half of the volume, still available at $3.95 in paperback from Collier Books under the title: *The World Since 1939: A History*." Georgetown alumni who have lost their copies of *Tragedy and Hope*," Dr. Quigley said, "can buy the 676-page paperback if they want to check my quotations."

His eyes twinkled and his accent from his Boston Latin School and Harvard days became even more pronounced: "You know, if enough people buy the paperback, maybe I will be rich. But not as rich as the right-wingers think I am, with all my supposed 'inside' Wall Street connections."

THE PROFESSOR WHO KNEW TOO MUCH

The Washington Post Sunday Magazine
23 March 1975

Borrowing a few crucial pages from his book, the ultra-right made a scholar an unwilling hero.

By Rudy Maxa Collage (below) by Allen Appel, based on a photo by Matthew Lewis.

Greetings, Dr. Quigley: With reference to your book, *Tragedy and Hope*, at which I am presently directing much of my energies, I would appreciate a short explanation as to why you generally approve of the conspiracy. I enclose a self-addressed envelope for your convenience.
— from a letter postmarked Rahway, N.J.

In 1966, Macmillan Company published the history of the world between 1895 and 1965 as seen through the cool, gray eyes of Carroll Quigley, a professor of history at Georgetown's School of Foreign Service. The 1,348-page tome, called *Tragedy and Hope*, was a commanding work, 20 years in the writing, that added to Quigley's considerable national reputation as a historian.

But though he had no way of knowing it, Quigley had just written his own ticket to a curious kind of fame. He was about to become a reluctant hero to Americans who believe the world is neatly controlled by a clique of international bankers and their cronies. He was about to learn of the country's awesome appetite for believing a grand conspiracy causes everything from big wars to bad weather.

Strangers would soon call to bend Quigley's ear about secret societies. Insistent letters from Rahway, N.J., among other places, would clutter his desk. And eventually, *Tragedy and Hope* would be pirated by zealots who would sell the book in the same brochures that advertise such doomsday products as "Minutemen Survival Tabs," concentrated vitamin tablets to help patriots survive sieges by foreign enemies.

It was the John Birch Society that really catapulted — or dragged — Quigley front-and-center into the conspiracy picture. Just before the 1972 primary, voters in New Hampshire opened their mail and found copies of a breathlessly-written paperback, *None Dare Call It Conspiracy*. The book, researched, written and recommended by Birch Society members, warned that public figures as different as John Gardner and Henry Kissinger were part of a conspiracy centered around the Establishment's unofficial club, New York's Council on Foreign Relations.

For identifying "a power-mad clique (that) wants to control the world," Quigley was labeled "the Joseph Valachi of political conspiracies."

None Dare Call It Conspiracy used exclamation points, charts of power networks and heavy rhetoric to awaken Americans to their diminishing freedoms. And much of the hoopla was based on a mere 25 pages from Quigley's book which, *None Dare Call It Conspiracy* said, "revealed the existence of the conspiratorial network" of a "power-mad clique (that) wants to control and rule the world." Quigley was "the Joseph Valachi of political conspiracies" for fingering the bankers and power brokers—the Insiders." And a photograph of Quigley shared a page with no less than financier J. P. Morgan.

John Birch Society President Robert Welch predicted distribution of 15 million copies of *None Dare Call It Conspiracy*, part of a "gigantic flare from educational materials called forth by the emotions and events of a crucial election year." As copies began to spread across the country, Quigley began to grasp what the selective, unauthorized quotation from his work could mean. The approach to history taken by the authors of *None Dare Call It Conspiracy* offended Quigley's scholastic sensibilities. Worse, he found he could not fight back against the misinformation he felt was being disseminated with the aid of his research and his name. "It blackened my reputation," Quigley said, "amongst scholarly historians who are going to say, 'Oh, he's one of those right-wing nuts.'"

Professor Carroll Quigley—B.A., M.A., and Ph.D., all from Harvard in the '30s—is a trim, engaging man who points to his good-sized nose and broad, high forehead with some pride. The physical characteristics mark him as a Carroll and a stroll past the statue of Georgetown University's founder, John Carroll, points up the resemblance.

Quigley does not descend directly from those Carrolls, the landed Marylanders who were influential enough in the Revolutionary years to have a signature on the Constitution. Instead, Quigley's maternal ancestors were the less affluent Carrolls left behind in Ireland who only got around to making it to Halifax a few generations ago. On his father's side, the Quigleys were so poor they couldn't even wait for the potato famine to leave Ireland for Boston in 1828.

Quigley talks genealogy with a historian's precision, spins family stories like a true Irishman, and more: he understands, and tells his listener he understands, how his past shaped him. Young Carroll Quigley lived on the edge of the Irish ghetto in Boston and mixed it up in the streets with Yankees, Italians, Russian Jews and a few blacks, a melting pot of a childhood that Quigley says cast a strong base for his adult writings and teachings.

He cultivated the spirit of the Irish and honed the intellectual interests of the Yankees while attending the Boston Latin School, whose list of distinguished graduates stretches from Benjamin Franklin to Leonard Bernstein. Harvard came next in a natural sort of way and Quigley intended to go into science until he decided "there were a lot a good people in science but nobody good in history."

He kept current in science but formally attacked history; he was no slouch in either. Quigley's Harvard tutor in medieval and ancient history, the late Donald McKay, told him he could be Harvard's first *summa cum laude* graduate in history in seven years—"You could be a summa!" he exhorted Quigley—but the undergraduate chose instead to settle for a magna cum laude for fear of shortchanging his emotional development.

After teaching stints at Princeton and Harvard, Quigley came to Georgetown University in 1941 and became an on-line resource for Washington. He lectured at the Industrial College of the Armed Forces, the Brookings Institution, the Stare Department's Foreign Service Institute and consulted with the Smithsonian and the Senate Select Committee on Aeronautical and Space Sciences.

To those duties and to his teachings he brought his holist philosophy, the belief that knowledge cannot be divided into parts, that the world can be viewed only as an interlocking, complex system. The philosophy complemented his life: he had reveled in the traditions and contrasts of his neighborhood, eschewed the summa in favor of keeping his emotional and social development on track, and applied himself to science and economics as well as history. His passion to consider the "big picture" never cooled.

Quigley has no small regret that some of the best minds of his generation insist on treating the world in a 19th Century fashion by tinkering with its problems as a mechanic looks at an engine: spreading the separate parts on the floor and considering each one to find the malfunction. This reductionist way of thinking, Quigley maintains, has gotten Western civilization into all kinds of trouble.

We cluck our tongues about inflation while stores offer expensive Christmas goods with liberal credit schedules that don't call for a first payment until spring. We bellyache about accumulating trash and energy shortages but spend precious little discovering how garbage can become an energy source. That kind of small thinking annoys Professor Carroll Quigley. It annoys him almost as much as if someone took the narrow view that a clique of "Insiders" controlled the world.

The historian's mind remembers the summer of '43 well: the temperature topped 90 degrees 59 days that year, and one stretch lasted 15 days. Quigley, still so Boston formal that he kept his suitcoat on during lectures, was charged with teaching the history of the world to 750 military personnel who had just finished their heavy mid-day meal. Five days a week, for one year, Quigley stood in Gaston Hall and prepared the soldiers for the military occupation of the countries in the European theater that the Allied forces expected to conquer.

From those frenzied months of preparing for his crash courses grew Quigley's eight-pound *Tragedy and Hope*. The title reflects his feeling that "Western civilization is going down the drain." That is the tragedy. When the book came out in 1966, Quigley honestly thought the whole show could he salvaged; that was his hope. He will not say as much today.

The section in his history that was to fascinate the political right concerned the formation of the Council on Foreign Relations and the actions of several famous banking houses. Quigley broke some new ground in his research in the late 1940s; 20 years later the right seized Quigley's findings and drew some broad conclusions.

Quigley had noticed that many prominent Englishmen and outstanding British scholars were members of an honorary society called Fellows of All Souls College. While Quigley was studying the 149 members, a former Fellow visited Washington to speak with Quigley. Quigley began chatting with him about the Fellows of All Souls College: "You mean the Round Table Group.", the visitor said. What Quigley asked, "is it the Round Table Group?" After considerable research, Quigley knew.

"I learned the Round Table Group was very influential," Quigley says. "I knew they were the real founders of the Royal Institute of International Affairs and I knew they were the founders of the Institute of Pacific Relations. I knew that they were the godfathers of the Council on Foreign Relations. So I began to put this thing together and I found that this group was working for a number of things.

"It was a secret group. Its members were working to federate the English-speaking world. They were closely linked to international bankers. They were working to establish what I call a three-power world: England and the U.S., Hitler's Germany and Soviet Russia. They said, 'We can control Germany because it is boxed in between the Atlantic bloc and the Russians. The Russians will behave because they're boxed in between the Atlantic bloc and the American Navy in Singapore.' Now, notice that this is essentially a balance of power system," Quigley says.

None Dare Call It Conspiracy, using Quigley's data, attributed to the Round Table Group a lust for world domination. Its sympathies were pro-Communist, anti-Capitalist, said the Birch Society book.

"They thought Dr. Carroll Quigley proved everything." Quigley says. "For example, they constantly misquote me to this effect: that Lord Milner (the dominant trustee of the Cecil Rhodes Trust and a heavy in the Round Table Group) helped finance the Bolsheviks. I have been through the greater part of Milner's private papers and have found no evidence to support that.

"Further, *None Due Call It Conspiracy* insists that international bankers were a single bloc, were all powerful and remain so today. I, on the contrary, stated in my book that they were much divided, often fought among themselves, had great influence but not control of political life and were sharply reduced in power about 1931-1940, when they became less influential than monopolized industry."

Tragedy and Hope received mixed, though generally favorable, reviews. Opined the Library Journal: "Mr. Quigley ... has written a very remarkable book: very long, very detailed, very critical, very daring and very good.... His coverage of the world is amazingly encyclopedic and well-balanced." Saturday Review was less flattering: "For those who approve of this way of writing history, his rambling volume may have a certain excellence." Said the New York Times: "The book provides a business-like narrative in which an incredible amount of information is compressed—and in some cases presented—with drama and distinction."

But from the right, Quigley earned kudos for nailing the seminal data on the Round Table Group that helped found the Council on Foreign Relations. His dispassionate presentation, however, did not sit so well. While Quigley's findings earned him pages of quotation (in apparent violation of copyright laws), *None Dare Call It Conspiracy* sniped: "... the conspirators have had no qualms about fomenting wars, depressions and hatred. They want a monopoly which would eliminate all competitors and destroy the free enterprise system. And Professor Quigley of Harvard, Princeton and Georgetown approves!"

"You see," Quigley says, "originally the John Birch periodical had me as a great guy for revealing everything. But then they became absolutely sour and now they denounce me as a member of the Establishment. I'm just baffled by the whole thing."

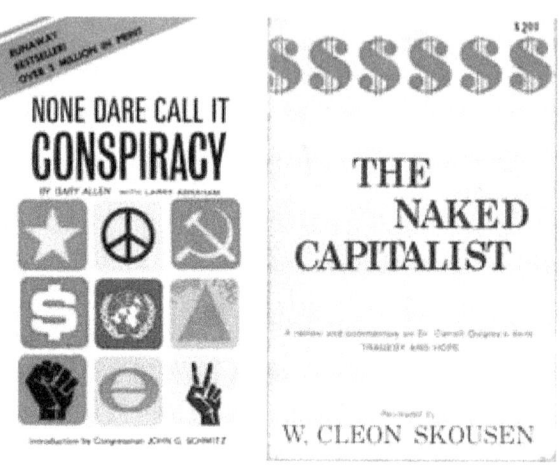

None Dare Call It Conspiracy The Naked Capitalist

Quigley was first quoted by Gary Allen, the author of *None Dare Call It Conspiracy*, in a 1968 book called *Nixon: The Man Behind the Mask*. Then, an instructor at Brigham Young University in Utah, a Cleo[n] Skousens, wrote *The Naked Capitalist* and again quoted Quigley extensively. But *None Dare Call It Conspiracy* was the big seller. Nearly five million copies of the book have been sold to date, according to the publisher, Concord Press in California, and a new German language edition is selling well.

Author and Birch Society member Gary Allen is one of Quigley's biggest fans, but he laughs a huge laugh when told Quigley is the most reluctant of heroes. Of course, says Allen good-naturedly, the Establishment could not be pleased Quigley revealed so much about a Council on Foreign Relation, which prefers to swing its weight quietly.

"They don't like this thing talked about because it is the real power structure," Allen says from California. "Dr. Quigley let the cat out of the bag. He had the liberal academic credentials. I'm sure a lot of people are very unhappy with him for telling tales out of school.

Allen did not talk to Quigley before he began quoting from *Tragedy and Hope* because Allen understood from "some intelligence people in Washington" that Quigley was arrogant and unapproachable. "So I took him at his word that he had had access to the private records of the Round Table Group," Allen says. "Now he's trying to duck the importance of what he wrote by saying we picked only a few pages out of a 1,400-page book."

After the books came the letters. Brother Nelson Goodwin, a self-styled Nevada "hobo" evangelist was moved last summer to take pencil in hand and write, "Brother Carroll: I have heard somewhere that 'Snake Eyes Joe Enlai' and 'Mousey Dung' and 'Snake in the Grass Fidel Castro' all received their poison atheistic doctrine in the Universities and Colleges of America. Thank God for Men like you who love our Beautiful United States, the finest nation on the earth. Others, like the writer from Rahway, wanted to know why Quigley "approved of the conspiracy." Quigley has gotten handy at fielding the curve balls.

"You can't believe what people think," he says. "Some believe it is all a Jewish conspiracy, that is part of the Protocols of the Elders of Zion which we now know were perpetuated by the Czarist Russian police force in 1904. And that this conspiracy is the same thing as the Illuminati, a secret society founded in 1776 in Bavaria. And that the Illuminati are a branch of the Masons. There are some people who say the Society of Cincinnati, of which George Washington was a member during the American Revolution, was a branch of the Illuminati and that's why the Masons built their monument in Alexandria to George Washington, since he was a Mason and head of the Illuminati before he helped start the Society of Cincinnati. See what I mean?"

If he chose to, Quigley could probably spend the rest of his life battling the people who are using his research to bolster their own conclusions. But he has narrowed the battle to stopping the illegal publication of *Tragedy and Hope*.

For reasons not clear to Quigley (but he does not attribute it to any conspiracy), Macmillan stopped publishing *Tragedy and Hope* alter it sold 9,000 copies. Suddenly pirate editions began appearing, almost exact photo-reproductions with identical dust jackets and binding. The original book had yellow-edged pages, a touch either missed or considered too costly by whoever decided to begin offering *Tragedy and Hope* on the sly. Carroll Quigley quickly became a right-wing underground sensation.

"We have discovered a limited quantity which we offer to informed patriots on a first come, first served basis for only $20 each," read one brochure offering the pirate copies. "For the first time, one of the 'insiders' of the international 'elite' gives a candid account of the world of monopoly capitalism. Not easy reading, but it is essential reading for those who consider themselves in-depth students of the conspiracy."

Quigley hired a lawyer who managed to stop at least one of the pirate presses. Then, working through an intermediary, Quigley sold a West Coast press the right to re-print 2,000 copies of his book to retail for $25 each, from the Georgetown University bookstore. As long as the right insists on selling his book, Quigley reasons he might as well get his piece of the action. He has no such interest in jumping aboard the conspiracy bandwagon.

"I generally think that any conspiracy theory of history is nonsense," Quigley says, "for the simple reason that most conspiracies that we know about seem to me to be conspiracies of losers, people who have been defeated on the historical platforms of public happenings. The Ku Klux Klan had its arguments destroyed and defeated in the Civil War but because it was not prepared to accept that, the KKK formed a conspiracy to fight underground.

"Now, there is not the slightest doubt that the international bankers have tried to make banking into a mystery. But we are dealing with two different things. I don't think that is a conspiracy; because something is a secret does not mean it is a conspiracy."

The seductive beauty of believing the world is in the grip of one conspiracy or another, however, is that any argument against a conspiracy is simply proof of how clever the conspirators are; red herrings are only a mark of the cunning of the conspirators, says the true believer.

Quigley is weary of tilting with conspiratorial windmills. He is 65 and intends to retire after this academic year. He has books unfinished. None of which, he hastens to add, have to do with conspiracy.

On his farm in West Virginia, Quigley is working on a book on the relationship of weapon systems to the stability of the world. He rests there on weekends and gardens between writing. But still the calls come, many from Texas, Florida and California, Quigley notices. One conspiracy hound called and talked for 20 minutes. Quigley finally said he had to return to his work.

"Just one more question," the caller said. "Just tell me this: why is Nelson Rockefeller a Communist?"

"I don't know," replied Quigley evenly. "I don't think he is but if you know he is and you want to know why he is, why don't you call him up and ask him."

QUIGLEY: ANOTHER SIDE OF A REFLECTIVE MAN

by Helen E. Veit
(Introduction by Terrence Boyle)
Washington, D. C., SFS '69

Helen Elizabeth Veit was the person closest to Carroll Quigley during the last ten years of his life. No one living today has a better understanding of the man and of his thinking.

Sadly, the last few years of Dr. Quigley's life as a teacher coincided with the late 1960s and early 1970s, when student unrest and anti-intellectualism unsettled college campuses all over this country. In 1969-70 that spirit came violently to Georgetown University and focused especially on the very few teachers like Prof. Quigley who adamantly refused to lower academic standards, no matter what political *cause du jour* was being offered as a reason.

When, therefore, in May 1970, Dr. Quigley and a very few other G.U. professors refused-with, by the way, no support from the craven University Administration of the day-to accede to demands that all classes and examinations be canceled in supposed support of "a nationwide protest" against American military involvement in Indo-China, a band of student activists vowed to prevent classes and examinations from being held, no matter what. Several of these protesters invaded Dr. Quigley's classroom, physically roughed him up, and prevented his final examination from being given that day.

Much of the joy of teaching left Carroll Quigley in the next few years. He complained bitterly that his 1970s college students were woefully under-educated and ill-prepared for college level work and that too many of them had their minds elsewhere, fixated more on bringing about a social revolution than on achieving an education.

And then, when a few years later Dr. Quigley died suddenly, just months after retiring from teaching, some remaining leftist students at G.U., who had so strongly opposed Quigley's tough grading standards, his teaching of the detested "canon of dead white males," and especially his insistent reliance on logic and reasoning, rather than on emotion and intuition, decided they would have the last word on this man by writing in the school newspaper a shallow obituary criticizing Quigley for not having been more a part of their "real" lives.

Helen Veit wrote a most fitting and irenic reply, which we reproduce here:

> To the Editor:
>
> As a student, academic assistant, and friend of Carroll Quigley, I am unhappy to think that Bob McGillicuddy's article, "Carroll Quigley: A Student's Elegy" (the Voice, Feb. 8, 1977), should be the Georgetown student's last picture of this man.
>
> Surely, after his long and dedicated service to Georgetown and its students, he deserves a more sympathetic understanding in the personal sense, to complement McGillicuddy's insights into his thought. I do not seek to make excuses for him. He would be the last person to want that: accepting personal responsibility for one's actions was one of his first principles. But a better perspective may be gained by viewing recent events in the context of his whole career.
>
> Until 1969-71, teaching Georgetown students was one of the most important and rewarding aspects of his life. Then came the campus disturbances, which, for reasons related more to his dynamic and outspoken personality than to any substantive grievance, focused disproportionately on him. At that point, he did, indeed, "turn inward," to concentrate on his writing and live his private life. After more than thirty years of almost uninterrupted teaching, it seems only reasonable that he should want time for other things, for activities made difficult or impossible by his commitment to lecture to hundreds of students a year.
>
> It is understandably difficult for a student to see that teaching was not the only thing in Carroll Quigley's life, but anyone who listened to him must remember his frequent references to the books he wanted to write when he had time, and must know how much he loved and learned from his West Virginia farm. As an undergraduate, I, too, believed teaching was all-important to him; later I learned that he wanted his retirement to be virtually a second career, during which he would write books summing up a lifetime of intense study and experience. Sadly, in the event, his life of teaching was his only life.

Impatient he may have been; arrogant he was not. His emphatic manner derived from his experience of teaching large classes and the need for catching and retaining their attention. But he never believed that he had "answers"; what he taught was methods of approaching problems. He often stressed how little we know about the important things of life, especially human relationships. What he sought above all was to help people to become mature, by realizing their potentials and understanding that material things, however necessary, should never be ends themselves, while what is important is seeking the truth in cooperation with others, with the knowledge that one will never find it.

Nor was he ever cynical, much as he deplored inefficiency and ignorance. His beliefs and principles were of the highest order; his greatest joy came from finding people who could meet his standards, and from whom he could learn.

Students should grant to others the same degree of understanding they ask for themselves; they should realize that even professors have private lives and the need for intellectual activities outside the classroom. Carroll Quigley's impatience came from his deep awareness that a man who wants to do so much can never have enough time. He was a man in a hurry — events have proved him right.

THE EVOLUTION OF CIVILIZATIONS

by Harry J. Hogan to the second (1979) edition of Carroll Quigley's The Evolution of Civilizations: An Introduction to Historical Analysis.

Dr. Hogan, now retired, has been a professor, administrator, and lawyer.
He received his B.A. magna cum laude from Princeton University, his LL.B. from Columbia Law School, and his Ph.D. in American history from George Washington University.
His articles have appeared in the American Bar Association Journal, the Journal of Politics, and other periodicals.

The Evolution of Civilizations expresses two dimensions of its author, Carroll Quigley, that most extraordinary historian, philosopher, and teacher. In the first place, its scope is wide-ranging, covering the whole of man's activities throughout time. Second, it is analytic, not merely descriptive. It attempts a categorization of man's activities in sequential fashion so as to provide a causal explanation of the stages of civilization.

Quigley coupled enormous capacity for work with a peculiarly "scientific" approach. He believed that it should be possible to examine the data and draw conclusions. As a boy at the Boston Latin School, his academic interests were mathematics, physics, and chemistry. Yet during his senior year he was also associate editor of the Register, the oldest high school paper in the country. His articles were singled out for national awards by a national committee headed by George Gallup.

At Harvard, biochemistry was to be his major. But Harvard, expressing then a belief regarding a well-rounded education to which it has now returned, required a core curriculum including a course in the humanities. Quigley chose a history course, "Europe Since the Fall of Rome." Always a contrary man, he was graded at the top of his class in physics and calculus and drew a C in the history course. But the development of ideas began to assert its fascination for him, so he elected to major in history. He graduated *magna cum laude* as the top history student in his class.

Quigley was always impatient. He stood for his doctorate oral examination at the end of his second year of graduate studies. Charles Howard McIlwain, chairman of the examining board, was very impressed by Quigley's answer to his opening question; the answer included a long quotation in Latin from Robert Grosseteste, bishop of Lincoln in the thirteenth century. Professor McIlwain sent Quigley to Princeton University as a graduate student instructor.

In the spring of 1937 I was a student in my senior year at Princeton. Quigley was my preceptor in medieval history. He was Boston Irish; I was New York Irish. Both of us, Catholics adventuring in a strangely Protestant establishment world, were fascinated by the Western intellectual tradition anchored in Augustine, Abelard, and Aquinas that seemed to have so much more richness and depth than contemporary liberalism. We became very close in a treasured friendship that was terminated only by his death.

In the course of rereading *The Evolution of Civilizations* I was reminded of the intensity of our dialogue. In Quigley's view, which I shared, our age was one of irrationality. That spring we talked about what career decisions I should make. At his urging I applied to and was admitted by the Harvard Graduate School in History. But I had reservations about an academic career in the study of the history that I loved, on the ground that on Quigley's own analysis the social decisions of importance in our lifetime would be made in ad hoc irrational fashion in the street. On that reasoning, finally I transferred to law school.

In Princeton, Carroll Quigley met and married Lillian Fox. They spent their honeymoon in Paris and Italy on a fellowship to write his doctoral dissertation, a study of the public administration of the Kingdom of Italy, 1805-14. The development of the state in western Europe over the last thousand years always fascinated Quigley. He regarded the development of public administration in the Napoleonic states as a major step in the evolution of the modern state. It always frustrated him that each nation, including our own, regards its own history as unique and the history of other nations as irrelevant to it.

In 1938-41, Quigley served a stint at Harvard, tutoring graduate students in ancient and medieval history. It offered little opportunity for the development of cosmic views and he was less than completely content there. It was, however, a happy experience for me. I had entered Harvard Law School. We began the practice of having breakfast together at Carroll and Lillian's apartment.

In 1941 Quigley accepted a teaching appointment at Georgetown's School of Foreign Service. It was to engage his primary energies throughout the rest of his busy life. There he became an almost legendary teacher. He chose to teach a Course, "The Development of Civilization," required of the incoming class, and that course ultimately provided the structure and substance for *The Evolution of Civilizations*. As a course in his hands, it was a vital intellectual experience for young students, a mind-opening adventure. Foreign Service School graduates, meeting years later in careers around the world, would establish rapport with each other by describing their experience in his class. It was an intellectual initiation with remembered impact that could be shared by people who had graduated years apart.

The fortunes of life brought us together again. During World War II I served as a very junior officer on Admiral King's staff in Washington. Carroll and I saw each other frequently. Twenty years later, after practicing law in Oregon, I came into the government with President Kennedy. Our eldest daughter became a student under Carroll at Georgetown University. We bought a house close by Carroll and Lillian. I had Sunday breakfast with them for years and renewed our discussions of the affairs of a disintegrating world.

Superb teacher Quigley was, and could justify a lifetime of prodigious work on that success alone. But ultimately he was more. To me he was a figure — he would scoff at this — like Augustine, Abelard, and Aquinas, searching for the truth through examination of ultimate reality as it was revealed in history. Long ago, he left the church in the formal sense. Spiritually and intellectually he never left it. He never swerved from his search for the meaning of life. He never placed any goal in higher priority. If the God of the Western civilization that Quigley spent so many years studying does exist in the terms that he saw ascribed to Him by our civilization, that God will now have welcomed Quigley as one who has pleased him.

In an age characterized by violence, extraordinary personal alienation, and the disintegration of family, church, and community, Quigley chose a life dedicated to rationality. He addressed the problem of explaining change in the world around us, first examined by Heraclitus in ancient Greece. Beneath that constant change, so apparent and itself so real, what is permanent and unchanging?

Quigley wanted an explanation that in its very categorization would give meaning to a history which was a record of constant change. Therefore the analysis had to include but not be limited to categories of subject areas of human activity — military, political, economic, social, religious, intellectual. It had to describe change in categories expressed sequentially in time — mixture, gestation, expansion, conflict, universal empire, decay, invasion. It was a most ambitious effort to make history rationally understandable. F. E. Manuel, in his review of this book for the *American Historical Review*, following its first publication in 1961, described it as on "sounder ground" than the work of Toynbee.

Quigley found the explanation of disintegration in the gradual transformation of social "instruments" into "institutions," that is, the transformation of social arrangements functioning to meet real social needs into social institutions serving their own purposes regardless of real social needs. In an ideologically Platonistic society, social arrangements are molded to express a rigidly idealized version of reality. Such institutionalization would not have the flexibility to accommodate to the pressures of changing reality for which the ideology has no categories of thought that will allow perception, analysis, and handling. But the extraordinary distinction of Western civilization is that its ontology allows an open-ended epistemology. It is engaged in a constant effort to understand reality which is perceived as in constant change. Therefore, our categories of knowledge are themselves always subject to change. As a consequence reform is always possible.

The question today is whether we have lost that Western view of reality which has given our 2,000 years of history its unique vitality, constantly pregnant with new versions of social structure. In Evolution, Quigley describes the basic ideology of Western civilization as expressed in the statement, "The truth unfolds in time through a communal process." Therefore, Quigley saw the triumph in the thirteenth century of the moderate realism of Aquinas over dualistic exaggerated realism derived from Platonism as the major epistemologic triumph that opened up Western civilization. People must constantly search for the "truth" by building upon what others have learned. But no knowledge can be assumed to be complete and final. It could be contradicted by new information received tomorrow. In epistemology, Quigley always retained his belief in the scientific method. Therefore, he saw Hegel and Marx as presumptuous, in error, and outside the Western tradition in their analysis of history as an ideologic dialectic culminating in the present or immediate future in a homeostatic condition.

Quigley comments upon the constant repetition of conflict and expansion stages in Western history. That reform process owes its possibility to the uniquely Western belief that truth is continually unfolding. Therefore Western civilization is capable of reexamining its direction and its institutions, and changing both as appears necessary. So in Western history, there was a succession of technological breakthroughs in agricultural practice and in commerce. Outmoded institutions like feudalism and—in the commercial area—municipal mercantilism in the period 1270-1440, and state mercantilism in the period 1690-1810 were discarded. Similarly, we may also survive the economic crisis described by Quigley as monopoly capitalism in the present post-1900 period.

Yet Quigley perceives—correctly in my view—the possible termination of open-ended Western civilization. With access to an explosive technology that can tear the planet apart, coupled with the failure of Western civilization to establish any viable system of world government, local political authority will tend to become violent and absolutist. As we move into irrational activism, states will seize upon ideologies that justify absolutism. The 2,000-year separation in Western history of state and society would then end. Western people would rejoin those of the rest of the world in merging the two into a single entity, authoritarian and static. The age that we are about to enter would be an ideologic one consistent with the views of Hegel and Marx—a homeostatic condition. That triumph would end the Western experiment and return us to the experience of the rest of the world—namely, that history is a sequence of stages in the rise and fall of absolutist ideologies.

America is now in a crisis-disintegrating stage. In such a condition, absent a philosophy, people turn readily to charismatic personalities. So at the beginning of our time of troubles, in the depression of the 1930s, we turned to Franklin D. Roosevelt. He took us through the depression and World War II. We were buoyed by his optimism and reassured by the strength and confidence of his personality. Within the Western tradition he provided us with no solutions; he simply preserved options. When he died, all America was in shock. We had lost our shield. Carroll came over to my place that night. We talked in the subdued fashion of a generation that had lost its guardian and would now have to face a hostile world on its own.

Since then we in America have been denied the easy-out of charismatic leadership. It may just be that we shall have to follow the route that Quigley has marked out for us in this book. We may have to look at our history, analyze it, establish an identity in that analysis, and make another try at understanding reality in a fashion consistent with that open-ended tradition.

If so, America, acting for Western civilization, must find within the history of that civilization the intellectual and spiritual reserves to renew itself within the tradition. Striking as was the impact of this book at the time of its first publication, in 1961, its major impact will be in support of that effort in the future. There is hope that in Western civilization the future ideology will be rational. If so, it would be consistent with an epistemology that accepts the general validity of sensory experience and the possibility of making generalizations from that experience, subject to modification as additional facts are perceived. It is that epistemology which was termed moderate realism in the thirteenth century and, in its epistemologic aspects, is now known as the scientific method. Such a rational ideology is probable only if it is developed out of the special history of the West. As appreciation of that spreads, the kind of analysis that Carroll Quigley develops in this book is the analysis that the West must use.

Such as effort would be consistent in social terms with Quigley's view of his own life. He greatly admired his mother, a housewife, and his father, a Boston firechief, and described them as teaching him to do his best at whatever he chose to put his energies. That was their way of saying what Carroll would have described as man's responsibility to understand and relate actively to a continually unfolding reality. He dedicated his life to that purpose.

THE EVOLUTION OF CIVILIZATIONS: A REVIEW

The Evolution of Civilizations, by Carroll Quigley.
(New York, The Macmillan Company, 1960. Pp. x, 281, S5.95)

Reviewed by Elmer Louis Kayser.

A work of the importance of *The Evolution of Civilizations* deserves much more than the hurried first reading that a deadline has imposed. Reading Professor Quigley's volume is a pleasant, but rather exacting exercise. He demonstrates Toynbeean erudition and non-Tonybeean brevity.

It is fortunate that a brief review is expected, for a truly critical review would have to be longer than the book itself. A vast time span, a tremendous area and an amazing diversity of fields are involved. A high degree of selectivity must be exercised in determining what material is to be presented. The sector is small within which anyone could claim the competence of a specialist. The work of others must be used and judgments made. A detailed criticism under these circumstances becomes a race between author and critic to see who has read the latest monograph or special study and made the soundest evaluation of it. Toynbee in reconsidering the first ten volumes of *The Study of History* in the recent twelfth volume found that there had been new writing while he was publishing which made it desirable that he makes changes. The blurb (author unknown) on the jacket of the latest Toynbee volume goes so far as to assert that, during the publication of the First Decade of Toynbee, new discoveries in some fields "have changed the picture almost out of recognition."

The present reviewer accepts the historical data which Professor Quigley uses as what a competent scholar selected at the time of writing as valid supports for the ideas that he presents. The reviewer makes no attempt to examine these individually and critically. His interest is in what the author was trying to do, in the patterns of thinking that he sets up.

The author is thinking of aggregates of human beings as they constitute themselves in social groups and various types of society: parasitic societies, producing societies, and civilizations, depending upon whether the members have the major portion of their relationships outside the group or within it. He finds "two dozen civilizations," living and dead, within the last ten millennia and suggest various groupings. Before discussing historical change, he considers methods of analyzing the evolution of a society, the resultant of development and morphology. Civilizations pass through seven stages: mixture, gestation, expansion, age of conflict, universal empire, decay, and invasion which he offers as a convenient way of breaking into segments an intricate historical process.

A very interesting chapter devoted to the physical setting of the earliest civilizations is followed by a detailed discussion of Mesopotamia, Canaanite and Minoan, Classical and Western Civilizations. These discussions of the civilizations which relate directly to the stream of Western Civilization through historic time occupy the major portion of the study. In a final word of conclusion, Professor Quigley states his belief that six points have emerged from his study. The first three, he points out, merely underscore well-recognized and long accepted points of view. The last three, he feels, represent a real contribution. They are: the seven stages (which proves as Toynbee's does not, a basis for an analysis of the whole course of the evolution of a civilization including the earliest phases), an improved nomenclature and techniques for dealing with historical problems.

Professor Quigley's indebtedness to his predecessors is obvious and acknowledged. While he lacks the Wagnerian tone of Spengler and the severely classical attitudes of Toynbee, he does have the more direct approach of the social scientist. His heavy emphasis on scientific method in the first chapter, even though he concludes by pointing out the difference between the natural and social sciences in the subjective factor, leads us to expect a much more rigorous method than the one applied. In this case, we notice such statements as "To be sure there are difficulties, but in some cases, at least these can be explained away." You wonder again at the grading system applied to Western society in the chart on page 81. The reviewer is not sure just how it is determined when a civilization reaches "its peak of achievement" and how this is related to the seven stages of development.

All of these are matters of detail. The important fact is that the author has distilled from a vast store of historical knowledge a highly suggestive approach for the systematic study of major historical movements. The real review will probably have to wait until that traveler from New Zealand in the midst of a vast solitude, standing on a broken arch of London Bridge, has finished his sketch of the ruins of St. Paul's.

Elmer Louis Kayser is the Dean of University Students and Professor of European History at The George Washington University. Born in Washington, Dean Kayser holds his A.B., M.A., and LL.D. from George Washington, and a PhD. from Columbia University. Vitally interested in International Affairs, Dean Kayser is the author of several boobs, an Associate Editor of World Affairs, and a director of the American Peace Society.

CARROLL QUIGLEY: SOME ASPECTS OF HIS LAST TWELVE YEARS

Recollections from Personal Correspondence by
Carmen Brissette-Grayson
School of Foreign Service, 1962

In the last 12 years of his life, from 1965 to 1977, Carroll Quigley taught, observed the American scene, and reflected on his basic values in life. He was simultaneously pessimistic and radically optimistic. Teaching was the core of Quigley's professional life and neither his craving to write nor his discouragement with student reaction of the early seventies diminished his commitment to the classroom. "I am sure that you will enjoy teaching increasingly, as I do," he had written in 1965:

> "it is the one way we can do a little good in the world. The task is so important, the challenge so great, and the possibilities for improvement and for variation as infinite that it is the most demanding and most difficult of human activities. Even a virtuoso violinist can be made to order easier than a good teacher."[1]

Six years later, in his 30th year of teaching at Georgetown, he was less hopeful. "I find teaching harder every year, as the students are less and less receptive. ..."[2] The turmoil of the Vietnam years spilled into the lecture hall and, on at least one occasion, students disrupted a class. He worried about the dilution of academic standards and feared the increasing bureaucratization of education. Such problems, he lamented, "will give you a glimmering of what teaching has become in the tail end of a civilization...."[3]

Despite these pessimistic readings of student responsiveness, the School of Foreign Service senior classes of 1973 and 1974 both honored him as the outstanding professor of the year. Quigley himself continued throughout this period to address a variety of audiences—bureaucrats, scientists, an Irish-American club, even a Catholic high school religion class. "A rather daring experiment in religious enlightenment," he concluded in describing that encounter with Catholic adolescents."[4] "I accept... outside lectures (and also ... I give courses I never gave before in my final year of teaching) because," he explained, "it makes me clarify my own thoughts about what is really important. I often say things in my lectures that I never realized before."[5]

Quigley revised his lectures to the end of his teaching days even in classes which he had taught for over a decade. "I am never satisfied with my courses, so keep working on them."[6] In his final weeks at Georgetown he broke off just before Thanksgiving and told his students in "The World Since 1914" class that there was little point in discussing the Third World when they knew so little about how their own society works:

> "So I told them about the USA — really very hair-raising when it is all laid out in sequence: .... 1. cosmic hierarchy; 2. energy; 3. agriculture; 4. food; 5. health and medical services; 6. education; 7. income flows and the worship of GROWTH; 8. inflation... showing how we are violating every aspect of life by turning everything into a ripoff because we... have adopted the view that insatiable individualistic greed must run the world."[7]

He feared "that the students will come to feel that all is hopeless, so I must... show them how solutions can be found by holistic methods seeking diversity, de-centralization, communities...etc."[8] Pleased with the class response, he later recalled:

> "The students were very excited and my last lecture in which I put the whole picture together was about the best lecture I ever gave. That was 10 Dec. [1975], my last full day of teaching after 41 years."[9]

Unlike his underlying faith in the efficacy of teaching, Quigley found little basis for optimism about the future of American society. A journal asked him in 1975 to write an upbeat article on the country's prospects. "I told the editor that would be difficult, but I would try. I wrote it and they refused to publish it because it was not optimistic enough..."[10] In 1976 he wrote congratulating my husband for his decision to give up any idea of leaving state politics for the federal arena. "It is futile," Quigley concluded, "because it is all so corrupt and the honest ones are so incompetent. I should not say this, as students said it to me for years and I argued with them."[11]

It was more than the institutionalization of the American political system which concerned him: "We are living in a very dangerous age in which insatiably greedy men are prepared to sacrifice anybody's health and tranquility to satisfy their own insatiable greed for money and power." [12] He feared that these values had virtually destroyed the roots of the Western outlook and had made the creation of a satisfying life in contemporary America a hazardous undertaking. "I am aghast at what... selfishness, and the drive for power have done to our society.... I worry... as I find the world so increasingly horrible that I do not see how anything as wonderful as... your life can escape." [13] Less than six months before he died he advised: "The best thing you can do is... to keep some enclaves of satisfying decent life." [14] Yet pessimism about American society did not weaken a radical optimism rooted in his essential values: nature, people, and God.

The greatest source of pleasure for Quigley, outside of his scholarly pursuits and his personal life, came from his profound love of nature. In 1968 he bought an 82-acre farm near the small town of Glengary, West Virginia:

> "in the case of the permanent residents they are the same individuals (or their offspring) that we have known for years. We are chiefly impressed with their distinctive personalities, and intelligence... marvelous, so steady, hard-working... and unafraid... [others] were really neurotic, afraid of everything..." [15]

This sounds like unremarkable country gossip until one realizes that the "permanent residents" to which he refers were several generations of bluebirds which he had been studying.

I once made the mistake of writing to him about my war of attrition with racoons who were foraging in our trash. Quigley rushed back a reply to prevent me from making any further intrusions in the cosmic hierarchy:

> "If the racoons make your trash disposal a problem, why not cooperate with nature instead of resisting it? The big solution to our pollution problems is to increase the speed of biodegradation, and what is more natural than for animals to eat? Here I feed a fox every night if our local skunk does not get to it first (I buy chicken backs and necks for 19 cents a pound, but am afraid to give these too frequently for fear they may have injurious hormones injected into the live chickens)... My fox never leaves a crumb or a mark on the concrete platform where he eats.... Last

summer when he had a mate and young ones, we gave him more food and he always took the best... away to his family. We used to time him: it took 4 minutes before he was back for something for himself...We have found that wild things are so wonderful." [16]

He concluded with a revealing description of what to him was a particularly satisfying weekend—writing, observing birds, and on Saturday night: "Beethoven's birthday, we sat... reading near the fire, while the radio played all nine of HIS symphonies." [17]

Thus, discouragement about the course of American life existed simultaneously with happiness derived from those aspects of life he knew to be lasting: "I am fed up with... everything but God and nature... and human beings (whom I love and pity, as I always did)." [18]

His loyalty was to a religious-intellectual outlook: "I feel glad I am a Christian," he wrote, "glad I am... without allegiance to any bloc, party, or groups, except to our Judeo-Christian tradition (modified by science and common sense)." [19] Over the years he usually closed such letters with what could serve as a characteristic valedictory: "God keep you all... and help you to grow." [20]

References—from personal correspondence between Carroll Quigley and Carmen Grayson, 1965-1976.

1. April 1, 1965. On Quigley's writing and the evolution of this manuscript, see the Foreword by Harry Hogan to "Weapons Systems: A History".
2. October 6, 1971.
3. Ibid.
4. January 5, 1972.
5. April 13, 1975.
6. January 2, 1975.
7. January 2, 1976; December 4, 1975.
8. December 4, 197 5.
9. January 2, 1976.
10. October 8, 1975.
11. June 28, 1976.
12. May 4, 1976.
13. November 29, 1973; May 20, 1974.

14. November 8, 1973.
15. May 24, 1975.
16. January 10, 1973; December 17, 1972.
17. December 17, 1972.
18. November 8, 1973.
19. November 29, 1973.
20. November 7, 1974.

RECENT OFF-CAMPUS ACTIVITIES OF PROFESSOR CARROLL QUIGLEY

History Department 16 May 1973

17 August 1972: As one of three original members of the Honorary Faculty of the Industrial College of the Armed Forces, Department of Defense, gave a lecture to about 250 officers at Fort Lesley J. McNair, on "The American Democratic Tradition". The lecture will be published in PERSPECTIVES IN DEFENSE MANAGEMENT in December.

12 September 1972: Gave two lectures to about eighty officers from the defense forces of Latin American countries at the Inter-American Defense College, Fort Lesley J. McNair, on the subject "Man in the Contemporary World", using a General Systems approach.

19 September 1972: Gave a lecture with subsequent discussion to the National War College of U.S.A., Fort Lesley J. McNair, on "Dissention in the United States", in elaboration of my previous lecture on the same subject given at ICAF on 24 August 1970 and published in ICAF's PERSPECTIVES IN DEFENSE MANAGEMENT of December 1970. This time, however, I used a new General Systems approach.

9 November 1972: Repeated the lecture of 12 May 1972 on "Cognitive Systems and Cultural Shock" to Wives Seminar, Foreign Service Institute, U.S. Department of State.

27 November 1972: At invitation of Professor Dorothy Brown, I lectured to Georgetown University seniors majoring in history on "Macro-history."

5 December 1972: Conducted one session of the week-long seminar of the U.S. Department of Agriculture Graduate School Program on Critical Issues and Decisions, at Williamsburg, Virginia, Conference Center, on "Man, Society, and the State". The participants consisted of upper-middle level government officials.

27-30 December 1972: Gave three papers at Annual Meeting of American Association For Advancement of Science, Washington, D.C., on:
(1) "Cognitive Factors in the Evolution of Civilizations";
(2) "General Crises in Civilizations";
(3) "The Civilizational Process: A General Systems Approach".
The first paper was published immediately in the December 1972 issue of MAIN CURRENTS IN MODERN THOUGHT. The advance interest in the second paper was so great that the AAAS sent out ISO copies of the complete paper to news media around the world in November. As a result of the third paper, I was asked to join the SOCIETY FOR GENERAL SYSTEMS RESEARCH.

7 March 1973: Participated in a four-speaker, hour-long debate over radio station KXss, Salt Lake City, on "The Conspiracy Theory of History". The discussion was sponsored and moderated by Professor Philip C. Sturges, chairman, Department of History, University of Utah; my chief opponent was Gary Allen, author of NONE DARE CALL IT CONSPIRACY.

10 April 1973: Gave a dinner talk, with subsequent discussion, to 25 executives of American business corporations on the Club of Rome thesis about "The Limits of Growth", at Brookings Institution.

11 April 1973: Repeated lecture of 5 December 1972 on "Man, Society, and the State" at U.S. Department of Agriculture Graduate School, National Press Building, Washington, D.C.

16 April 1973: Gave a paper on "Can Man Survive at a High Standard of Living?" at Presidential Plenary Session of Association of American Geographers Annual: Meeting, held at Hyatt Regency Hotel, Atlanta, Georgia, before an audience of about 500 persons in main ballroom.

18 April 1973: Spoke to about 80 students and faculty of the GIT History Majors Association on "The Crisis in the Historical Profession."

15 May 1973: Gave a lecture on "Cultural Shock and Overseas Enterprise: Its Nature and Cure" to about 70 executives of the Overseas Branch of the Pharmaceutical Manufactures Association, at Innisbrook Resort and Golf Club, Tarpon Springs, Florida.
Spring 1973: Made an evaluation of a sixth grade social science course, MAN:

A COURSE OF STUDY, for Montgomery County, Maryland, Public Schools. The course, developed by the Educational Development Center of Cambridge, Massachusetts, with funds provided by the National Science Foundation, has aroused soma controversy among parents and citizens of Montgomery County on the grounds that "The course teaches and promotes secular humanism and moral relativism."

5-7 June 1973: Spoke to students and faculty at three high Schools of Montgomery County, Maryland, on "The Crisis in United States Foreign Policy."

20 August 1973: Spoke to about 47 visiting historians from Great Britain on "Methodology in Comparative History: the United States and the United Kingdom", at Department of State."

21 August 1973: Dinner followed by ray lecture to the students and their wives, at Industrial College of the Armed Forces, repeating the lecture of last year on "The American Democratic Tradition: Myths and Reality."

22 September 1973: Gave a paper on "A General Systems Approach to Historical Change in Civilizations" to about 100 persons at session of The Middle Atlantic Chapter of The Society for General Systems Research at University of Maryland, College Park.

13 November 1973" Conducted a seminar for $3^{1/2}$ hours with about 25 government officials on "the Crisis in American life" at U.S. Department of Labor.

26 November 1973: Conducted a session with the History Senior Seminar of Georgetown College on "Macrohistory".

4 December 1973: Repeated the seminar of 13 November on the American Crisis for U.S. Department of Agriculture Graduate School at Williams-burg, Virginia to 37 government officials.

CARROLL QUIGLEY ENDOWED CHAIR BROCHURE

For forty years Professor Carroll Quigley's teachings quickened and disciplined the minds of students of the School of Foreign Service. His inspired lectures in Development of Civilization, for four decades and for as many thousands of students, literally defined the School, their education and themselves.

Professor Quigley's pedagogy was synonymous with discipline and with methods of analysis and interpretation. He was justly known – even reknowned – for his determination to make students think. The result was not always immediately or fully appreciated (as the next paragraph recounts!) but no teacher has been more respected by alumni who daily, in their working lives, progressively discover the value of a Quigley education.

One day in the Walsh Building a colleague of Professor Quigley's saw a sign that said "Jesus Loves You." Written below the sign was the following plaint by a student: "If that is true, why did Professor Quigley give me an F?" Those who recall Dr. Quigley's lectures on the providential deity will know that there is no logical inconsistency between Jesus's love and a low grade from Professor Quigley!

To say that Professor Carroll Quigley is an institution inseparable from the School of Foreign Service is to state a fact. His retirement from full time teaching at the age of 65 in no way diminished this fact. But it does provide his former students with an opportunity to contribute to a fund in Professor Quigley's name. Our goal is a fund of $500,000 to endow a Carroll Quigley Professorship. This Professorship will stand at the center of the School of Foreign Service as a permanent, inspiring testimony to the legend of this master teacher.

This fall Professor Carroll Quigley delivered a series of lectures entitled "Public Authority and the State in the Western Tradition: A Thousand Years of Growth, 976-1976." These published lectures, inscribed by Professor Quigley, will be sent in appreciation to contributors to the Carroll Quigley Fund.

Peter F. Krogh
Dean, School of Foreign Service

———————————

I have known Carroll Quigley as a colleague and friend for three decades at Georgetown University. His name will be indelibly identified with the School of Foreign Service, but his presence has equally enriched the History Department faculty and the University. It is fitting that an endowed chair should be dedicated in his honor to commemorate the excellence of his teaching and the many contributions he has made to keep Georgetown University's academic standards high.

Dr. Quigley has always been concerned with the attainment of quality education at Georgetown and with inspiring in his students a desire for knowledge. He has not only stimulated the imagination of his students, but compelled them to think independently, and to challenge accepted concepts and traditional historical interpretations. This process sometimes was painful for some students, but many who were able to take advantage of his teaching techniques and methodology of approach were grateful for the experience. Most alumni who look back on their college years at Georgetown and took Dr. Quigley's course in Development of Civilization say they will never forget him. His influence remains with them, and they recall vividly how much he taught them.

The key to Carroll Quigley's success as a teacher and as a scholar lies in his creative intellect, the depth of his perceptions, and the wide interdisciplinary range of this interests, which encompasses the fields of history, economics, philosophy, and science. An iconoclast and a person of insatiable curiosity, as well as keenness of mind, Dr. Quigley stands apart from the specialized scholar who plows diligently in the rutted grooves of narrow disciplines.

What has most disturbed Carroll Quigley is the deterioration that has occurred in college education. While universities have produced an ever increasing number of specialists, technicians, scholars, and researchers in a wide variety of fields, institutions of higher education have been affected by a philosophical myopia. This has caused a serious erosion of the highest ideals associated with intellectual pursuits and professionalism. Throughout his life, Dr. Quigley has fought against this trend. A chair in Carroll Quigley's name will stand for quality education for as long as it is endowed.

Dr. Jules Davids
Professor of Diplomatic History

LECTURES

THE HOLISTIC, MORPHOLOGICAL, & COGNITIVE QUALITIES OF CARROLL QUIGLEY'S HISTORIOGRAPHY

Glenn E. Bugos
Introduction to Historiography
and Historical Method January 12, 1982

There is truth and it can be found; it has been found, to some degree, by men in the past, and by men in other societies. The task of finding it is life-long, and probably continues after bodily death. And the greatest joy of living is the search for it. That is why we are here.[1]

Carroll Quigley seldom used terms such as "truth" in his academic works. Forever scientific, even in his discussions of abstract and moral concepts, he preferred to use the more easily definable term "Cognitive sophistication" to explain his educational goals. Quigley felt that each person had a cognitive system that classifies, critiques, and prioritizes all the phenomena one encounters, and when one is able to recognize one's own unconscious cognitive prejudices by comparing cognitive systems with the systems of other people in other times, one is then cognitively sophisticated. Quigley's goal as an academician, then, became that of making Western man aware of his cognitive assumptions by constantly critiquing this cognitive system from every possible perspective. The all-encompassing nature of the critique, the necessity of recognizing perspectives, and the personal force with which "The Great God Quigley" presented his theory makes his biography an important factor in understanding his historiography.

Born to an upper-middle class Irish Catholic family in 1911, Quigley developed a strong sense of ethnicity and community that greatly influenced his concepts of community and culture. He showed early academic progress at the Boston Latin School and served as editor for the school's award winning newspaper. His early interests, however, were in science and mathematics. When he entered Harvard University his declared major was biochemistry. His early immersion in scientific method profoundly influenced his approach to history, which he adapted as his field of study before graduating *magna cum laude* in 1933. He continued his studies in European history at Harvard, receiving his A.M. in 1934 and his Ph.D in 1938 with a dissertation on the Risogimento during the Napoleonic era.

His education continued as he presented his historiography in numerous lectures to students whose critique compelled him to recognize that his way of looking at the world was "not necessarily the only way, or even the best way to look at it" [3]. During his three years as a tutor in history and government at Princeton and Harvard Universities and his 35 years as a Professor at the Georgetown University School of Foreign Service, he gained insight into the psychological structure of modern society and developed a reputation as an outstanding teacher. His course on "The Development of Civilizations" was cited by School of Foreign Service Alumni from 1941 to 1969 as the most influential course in their undergraduate careers and so received four faculty awards for distinguished teaching[4]. His years of teaching compelled him not only to constantly reexamine his historiography, but to produce lectures general in approach, which provided the base for his two major works, *The Evolution of Civilizations* and *Tragedy and Hope*, thereby facilitating the expression of his generalist history. By 1971, he had a very clear idea of where his responsibilities and curiosity, had led him; "I am a 'macrohistorian' specializing in the processes of change in advanced societies, with a special interest in methodological questions" [5].

His generalist approach to history necessitated his keeping abreast of many academic disciplines, which he did through membership in the American Anthropological Association, the American Economic Association, the American Association for the Advancement of Science, and the American Historical Association, as well as serving as a consultant to the Department of Defense and the House Select Committee on Astronautics and Space Exploration. But Quigley's interdisciplinary interests resulted not from dilletantism, but from a distrust of reductionism as a means of understanding society and an insatiable curiosity he synthesized into a revolutionary holistic epistemology.

Quigley's explanations of his historiography changed during the tumultuous 1960's as new scientific and psychological concepts were introduced that aided him in clarifying his definitions. However, he continued to practice a holistic scientific historiography towards a moral goal of global peace and understanding through cognitive sophistication. To understand this unique historiography, one must first understand its roots in the scientific methodology of what has come to be known as' "general systems theory." Quigley's wide-ranging knowledge of numerous civilizations gave him material from which to discern patterns in the system of evolution of civilizations, allowing him to extend his general systems theory to "morphological history". Then, by critiquing contemporary society in the context of his morphology of history, Quigley sought to bring about a revolution in thinking.

Always the teacher, Quigley emphasized the study of tools of analysis to develop a useful epistemology. In epistemology he always retained his belief in the scientific method.[6] Quigley's explanation of scientific method as an analytical tool in the social sciences is original with him only in that he recognized the real limitations of the physical sciences, as opposed to the scientific extremism of Langlois and Seignobos. The scientific method Quigley subscribed to consists of gathering evidence, making a hypothesis, and testing the hypothesis.

The laws arising from the use of scientific method in both the physical and social sciences are idealized theories reflecting observed phenomena only approximately, but Quigley felt laws must be based on observation and must be amended to account for any observed anomalies. After these laws were scientifically constructed, Quigley used them as conceptual paradigms to explain historical phenomena through comparison, in contrast to rationally derived laws of the theorists which will not adapt to anomalies of observation. "Theory must agree with phenomena, not vice versa."[7] Thus, Quigley puts the historian at ease with scientific methods by explaining that physical laws have as many exceptions as the historicists claim historical laws do.

Quigley's methodology emphasizes observation as a technique because the inconclusive nature of historical observation makes any attempt to establish laws as opposed to paradigms, impossible. He also demanded that the historically "observed" phenomena be authenticated and verified in a scientific fashion, although in his sparsely footnoted works he always emphasized the synthesis of all the observations and not the authenticity of any one fact.[8] As more evidence is observed, scientists seek "advances by a series of successive (and one hopes, closer) approximations to the truth." Thus, only the communal effort of scholars can achieve the truth. Observations are then synthesized into hypotheses which must explain all the observations in the simplest way possible. Simplicity in the sense that the hypothesis makes the fewest assumptions and infers the simplest relationships actually makes the hypothesis scientific. Also, it is simpler to prejudge that a hypothesis is invalid until proven valid through checking back for evidence, foretelling new observations, and by experimenting with controls, to complete the method of propounding tentative paradigms.

Quigley's quest for simplicity in history did not preclude his recognition of its complexity. Instead of surrendering to historical complexity as an insurmountable obstacle and retreating to an historicism that would obviate the development of paradigms, Quigley confronted complexity head-on and sought to recognize it as an integral part of historical method. He realized that while reductionism is possible with the physical sciences, any such attempt at dissecting an historical phenomena and isolating and analyzing only one factor as an independent variable is impossible in the social sciences. Thus, Quigley studied the whole context of a phenomena, a method developed by the theoretical biologist Ludwig von Bertalanffy termed "general systems theory" [10] This "generalism" became known as "holisticism" and operationalized as "macrohistory." By "holisticism", Quigley meant that the "whole" of reality held greater meaning than the sum of its parts, thus scholars should tend towards general studies to understand general and comparative historical concepts and paradigms rather than the hyperspecialization pervading the discipline of history.[11]

Other generalists Quigley respected were Kenneth Boulding and Robert Solo in economics, Amitai Etziani in sociology, and William McNeill, Frederick William Maitland, and Charles McIlwain in history. He felt these academicians were top-quality generalists because they had a clear system of values rooted in the Western Hebreo-Christian tradition and a sophisticated understanding of epistemology.[12]

Here, Quigley shows the profound influence the teachings of the founders of the Western Hebreo-Christian tradition had on his own cognitive system. Quigley found the "medieval synthesis" of Occam's holism with the moderate realism of Abelard and Thomas Aquinas as the root of the Western intellectual tradition which triumphed over the exaggerated rationalism of the Platonists. It was not a complete triumph, however, and Western epistemology developed with a moderateness and duality of accepting both rationalism-materialism and religiosity-holisticism whenever a situation requires a certain way of thinking.[13]

This "medieval synthesis" added two dimensions to the rationalist's three-dimensional spacial and materialist configuration of human experience, the two dimensions of time and of abstraction. Even this fifth-dimension of time is divisible into chronologically sequential levels of evolution, namely physical evolution (the materialist, three-dimensional stage), organic evolution (as the physical elements combine for survival), and social evolution (as the organism becomes more complex as on the level of states, and the society molds the personality of the individuals within it), which leads to the increasing sophisticated levels of cognition, the emotional, spiritual, and rational levels.[14] Man is a consequence of this process of evolution, and therefore, so is his history.

Quigley believed that as Western man becomes more cognitively sophisticated and is more able to determine his hierarchy of needs according to these levels of abstraction, then he will overcome the exaggerated rationalism of the historical methodology of the 19th century. In a table prepared for a conference on the philosophy of history contrasted the catch-words of the historical methodology of two eras:[15]

1880	1980
reductionist	holist
isolation of problem	contextual
specialist	generalist
analytical	ecological
quantification	qualification
seeking laws	making models
chain-causation	network causation
technicians	scientists
knowledge	understanding

Quigley notes the evolution of historical methodology to the more sophisticated modern approach but would disagree that it is the final, immutable approach. He feels Western man's realization that all present knowledge (in his case of epistemology) will be superceded in the future and this will save Western society from dissolution or stagnation from within while allowing innovation for growth. Thus, Western man's epistemology, because of its future preference and scientific deviation, is an important factor in the development, control, and future prospects of the powerful Western civilization, just as the epistemology of past civilizations hindered their ability to cope with the changing physical world and thus was an important factor in their demise.[16]

But epistemology also played a dominant role in determining several other aspects of life. As with all of Quigley's concepts, however, "epistemology" must be clearly defined before its role in shaping history can be understood. The operational definition Quigley gives "epistemology" is "cognitive system" that is, the ways in which "the language of a society classifies human experience in order to think or to communicate and the values which a particular society puts upon these categories, determining the most fundamental engines of human motivation."[17] The generic morphology of a cognitive system consists of those five levels on the continuum of the fifth dimension of abstraction, that is, feelings, emotions, self-awareness, rationality, and spirituality.

In his book *Tragedy and Hope*, Quigley examines the categories and valuations of human experience along this continuum of abstraction by man in Western society in order to show how this cognitive system was a precondition to the economic and military development of Western society, as well as to the seeds of disintegration it planted which reach fruition in two world wars sandwiching a global depression. Given time, Quigley would have investigated the cognitive system of each civilization in history along this conceptual paradigm exhibited in the Western system so that we could truly understand that society. This is because the society's cognitive system "is the most important we can know about any society and the most difficult to learn. It is also difficult to recognize that we ourselves have a cognitive system, a distinctive way of looking at the world that is not the way the world actually is, but is simply the way our group conveniently looks at the world."[18] Quigley's recognition that scientific method engenders a morphology or pattern in which we have always and will always perceive human experience provides the transition to what he terms "historical analysis", that is, a cognitive system specific to the task of understanding human experience through historical paradigms. Whereas scientific methods can provide Western man with an all-purpose epistemology with which to assess and react to any given situation, the scientific method when applied to the historians task of developing historical paradigms is afforded the added sophistication of the perspective of time (Quigley's fourth dimension of human experience), and thus is closer to achieving the true aim of the human experience, that of understanding human experience.

Quigley believed that general and morphological histories were necessary to develop the conceptual paradigms to understand historical phenomena. Quigley believed that every event, every human experience is unique and "occurs at a certain place, at a certain moment, to persons at a specific age and condition and in an arrangement of all these which will never be repeated."[19] And to a certain extent, an historical interpretation is unique to a certain configuration of conditions which bias its findings, such as nationalism-biased sources in Risorgimento history, or such as academic specialists who isolate one historical factor as an independent variable to protect and enhance the worth of their particular discipline.

Quigley felt inexorable accrual of knowledge would obviate belief in historical relativism. More importantly, Quigley denounced historians who carried relativism to extremes because he felt they exaggerated rationalism in regards to scientific method to make it appear ridiculous.[20]

Quigley believed events were unique, but that events form patterns, which can be perceived, conceptualized, communicated, and understood, but only to the degree that they are not unique. In this sense, Quigley is a comparative historian searching not for the unique character of civilizations, but for resemblances, much like the historians of medieval Catholicism and Leopold von Ranke who seek a "Universality" in the past. The most important area of commonality unique events can share is if they both involve a given society. Events that can be examined in the context of a given society give insight into the life cycle of that society, thus allowing it to serve as an historical paradigm. For Quigley, a society is more than a well-defined aggregate of people, rather, it "is a group whose members have more relationships with one another than they do with outsiders. As a result, at society forms an integrative unity and is comprehensible." [21] The unity of interrelationships within this society operationalizes itself to the historian in the form of culture, or if the interrelationships make the society a producing and expanding one, then it is also operationalized in the form of civilization.

Perhaps the single most important factor making Quigley's historical analysis more useful than those of other historians who studied the life-cycle of civilizations, namely Giovanni Battista Vico, Nikolai Danilevsky, Oswald Spengler, and especially Arnold J. Toynbee, is that Quigley readily defined his historical concepts and terms. His definitions of concepts, like Leontief's Input-Output analysis of a modern economic system, recognizes that all elements in a general system are dynamic and that the definition of any element must be contextual rather than denotative. The earlier historians often saw Classical antiquity as the prime example of historical culture, society, and civilization although Quigley shows that it encompasses a number of anomalies from the historical paradigms he deliniates.[22] Whereas these historians used simplistic biological and Darwinian terms as analogies to the life cycles of civilizations, Quigley drew upon his perhaps more sophisticated understanding of anthropology, sociology and psychology to deliniate his concepts more clearly.

His definition of "culture" in *The Evolution of Civilizations* is one such notable concept. It is a multifaceted definition, stating:

> "From one point I view (culture) is the cushion between man's purely animal nature and the natural environment. From another point of view it is the social heritage passed down from generation to generation. From another point of view it is a complex medley of personalities, material objects, patterns of behavior, subtle emotional relationships, accepted intellectual ideas and intellectual assumptions, and customary individual actions. From any point of view it is constantly changing, and forms the chief subject of study in all the social sciences."

To reproduce and survive, societies must act as a buffer between the human infant and his physical environment and must train that infant to become a productive and accepting member of that society. The acculturization during the training process is what transforms the vast spectrum of his human nature (the sum of his potential qualities) into the much narrower spectrum of his human personality (actually developed qualities). Culture would therefore equal artifacts plus organization into patterns of actions, feelings, and thoughts among persons and artifacts. Thus, while a basic human need is food, it is the culture that determines beef and broccoli are foods as opposed to locusts and seaweed. This added influencing dimension of culture on the human personality differentiates man from beasts, who have only their natural environment to shape their personality because they can survive without culture. Quigley, with his scientist's passion for diagrams, displayed the human interrelationship as follows:

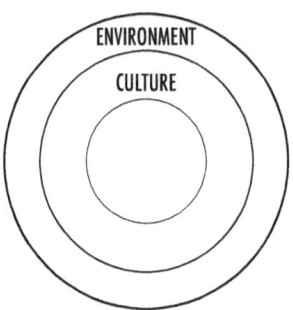

The hereditary aspect of culture makes it "integrative" which means that the different parts of a culture adapt themselves to one another and tend to become an increasingly interlocking unified system in which each part fits snugly into all the surrounding parts. But because culture is made up of loose-fitting parts that are only partially adapted to one another, and to the adjacent influence of the environment and human needs, it is both adaptive and persistent and thus serves as a trigger mechanism to keep the three circles operating in coordination.

In this model of interrelationships, human nature certainly shapes the culture but in a very nebulous manner which social scientists have difficulty observing. They can more easily observe how the culture shapes human potentialities into human personality. While Quigley deliniates the generic factors comprising human personality along his five level continuum of abstraction, the most important are those one thinking on the "rational" level should consider. This division of human needs into a hierarchy of levels from the more abstract to the more concrete parallels the division of the elements of culture and are here presented with their operational definition:[25]

8	Intellectual	Rational Explanations and Communication	
7	Religious	Psychic Certainty	Internal Controls
6	Emotional	Existential Relation with Nature and People	
5	Social	Gregariousness	

4	Economic	Energy, Materials	
3	Political	Domestic Tranquility	External Controls
2	Military	Foreign Security	
1	Physical	Space, time, oxygen	

Quigley considers the fulfillment of these factors a similarity shared by all civilizations and thus important to discerning historical patterns. To the degree that a civilization is able to fulfill these fundamental needs, it is able to exert control over the people that comprise the society, either through controls of acculturization internalized in the psyche of the individuals which comprise that civilization, or more concrete controls, such as economic and military leverage, which are external to the individuals in a civilization and imposed upon them through some societal process located in another level of the culture. This is known as morphological tension. For instance, a change on the intellectual level exacerbating the separation of man from nature on the emotional level could lead to that culture's inability to satisfy needs on the physical level if this culture has the economic infrastructure to manifest that change which started on the intellectual level. Thus, Quigley showed that cultures satisfy human needs by socializing them into human desires along a complex nexus of societal (and historical) factors.

This description of culture by its functions is more than a temporalized physiocracy expounding needs as the driving force in history; indeed the needs a culture must satisfy, with the exception of those on the physical level, result primarily from the culture's cognitive system. Nevertheless, Quigley's major contribution to historiography was in his analysis of the evolution of civilizations, and in this analysis he determined that the culture's ability to create needs it can fulfill is the primary factor transforming that culture into a civilization. Quigley defines "civilization" as "a producing society with an instrument of expansion."[26] Seventeen societies meet this definition of civilization, including the two currently existing Western and Orthodox (Russian) civilizations. Each of these civilizations had a unique culture and a surplus producing instrument of expansion.

The earliest civilizations depended on their proficiency in growing a carbohydrate plant as an energy food and they can be classified into the maize, rice, and grain groups. However, this dependency is only part of the spatial dimensions, which along with time and abstraction, comprise the matrix on which all civilizations are found. Quigley saw the matrix of early civilizations influenced primarily by geographical and meteorological changes in man's prehistory. The demographic flows and agricultural systems resulting from these changes found the matrix of subsequent civilizations, although the evolution of the instrument of expansion makes the civilization historically unique.

Quigley defines the spatial dimensions of the matrix of civilization in terms of geography, the abstract dimension as the cognitive system embodied in culture, and the dimension of time in terms of continua of phenomena. Quigley shares Marc Bloch's fascination with time as that perspective which makes history a unique and fruitful discipline.

Quigley's continuum in the context of history is:

> "a heterogeneous unity each point of which differs from all the surrounding points but differs from them by such subtle gradations in any one respect that no boundaries exist in the unity itself, and it can be divided into parts only by imaginary and arbitrary boundaries." [27]

He uses the example of the colors on the prism to explain the irrational quality of space; orange is not a single, definable color on the prism but rather the gamut of colors between red and yellow. Because only a rational and logical construct of the spectrum could produce colors that are both perfectly definable and commensurable, Quigley denounces attempts to use mathematical rationalism to determine the periodizations of historical paradigms. But history deals with changes and all changes, occurring in time, involve continua. Thus, the practice of slicing continua into periods or dual poles and giving names to these artificial categories is necessary if one is to think or talk about the world. However, one must always remain alert to the danger of believing that those terms are real or refer to reality except by rough approximation. But "only by making such divisions can we deal in a rational way with the many non-rational aspects of the world." [28] And Quigley sought to elucidate as many divisions as necessary by approximating dates for all relevant phenomena and transitory periods.

Thus, added to the five-dimensional continuum of human experience and the eight-leveled continuum of human needs and cultural tasks, is a seven-stage civilization life cycle along a continuum of time. To comprehend this continuum, "the periodization should, ideally, depend on the causes of the cultural changes." [29] Whereas Toynbee, Spengler, and Vico saw change resulting from Darwinian strife, Quigley sought to understand the patterns in the conditions causing the strife. Quigley saw the strife occurring at the point where a social instrument becomes an institution and fails to respond adequately to societal needs. An instrument is a social organization that is fulfilling effectively the purpose for which it arose, to satisfy one of the eight basic human needs of the individuals in the society. An institution is an instrument that has taken on activities and purposes of its own, separate from and different from the purposes for which it was intended, and as a consequence it achieves its original purposes with decreasing effectiveness. That is, in an institution the organizational relationships become ends in themselves to the detriment of the ends of the whole organization. Quigley clarifies the evolutionary process leading inexorably to tension as the aggregate of the process transforming instruments into institutions, a process pervading all social phenomena.[30] As human needs are left unsatisfied by institutionalization struggle ensues between a group of discontents seeking to overthrow the institution and a vested-interest group seeking to continue benefitting from the institutionalization. This struggle is called the "tension of development" and from this tension and its ensuing controversy there may emerge any one of (or combination) among three possible outcomes: reform, in which the institution is reorganized and its methods of action are changed to become more of an instrument; circumvention, in which the institution is left with its privileges and vested interests intact, but its duties are taken away and assigned to a new instrument in society; or reaction, in which the vested interests triumph and the people of that society are doomed to ineffective achievement of their needs on that level for an indefinite period. Thus, historical development is concerned with the changes that take place on any single level of culture in a society.

This process of historical development takes place on innumerable levels of a society because there are innumerable levels to the culture. But "historical evolution" results from both historical development and "historical morphology", both acting simultaneously and reacting on each other. "Historical morphology" is concerned with the structures and the relationships between the different levels of society. Because of these structural interrelationship between the levels of the culture, there is an optimum point of historical development on each level of culture. When each level in relationship to the development of each other level is at the optimum point where morphological tension between the levels is minimal, then that society is responding to needs with the most efficient resource expenditure. Having established that the evolution of a society is a resultant of the two kinds of change termed development and morphology, Quigley can then concentrate on the historical evolution of a certain type of society, the civilization.

The pattern of change in civilizations Quigley presents consists of seven stages resulting from the fact that each civilization needs an instrument of expansion, which becomes an institution. The civilization rises while this organization is an instrument and declines as this organization becomes an institution. By "instrument of expansion", Quigley means that the society must be organized in such fashion that it engenders the three essential factors of "incentive to invest, accumulation of surplus, and application of this surplus to the new inventions."[31] The most important organization is that for capital accumulation which serves as the surplus-creating instrument, although there is not expansion unless the elements of invention and investment are also present. This surplus-creating instrument need not be economic organization, but can be a religious organization such as the tribute collecting Sumerian priesthood in the Mesopotamian civilization, a political organization such as the Egyptian state which collected taxes, or a social organization such as slavery in the Classical Age. Quigley, of course, finds many sources of capital accumulation in any society, a result of society's complexity, but there is generally only one of significance.

Like all instruments, an instrument of expansion in the course of time becomes an institution and the rate of expansion slows down. Though this processes of institutionalization is much more detrimental, it is the same as the institutionalization of any instrument, and appears specifically as a breakdown of one of the three necessary elements of production, usually in a decrease of the rate of investment. This decrease in the rate of investment occurs chiefly because the social group controlling the surplus ceases to apply it to new ways of doing things because they have a vested interest in the old way of doing things. Moreover, by a natural and unconscious self-indulgence, they begin to apply the surplus they control to non-productive but ego-satisfying purposes. When discussing the manners in which the vested interests prevent the fulfillment of human needs in a society, Quigley writes without the sobriety characteristic of most of his exposition. His scathing attacks on "the Establishment" in *Tragedy and Hope* made him the darling of John Birchers in America who saw him as "the Joseph Valachi of political conspiracy,"[32] And though he stated "I generally think that any conspiracy theory of history is nonsense"[33] the vehemence with which he blames the establishment for America's energy crisis[34] and financial problems among other things indicates that he considers them a powerful opponent blocking progress in contemporary western society. This stage of conflict, while clearly the most important, is only one of the seven stages of evolution for a society.

This process of the institutionalization of an instrument of expansion allows the understanding of why civilizations rise and fall by permitting the division of the process into seven stages. These stages are Mixture, Gestation, Expansion, Age of Conflict, Universal Empire, Decay, and Invasion.[35] Quigley's historiographical work on conceptualizing change in civilization is operationalized by examining a civilization through its correlation with this paradigm of seven stages.

Every society begins with the mixture of two or more cultures along their shared borders. But such casual cultural mixture is of little significance unless there comes into existence in the zone of mixture a new culture, arising from the mixture but different from the constituent parts. Also since cultural mixture occurs on the borders of societies, civilizations rarely succeed one another, but undergo a displacement in space. But more importantly, this new society undergoes a displacement of culture that necessitates it making choices on how to fulfill its needs free from the acculturization process of their original societies. The specific choices they make are unimportant so long as they are morphologically compatible to give rise to social custom and so long as enough members of the society subscribe to them. What is important is that if these choices can engender the necessary elements of an instrument of expansion in the formulative stage of gestation, that society can evolve into a civilization.

The next stage of a civilization is the exercise of its instrument of expansion through increased production of goods, increase in population of the society, increase in the geographic extent of the civilization, and in increase in knowledge, all of which comprise the Stage of Expansion. It is generally a period of vigorous change in political order and science. As the vigor promoting growth through the instrument of expansion in the society diffuses from the core area to the peripheral area of the society, the rate of expansion in the core area slows and it enters the Age of Conflict. This age is marked by growing tension of evolution and class conflicts, increasingly frequent and increasingly violent imperialist wars, and growing irrationality, pessimism, superstition, and other-worldliness. It is also marked by a shift from intensive expansion, that is by producing more goods with fewer resources but by better organization, to extensive expansion to satisfy increasing desires by using more resources with the same organization.

At this point the institution comes under attack by dissidents seeking reformation or circumvention to rejuvenate their instruments, which has seldom worked. The clearest case to be found is the evolution of our Western civilization where both reform and circumvention have occurred. As a result, Western civilization has had three periods of expansion, the first about 970-1270, the second about 1420-1650, and the third about 1725-1929. The instrument of expansion in the first was feudalism, which became institutionalized into chivalry. This was circumvented by a new instrument of expansion Quigley calls "commercial capitalism." When this organization became institutionalized into mercantilism, it was reformed into industrial capitalism, which became the instrument of expansion of the third age of expansion. By 1930 this organization had become institutionalized into monopoly capitalism, and the society was, for the third time, in a major era of crisis.[36]

As long a Western society is able to invigorate one instrument of expansion through reform or circumvention, it can remain viable. However, Quigley is not optimistic on our prospects of reform because of the nature of revolution as essentially a collision between power and law, the law supporting the numerous vested interests on all levels. These are challenged when some event suddenly crystallizes previously dispersed and disorganized discontents into a structure of power determined to a change obsolescent laws which are obstructing the satisfaction of needs. Success by the reformers depends on their ability to organize new organizational structures on all levels, structures which the population will recognize as instruments able to satisfy real needs, while "the success of the counter-revolutionary side depends on its success in persuading the people that their desires are true reflections of their needs and are to be identified with the existing structure of the vested interests."[37]

Quigley found the vested interests in contemporary society very strong. Thus, Quigley argued that:

"If Western Civilization reforms and again passes into Stage 3, it will be far too powerful to be defeated by Russian civilization; if Western Civilization does not reform, but continues through the Stage of Conflict into the Stage of Universal Empire, the threat fro^ Russian civilization will be much greater."[38]

This stage of Universal Empire is characterized by a single dominant political unit which stifles minor reforms of the other levels of society, thus making the society even less able to respond to the needs of its individuals. Even though this stage appears to be a period of relative peace and prosperity, it is illusionary and hides latent civil war and economic depression, which will reach fruition in the Stage of Decay. In the final stage, the Stage of Invasion, the civilization is no longer willing or able to defend itself and thus succumbs to outsiders from another younger civilization.

The seven stages thus presented are a convenient way of dividing a complex historical process, but this process is not relentlessly deterministic at all points but merely at some points, in the sense that men have power and free will but their actions have consequences nevertheless. Thus this historiography of morphological civilizations, which Quigley explores in many historical paradigms still places primary emphasis on cognition, a factor that above all others, man must understand.

The historical paradigms Quigley develops serve as the historian's cognitive system, much like any individual would use or misuse his general cognitive system; "Instead of dealing with life, we deal with our structuring of it."[39] Once the structure of the cognitive system is understood, as Quigley understood it, the resulting objectivity in methodology allows one to remain cognitive in assessing any human experiences.

Quigley believed his historical methodology was applicable to other academic disciplines, which he attempted to do in a number of articles.

One of the more controversial was his article on "Assumption and Inference on Human Origins" in which he challenged anthropologists to reappraise their sacrosanct paradigms on human origins, including the Darwinian construct of evolution resulting from materialist struggle:

> "The paradigms of the 19th century methods were analytical, isolating, quantitative, materialistic, objective, dualistic, etc. With these, great achievements were made, especially in the extension of factual knowledge and human powers. But this positivist, analytical method is now approaching marginal effectiveness, a condition in which relatively minor accretions of benefits will require gigantic allotments of resources."[40]

What he calls for is a dissolution of the consensus on materialist evolutionism by default of sufficient evidence on other hypotheses and a reappraisal of the basic cognitive assumptions on which this hypothesis is based. Quigley contends that the idea that man without artifacts is not human or that human relationships must take place through artifacts is the kind of dehumanized point of view against which the 20th century is in growing revolt; "The care of one person for another, leading to what Montagu has the courage to call 'love', is not only a reality of human experience but undoubtably a significant factor in human origins and human evolution."[41] Quigley's article was not intended as a general decrial of anthropology, as evidence in his remark that his professional work has rested primarily on an effort to apply anthropological methods to history. But he wished to compliment the holistic, comparative, and conceptualizing techniques prevalent in anthropology with the historian's perspective on the dimension of time and the processes of chronological change.[42]

A second such applied methodology article is "Our Ecological Crisis" in which he contends that "...the historical roots of our ecological crisis must be sought in the history of how our present attitudes towards nature and our fellow men came into existence."[43]

He begins the article with detailed definitions or degrees of "environmental pollution" as "the movement of objects by human action from places or conditions where they are natural or unobjectionable to places or conditions where they are unnatural, objectionable, and injurious."[44]

These detailed definitions exemplify Quigley's technique of extracting conceptual paradigms and then reenforcing or qualifying them with historical examples. After thus assessing and defining this contemporary phenomena, Quigley operationalizes it by asking "Why does our technology take such ecologically disruptive or destructive directions?"[45] a question stated in such a way as to avoid common assumptions and inferences. He then conceptualizes on how he will seek the historical roots of the crisis by stating that primary concerns are:

> "...organizational questions, the patterns of behavior in our society which form it into a functioning social system, together with our technology on one side (determining what we can do) and our outlook and value system on the other side (determining what we will want to do)... Thus *Outlook* acts on *Organizations* which handle *Technology* against the *Natural Environment*....This means: 1) that the causes and the remedies of our ecological crisis must be sought in changes in outlook; and 2) that changes in our technology and even in our organizational arrangements are at best, concerned with systems rather than with causes."[46]

It would perhaps come as no surprise to readers acquainted with Quigley that his historical analysis of the roots of the ecological crisis finds fault in the separation of man from nature by culture, Greek dualism, and the secularization of future preference, and the remedy in medieval Christian pantheism translated into contemporary ecological holism. But still his argument is compelling perhaps as much because of its structural simplicity as for the force of its historical examples. Quigley also uses this approach successfully on such diverse issues as American foreign policy, energy, African decolonization, and contemporary youth dissent, as well as in *Tragedy and Hope*.

A third example of his application of methodology is in his few attempts at foretelling new observations. Although Quigley was uncomfortable with predicting the future, he took the opportunity when reviewing Victor Ferkiss's book on *The Future of Technological Civilization*, to foretell the benefits or detriments of American society to reform itself along the lines he and Ferkiss present.[47]

Of much greater importance, however, is the work Quigley did as a consultant to the Department of Defense for many years on the development of weapons systems much of which is currently unavailable. Quigley recognized the military as an agent capable of effecting drastic change in society and thus it must be made compatible with the goals and existing structure of that society. Because of the lengthy lead time in developing weaponry systems, Quigley had to project the optimum weapon system by assessing how past civilizations influenced their weapons systems, how future civilizations will resemble past civilizations, the sociological impacts of past weapons systems, and the technological capabilities of future systems. Such a study exemplified the dynamic interrelationships among all factors in a certain aspect of civilization.[48]

Quigley clearly felt a proliferation of his cognitive insight into such diverse disciplines would bring about the change in outlook that could reform Western society. He felt our society has now largely lost its basic distinction between necessary and important, in which material things were necessary but spiritual things important. It is difficult to reform our old methods of thinking no matter how bankrupt they may be because standing in the way of reform are the pressures exerted by institutionalized establishments, the profits of powerful groups producing equipment based on old ways of thinking, the specialized scholars protecting their topic, and the need of bureauacratized organizations for persons with the narrow technical training of the older cognitive patterns. Because of this strong reaction by the vested interests, Quigley studied and sought to reform and strengthen the revolutionary tendencies of his students.

Quigley taught the historical methods he felt were the first step towards reform of the old methods of thinking. He told his students that he was trying to train executives rather than clerks, the distinction between the two being the distinction made between understanding and knowledge.[49] His forceful and wide-ranging lectures attacked the assumptions his students had perhaps never questioned.

Quigley intended these disquieting lectures to provide the cultural shock which leads to cognitive sophistication, which:

> "makes it possible to know both one's own cognitive system and that of any different group with which one works so that one may be able to translate both talk and action from one such system into the other, while recognizing the conventional and arbitrary nature of both."[50]

Any executive capable of using his vocabulary of talk and action with such cognitive sophistication is capable of understanding many things. While reflecting on the precarious position of our contemporary society coping with its third Age of Conflict, Quigley noted that "civilization is the race between education and catastrophe." Quigley, with his perceptive insight into our cognitive system, invaluably advanced the cause of education.

SELECTED BIBLIOGRAPHY

Works by Carroll Quigley:

- "America's Future in Energy." *Current History*. 69 (July 1975): 1-5.
- "Assumption and Inference on Human Origins." *Current Anthropology*. 12. (October-December 1971): 519-540.
- "Cognitive Factors in the Evolution of Civilizations." *Main Currents in Modern Thought*. 29 (November-December 1972): 69-75.
- "The Creative Writer Today." *Catholic World*. 206 (December 1967): 111-117.
- "The Evolution of Civilizations: An Introduction to Historical Analysis". *Indianapolis: Liberty Press*, 1979.
- "Falsification of a Source in Risorgimenta History." *Journal of Modern History*. 20 (September 1948): 223-26.
- "Letter to the Editor." *Washington Post*, 26 October 1974.
- "Major Problems of Foreign Policy." *Current History*. 55 (October 1968): 199-206.
- "Needed: A Revolution in Thinking." *National Education Association Journal*. 57 (May 1968): 8-10.
- "Public Authority and the State in the Western Tradition: A Thousand Years of Growth, 976-1976."The Oscar Iden Lectures. Washington: School of Foreign Service, Georgetown University, 1977.
- "The Search for a Solution to the World Crisis." *Futurist*. 9 (March 1975): 38-41.
- "Our Ecological Crisis." *Current History*. 59 (July 1970): 1-12.
- Tragedy and Hope: A History of the World in Our Time. New York: The Macmillan Company, 1966.
- Washington, D. C. Georgetown University Special Collections. Carroll Quigley Papers.

REFERENCES

1. Carroll Quigley, "Education and the Academic Process," memorandum to the Georgetown University School of Foreign Service Dean's Office, 1971, p. 3.
2. Quigley, "Letter to the Editor", Washington Post, October 26, 1974.

3. Quigley, Tragedy and Hope: A History of the World in Our Time (New York: The Macmillan Company, 1966), p. xi.
4. Obituary of Carroll Quigley, Washington Star, January 6, 1977.
5. Quigley, "Assumption and Inference on Human Origins", Current Anthropology 12 (October-December 1971): 536.
6. Quigley, The Evolution of Civilizations: An Introduction to Historical Analysis (Indianapolis: Liberty Press, 1979), p. 33.
7. Quigley, "Assumption and Inference on Human Origins", 538.
8. Quigley, "Falsification of a Source in Risorgimento History," Journal of Modern History 20 (September 1948): 223-26.
9. Quigley, Evolution of Civilizations, p. 34.
10. Ludwig von Bertalanffy, General System Theory: Foundations, Development, Applications (New York: George Braziller, 1968).
11. Quigley, "Public Authority and the State in the Western Tradition: A Thousand Years of Growth, 976-1976, The Oscar Iden Lectures (Washington: Georgetown University School of Foreign Service, 1977), p. 1.
12. An unpublished article for the Georgeqvy/5\n University Hoya, ca. 1972, p. 4.
13. Quigley, Evolution of Civilizations, p. 346.
14. Ibid.
15. Quigley, "Structuring History" (1971) mimeographed.
16. Quigley, Tragedy and Hope, p. 1233.
17. Quigley, "The Creative Writer Today," Catholic World 206 (December 1967): 111-112.
18. Quigley, "Needed: A Revolution in Thinking," National Education Association Journal 57 (May 1968): 42.
19. Ibid.
20. Quigley, Evolution of Civilizations, p. 296.
21. Ibid.
22. Ibid., p. 131.
23. Ibid., pp. 59-60.
24. Ibid., p. 64
25. Quigley, Notes to Papers Presented at American Association for the Advancement of Science Meeting? Washington, D. C, 1972.
26. Quigley, Evolution of Civilizations, p. 142.
27. Ibid., p. 95.
28. Ibid., p. 98.
29. Ibid., p. 128.

30. bid., p. 115.
31. Ibid., p. 132.
32. Gary Allen, None Dare Call It Conspiracy (Rossmoor, Ca: Concord Press, 1971), p. 22-3.
33. "The Professor Who Knew Too Much" Potomac magazine, The Washington Post, 23 March 1975, pp. 17.
34. Quigley, "America's Future in Energy." Current Hi story.69 (July 1975): 1-5. 25
35. Ibid.
36. Ibid., pp. 348-414.
37. Quigley, "The Structure of Revolutions, With Applications to the French Revolution," pp. 14-15.
38. Quigley, Evolution of Civilizations, p. 166.
39. Quigley, "Lecture to Inter-American Defense Council," (Washington, 1973), p. 6.
40. Quigley, "Assumption and Inference," p. 536.
41. "Falsification of a Source in Risorgimenta History." Journal of Modern History 20 (September 1948): 223-26.
42. Ibid. p. 536.
43. Quigley, "Our Ecological Crisis," Current History 59 (July 1970): 1
44. Ibid.
45. Ibid., p. 4.
46. Ibid.
47. Quigley, "The Search for a Solution to the World Crisis, "The Futurist" 9 (March 1975): 38-41.
48. Quigley, "A Historical Projection of Tomorrow's World" prepared for the Sea-Based Deterrence Summer Study-Panel 1, 1964, pp. 1-23.
49. Ibid., p. 420
50. Quigley, "Needed: A Revolution in Thinking," p. 42.
51. Untitled, unpublished article for Georgetown Hoya, p. 6.

COMPARATIVE NATIONAL CULTURES

Address given on November 13, 1957, at The Industrial College of the Armed Forces and later published as iCAF Publication No. L58-54.

INTRODUCTION
Colonel T. L. Crystal, Jr., USAF,
Member of the Faculty, ICAF

SPEAKER
Dr. Carroll Quigley, Professor of History,
School of Foreign Service, Georgetown University.

INTRODUCTION

Dr. Carroll Quigley, Professor of History, School of Foreign Service, Georgetown University, was born in Boston, Massachusetts, 9 November 1910. He was educated at Boston Latin School and at Harvard University, obtaining an A.B. (magna cum laude) in 1933, an M.A. in 1934 and a Ph.D. in 1938. He was an instructor in History at Princeton University from 1935 to 1937, leaving there to do research work at the public archives of Paris and Milan on the Woodberry Lowery Traveling Fellowship of Harvard University. While abroad he wrote his doctoral dissertation on "The Public Administration of the Napoleonic Kingdom of Italy, 1805-1814." From 1938 to 1941 he was instructor and tutor in the Division of History, Government and Economics at Harvard University. Since 1941 he has been at the School of Foreign Service at Georgetown University, first as lecturer in History and Civilization and now as Professor of European History. He is regarded as an authority on the comparative history of civilizations and the history of Europe in the 20th century.

He is a member of the American Historical Association, the American Economic Association, the American Anthropological Association, and other learned societies. He is engaged at present in writing a book on world history in the 20th century Europe. His most recent published work is "The Origin and Diffusion of Oculi" in *The American Neptune* for January 1958. This is Dr, Quigley's fifth lecture at the College.

COMPARATIVE NATIONAL CULTURES

13 November 1957

COLONEL CRYSTAL: Good morning.

We have the privilege this morning of welcoming back to this platform a friend of long standing. Until I met the Doctor this morning, I really was going to say "an old friend," because anybody who has done as much for as long a period as Dr. Quigley has for the Industrial College, I felt, must have a long gray beard. But in this age of DDT and penicillin he has preserved his facilities remarkably well.

I'd like to tell you a little bit about what his business is. He is a professional historian at the School of Foreign Service at Georgetown University. One of the methods they use there is to help the student to form an idea of the process of social development by obtaining a broader perspective and understanding of the past of our civilization, the meaning of great movements in the past, with special emphasis on their effects on our present civilization. And he has been trying to do this for some years with us.

Evidence of it is contained in some of the documents which have been published by us and to which I strongly recommend you: The pre-Revolutionary History of the Soviet Union, a brilliant presentation that lets you understand a little better where the Muscovites came from; The Development of the Soviet Economy—his lecture on this subject last year—and finally, and to me as a student, of even greater importance, is his bibliography on the economic potential of the Soviet Union and its satellites.

I'll give you one example of how a professional teacher helps students, because in an area which is difficult to find much about, labor in the Soviet Union, he has listed Deutscher, I., Soviet Trade Unions: Their Place in Soviet Labor Policy, an I.R.R.A. publication, and Hubbard, L. E., Soviet Labour and Industry. So in your research in this course of human resources don't neglect what the Doctor has already made available to us in our library.

He has also annotated it with critical comments on the biases of the authors, and this is that understanding perspective about which professional historians probably know more than most people in other areas of dispute and contention. History is one of those areas. In his biography you've probably read his latest contribution to scholarly work. I've not made arrangements with the magazine to get a specially reduced rate on the American Neptune for January, because I am one of those who is rather perplexed at exactly what the Origin and Diffusion of Oculi means. If any of you share my confusion, I want to admit that the amount of lexicographical research that I did last night only heightens my confusion, because I found the word "oculus" to mean, anatomically, an eye. In architecture, it's a circular hole in the middle of the western facade of most Gothic cathedrals. It is also the circular hole in the top of the dome of the Pantheon. In an astronomical manner it's the Corona Borealis. In botany it is a leafbud or an astringent plant. In chronology it's the third Sunday in Lent. In lapidology it's an opal, the *oculus mundi*. In zoology it can be called the crab's eye.

Well, without further ado, Doctor, you know you're among friends. We're very happy to have you here. I am proud to present to the class Dr. Carroll Quigley.

DR. QUIGLEY: I think it's a shame to interrupt that. He speaks very well, and it's the most fascinating subject I've ever heard discussed. But he's not a good man with the dictionary. I guess he didn't get the right dictionary.

The oculi I am talking about are the eyes painted on the front of ships in Asia and the East Coast of Africa. They have eyes painted so the ship can see where it is going, according to some people. One of the arguments in my article is that it is not to provide the ship with a way of seeing where it's going, but something else. But don't rush out and buy the American Neptune, because they'll run out. I don't think they publish more than a handful of them.

PART 1

Today I'm going to speak about the cultural development of two great areas. I don't expect to give you much new information. What, rather, I'd like to do is to define rather sharply some of the information you may have and above all to show the relationship between things that you already know.

I want to begin by pointing out that we have a world today consisting of three great parts. At the center is the Soviet bloc. Around that is the fringe of shattered cultures which I call the buffer fringe, running from the Islamic countries in the west through Afghanistan, India, Burma, and the rest of them to eastern Asia. I call that the buffer fringe. Outside of that we have our own Western bloc. Today I'm going to say nothing at all about the Soviet bloc except that I will say something about China, dealing with it as if it were a part of the buffer fringe, because as a historian I am always a decade or even centuries behind the times, and I'll be talking about China as it was a generation or more than a generation ago.

I'll speak, then, only of the buffer fringe and of our own Western civilization. What I'm going to do, very simply, is go through a series of developments in the order in which they appeared in our own Western civilization. Then I will examine the order in which these developments occurred in the buffer fringe and show you how the difference in order of occurrence is of major significance in creating the problems of the buffer fringe area.

Table 1. Development sequence in the Western World and the buffer fringe

The Western World	The Buffer Fringe
1. Western ideology	1. Weapons
2. Commercial revolution, 1440	2. Commercial crisis
3. Revolution in weapons (especially firearms), 1500	3. Transportation and communications
4. Agricultural revolution, 1720	4. Sanitation and medicine
5. Industrial Revolution, 1780	5. Demographic explosion
6. Revolution in sanitation, 1800	6. Industry
7. Demographic explosion, 1820	7. Agricultural revolution
8. Revolution in transportation and communications	8. Western ideology

On the left of Table 1 is shown the order in which they occurred in our civilization. When I speak of "our Western civilization" I am talking about that area of the globe which runs from Poland westward to New Zealand. The civilization that I have reference to, our own Western civilization, began about 550 A. D.; and thus it has existed for almost a thousand years and a half.

Now, the first occurrence in Western civilization, the first great development, is our ideology. It's something I could speak about endlessly, as you know. But I want simply to refer to certain basic things in the outlook of Western ideology, particularly in the first 1,000 years of its existence, because that 1,000 years of Western ideology became the foundation for many of these later developments.

When I speak of Western ideology I refer specifically to religion—Christianity—to such things as the scientific outlook; and to a third thing, which I will call the liberal outlook. It may not be clear to you as I speak, because in all of this I am oversimplifying most drastically; I hope you will understand that. But it would seem to me that there is a common element to all three of these—the Christian outlook, the scientific outlook, and the liberal outlook—and to sum it up, rather briefly the outlook is this:

All three believe that there is a truth somewhere. They all believe that it is worthwhile seeking that truth. They all believe that the process by which we seek that truth is a process in which we approach it in time; that is, truth is something which unfolds in time. Therefore we must constantly work and strive and discuss in order to get closer and closer and closer to the truth, which we perhaps never reach. This is why scientists don't stop work today in the smug idea that they have the truth; but they have to go on struggling, because what they have today is simply an approximation of the truth.

Another characteristic of all three of these is that the unfolding of truth in time results from a cooperative effort. That is, it's a social effort. It arises from discussion, criticism, and so forth; and from that emerges a kind of consensus, which is closer to the truth than would be the point of view of any single individual. So thus we have that there is a truth. This is not a skeptical outlook. It is not a dogmatic outlook because nobody now has the truth. It puts great emphasis on chronological development. It puts great emphasis upon social cooperation. Some of this may not seem convincing to you, and I imagine that the field in which it will not seem convincing is perhaps the field of religion. But the Christian religion basically does have this outlook.

It believes that religious truth has been unfolded in time. That is, we had a whole series of revelations and prophets. We have the Old Testament, that was not replaced but supplemented by the New Testament, and the New Testament has been interpreted and unfolded in the course of time to reveal additional truth. And the process of religious appreciation still goes on. Am I right?

Now, one other thing that I should emphasize about the Western ideology and particularly the Christian ideology is this: It is not a dualistic ideology. This is a point which many people, I think, misunderstand, because there has been a tendency, at least in the last 500 years, for the Christian or religious outlook to be dualistic. By that I mean that they oppose the material world to the spiritual world. But this was not fundamentally the point of view of the religious outlook of Western civilization for at least the first 1,000 years. During the first 1,000 years, they recognized the basic necessity of the material world. I could point this out in a number of ways. They made a distinction between what was necessary and what was important. Material things were necessary; spiritual things were important. But you could not achieve spiritual things except by working through the material world.

The Christians felt, for example, that we could not be saved except for the fact that God became man in a real body living in this world. We cannot be saved unless we supplement God's grace with good works in this world. So that the religious outlook is social. It is also materialistic. And in the first church council in 325, the Council of Nicaea, where the creed was first stated, they said most explicitly that they believed in the resurrection of the body, indicating their point of view, which is the really basic Christian point of view, that the body is not an evil or bad thing, but is indeed a good thing, made in the image and likeness of God, and a thing which is necessary to our salvation, because only with a body can we do good things to our neighbors in this world.

I have perhaps said too much about that, but the reason I'm emphasizing it is this: I feel very strongly that this point of view, which I am trying to describe here, which I will call the Western outlook, and which, as I showed you, appeared in religion, in the scientific outlook, and, I am sure you understand, in liberalism believes there is a truth, which can be reached by discussion, as a social achievement. Therefore there must be freedom of speech, freedom of discussion, and these other things, no one has the truth. Therefore no one has the right to impose his "truth" upon others. Rather, as we talk around the truth, each of us gets a fragment of it; and by contributing our fragment to a common discussion, we will get a truth which is closer to the ultimate truth than would be the point of view of any one of us. Now, this, it seems to me, this outlook, is the real explanation of why Western civilization has been so prosperous, so wealthy, and so powerful—because it has been the most wealthy and most powerful civilization that ever existed.

Now, I wish to go on to the next thing. But I must, before I speak of the commercial revolution, indicate the basic structure upon which the commercial revolution was imposed. That basic structure you must be familiar with, I am sure. In the Middle Ages, about the year 1000, Western Europe was organized in a series of self-contained, self-sufficient economic units. We call them manors. Each manor tried to produce everything it needed, and over it was a fighting man, a knight.

The serfs on the manor did no fighting, and were not really expected to be fighters; but they produced goods from the soil. The feudal lords, on the other hand, were fighting specialists and were never expected to till the soil. Thus you got a rigid class structure of an upper class, 2 percent of the population, the feudal knights; and a lower class, the serfs, perhaps 97 percent of the population. The other odd percent is going to the clergy, who were really to a certain extent part of the upper class or part of the lower class depending upon whether they were upper clergy or lower clergy. This system was a system of a rigid class structure and above all with economic self-sufficiency of the unit. A manor was a self-sufficient agrarian unit supporting a fighting knight. There was almost no commerce.

Beginning about the year 1440, although it had begun hundreds of years earlier in a small way, we got this tremendous development that we call the commercial revolution. That is, there was an influx of money. We got a substitution of money arrangements for personal arrangements, and the whole development which we call the commercial revolution.

Now, this commercial revolution—the growth of commerce, the growth of a money economy—led ultimately to specialization, economic division of labor, increasing exchange, and a higher level of economic efficiency. Manors could now specialize on those things that they could produce best and could exchange them for money, which could be used to command the products of other manors, other areas, or other social groups which were specializing on those things that they could best do. We call this the commercial revolution.

All right. That's obvious enough.

The next development is the revolution in weapons, particularly firearms. This is something with which you are certainly familiar—the arrival of gunpowder and the rest of it, the increasing efficiency of missile weapons.

But I wish to emphasize here one thing which some of you may never have thought of, and it is this: It seems to me, looking over the whole course of history, that the kinds of weapon a society possesses are a major factor in determining the structure of that society. To oversimplify once again a very complicated subject, I would like to divide weapons into two kinds—what I call amateur weapons on one side and what I call professional weapons or specialist weapons on the other hand. The distinction between these two is approximately this: Amateur weapons are cheap to obtain and easy to use. Specialist weapons are expensive to obtain and difficult to use.

To define those terms a little bit, when I say "cheap" and "easy" in reference to amateur weapons, I mean that an amateur weapon which can be obtained as a result of a few weeks or a few months of work I would call cheap. A weapon which could be used as the result of a few weeks or a few months of practice I would call easy to use. On the other hand, professional weapons can be so expensive that only a very small minority of the society can possess them. And now, as you well know, they can be so tremendously expensive that only very wealthy governments can possess them. So specialist weapons thus can be expensive, but they generally also are difficult to use, in the sense that they can be used only by trained personnel who have practiced at it not for weeks or months, but for years.

Now, this distinction between amateur weapons and professional weapons is of tremendous significance in forming the structure of a society, in this sense: When you have amateur weapons as the best weapons available in a society, you have as the best weapon something which can be obtained by almost everyone and can be used by almost everyone. In such a society, where the amateur form of a weapon is the best obtainable weapon, you would have a situation where people would be relatively equal in power, because each can have the best available weapon. In a society where people are in fact relatively equal in power, in a showdown the majority can compel the minority to yield.

In such a situation you ultimately will get some kind of a legal expression of the fact that people are equal in power and that a majority can compel a minority to consent. This leads us to democracy, it seems to me that if you look at the history of any civilization or even the whole history of mankind, you will see that if we were to graph a cycle between amateur weapons and professional weapons, we would see that the periods in which professional weapons become supreme, going upward, let us say, are generally followed by periods in which authoritarian governments are established. On the other hand, periods in which amateur weapons are supreme are generally followed by periods, and very closely followed, within a mere couple of generations, by periods in which more democratic regimes are established.

Now, to look at this in the whole of human history would take us much too much time. I do it sometimes in my courses at the university, but here I simply wish to look at Western civilization .

In Western civilization at the beginning, let us say back in the year 1000, you had, as I pointed out a moment ago, a very rigid class structure, in which the minority had the best weapons. In the year 1000 there were two outstanding weapons available—the mounted knight on horseback and the stone castle. The stone castle was a defensive weapon. Here is a strange situation—a society with two supreme weapons which cannot defeat each other—because a mounted knight on horseback could not capture a stone castle and a stone castle could not destroy a mounted knight on horseback. But in any case this was definitely a period of specialist weapons.

A castle was obviously expensive, but a mounted knight was also a very expensive thing. The horse of a knight was, back in the year 1000, worth 60 oxen, and an ox was too expensive for the ordinary peasant to afford. Thus a horse was more expensive, 60 times more expensive, than what an ordinary peasant could afford. And a knight of this kind had to have two horses. He had to have armor and weapons, all of them very expensive. He had to have a long period of training. He started to train at least by the age of 10, and he was regarded as a trained knight not much before the age of 20. Thus it would take 10 years of training. So you had thus a specialist weapon. The peasants couldn't possibly cope with it. They had no weapons which could possibly deal with it.

Furthermore, if that knight had a castle, he had a supreme defensive weapon. If anyone gave him orders: "Do this" or "Do that" he could get in his castle and say, "Nuts" and no one could make him obey, because they could not capture the castle. Now, I won't give you any reason for this except to say that a feudal knight such as I have described was expected to serve each year only 40 days or approximately that; and you could not capture a castle with feudal knights, even if you had a large number of them, because you couldn't starve a castle out in 40 days. Well, now changes occurred. But here you had a political and military system where the defense was supreme. The defense was extremely decentralized—with each castle becoming a nucleus of resistance to authority, and where the weapons were expensive, specialized weapons. Thus you had an authoritarian, decentralized political system.

Now, as you know, that was replaced later by an authoritarian, centralized system. And it was replaced because of the appearance of gunpowder and cannon, because fewer people could have gunpowder and cannon than could have castles and thus the nuclei of political organization became larger, organizing in each case around the center of whoever could afford cannon.

Now, those people who could afford cannon ultimately became kings. They took royal titles. They could knock down the castle of the knight. They could also raise more money with their weapons. They thus worked out a system whereby they hired knights. Hired knights could capture castles, because they could besiege them and starve them out, staying there as long as their pay continued to be paid. It's a very complicated process, but what I am trying to show you here is that you shifted from a defensive weapon which was supreme and decentralized but specialist, the medieval knight with a castle, 300 or 400 years later to a system where you had a still very expensive specialized weapon, much more centralized because fewer people could afford it and have it, but which was not defensive. It was much more offensive. And as a result, political units which previously had been organized around castles now began to organize in much larger areas. Ultimately those large areas became great duchies, principalities, and kingdoms.

Now, as this process continued, weapons became cheaper and cheaper. By the year 1800 approximately the best available weapon, or perhaps I should make it later, 1870, the best weapon available was cheap enough to be obtained by almost anyone. A rifle in 1860 or 1870 or a Colt revolver could be obtained from the work of a man over a period of a few weeks at most, and that was as good a weapon as employees of the government had. Thus you had a democratic amateur weapon. It could be widely dispersed, and in the political reflection of this military fact you got democratic regimes.

The last democratic uprising in this country, Dorr's Rebellion, in 1842, showed clearly, as earlier in Europe the French Revolution and other events had shown, that if the mass of the people have these weapons, they could not be compelled to obey by government troops who had the same weapons. Thus you got democracy.

Since then the trend in weapons has been definitely away from amateur weapons and toward specialist weapons, as you know. Today, a government certainly can have those weapons which are too expensive for people to have. Therefore governments today certainly can compel the people to obey.

And unless in the future, as I hope but I am not certain—perhaps I hope in vain—there is some development in the effectiveness of guerrilla warfare, so that it becomes once again difficult for a government to compel obedience of groups which wish to refuse obedience, unless that occurs, it would seem to me almost inevitable that political development would follow along behind the military development; specifically that authoritarian governments must replace democratic governments in most places, just as specialist weapons have replaced or are replacing amateur weapons.

I would hope that perhaps sometime, as I say, guerrilla weapons and guerrilla methods of warfare will make it impossible to compel obedience with the very expensive weapons which governments will possess. I do see some vague indications in that direction; but, being a historian rather than a fortune teller, I will say no more about it.

Well, now, that will give us the revolution in weapons. The next thing is the agricultural revolution. Here again is a very complicated subject, which I must go through quite rapidly. I spoke about the medieval manor. In the year 1000 the medieval manor had a three-field rotation system, a fallow-rotation system. They planted each field 2 years. The third year it was left fallow, unplanted; and this would recoup, presumably, some of the nutrient elements in the soil, particularly nitrogen from the nitrogen in the air.

Now, this system was a wonderful system back in the year 600. But by the year 1600 a better system was beginning to appear. And that second stage in the development of agriculture, the first stage being the self-sufficient manor on a fallow-rotation system, began to appear as early as 1600. The date I have given you here is 1720, when it really systematically began to be applied in eastern England, particularly Norfolk. This second stage is the leguminous-rotation system, in which a leguminous crop, whose roots trap the nitrates from the air, was put in the fallow part of the cycle. So thus you could plant your crops every year and not have to leave fields fallow. Instead of leaving them fallow, you put in some such leguminous crop as clover or alfalfa or something of that kind. This immensely increased the nitrogen content of the soil for the subsequent year, in which you planted grain or some other food crop.

Notice that when you put a leguminous crop into this fallow part of the old three-field cycle, you are planting a crop which is not consumable by men. Clover and alfalfa are not foods, but they can be feeds. And thus the agricultural revolution, by putting a leguminous crop into the old cycle, was providing great stores of fodder for farm animals. The results of this were revolutionary. In the Middle Ages farm animals had to go out and forage for themselves, looking for whatever hadn't been picked. Thus animals in the Middle Ages were excluded out from the arable field and had to shift for themselves outside. As a result of the agricultural revolution you now had lots of fodder, you had the fields all the time under crops each year, you could not permit the animals to range freely, so you included them in. You put fences around them; instead of, as in the Middle Ages, around the arable field, you now put the fence around the animal. And you could now feed him in a contained area with the leguminous crop to provide his fodder.

As a result of this, the slaughter weight of farm animals in Smithfield, England, approximately tripled in the space of 85 years. That is, from 1710-95 the slaughter weight of lambs, for example, went up from 18 pounds to more than 50 pounds. The sizes of all farm animals drastically increased. This is something that we don't generally think of, but in the Middle Ages animals were very small, and men were also quite small, which explains why modern man has such difficulty getting into medieval armor. If you had the armor of medieval horses, you would also discover that a modern horse couldn't get into it, because cattle and horses have all increased in size.

Now, that is the second stage in the agricultural revolution — the leguminous rotation.

About 1840 we got into a third stage. That was the chemical fertilizer stage. This chemical fertilizer had combined with it farm machinery. In Germany about 1840 a German chemist discovered or at least propagated the idea of putting a chemical fertilizer into the ground. And about the same time, as you know, in America and other places, McCormick and other people began to invent farm machinery, such as the famous invention of the reaper. This is the third stage — the chemical-machinery stage. The fourth stage in the development of this agricultural revolution has occurred in the present century — the use of hybrid crops which give immensely greater output, plus the use of all kinds of sprays and chemicals.

Thus we have four stages, successively, in the agricultural revolution. But the importance of the whole thing is that one man can produce today immensely more food than one man could 800 or 900 years ago. I don't know exactly how true these figures are, but I have read somewhere that if you were to go back 500 years, it took approximately 17 men to produce enough food for 21. That would mean that if you had 17 people tilling the soil as a full-time job, you could allow only four people to go off and do something else — governing the country, fighting in armies, or making handicrafts or whatever it might be.

Those figures have been more than reversed. Today four men, I would believe, under the best modern conditions could produce enough food approximately for close to a hundred people. What this means is that we have released by this tremendous agricultural revolution over the centuries enormous amounts of manpower for nonfood-producing activities.

All right. Now we go on to the next big development here, the Industrial Revolution. The Industrial Revolution is also something which goes through successive stages. I won't really annoy you with the stages, because you certainly must be familiar with them. I generally divide them at least into two — the external combustion engine — that's the steam engine — about the year 1780 or so; and then the internal combustion engine, about 120 or 125 years later. Then after that the revolution has continued, as you know.

Now, the Industrial Revolution allowed men to produce more and more and more nonfood products, industrial products, the craft products, with an hour of work. As you know, products per man-hour as a result of the Industrial Revolution greatly increased, because the essential feature of the Industrial Revolution is not the factory or the growth of cities or the use of capital or any of these other things which are so frequently mentioned, and should be mentioned; but the essential feature of the Industrial Revolution is the use of nonliving power for production — the power from nonliving sources, such as coal and ultimately oil, waterpower, and other sources, And we hope, I suppose, that ultimately we will have atomic sources.

Now, let me stop at this point very briefly to point out to you the wonderful sequence of events here. If we were to study the history of Europe, we would find in it, I am sure, much poverty, much hardship and misery — that is true — but the hardship and misery and poverty were more or less incidental in this process. They weren't intrinsic to the process. In order to demonstrate that I will simply ask: What is necessary for industrialism?

Well, for industrialism you need labor and food, which are approximately the same thing. You need capital. You need invention. These things are provided by the earlier stages here. Invention came out of this Western ideology and the whole urge to innovate and provide better ways of doing things. The capital which was necessary to finance the Industrial Revolution came out of the profits of earlier developments, out of the commercial revolution, where people made great fortunes, for example, in India and other places. The capital to a certain extent also came out of the agricultural revolution, where those people who first adopted the agricultural revolution were able to make extraordinary profits out of it, particularly in Norfolk, England, and other places. In spite of the fact that the soil of Norfolk is poor soil, the agricultural revolution gave a tremendous increase in output there, which gave large profits to the Coke family and other great families of that area.

The Industrial Revolution required food. The agricultural revolution provided the food. The agricultural revolution also provided the labor which was necessary, because if fewer people can produce more food, then you can release manpower to go into industry. Thus we see that each stage here to a very considerable extent is built upon the preceding stages. And it happens in an order which is not the result of any cleverness on our part. It's very much, it seems to me, the result of happy accident or the favor of God or something of that kind. It certainly wasn't, I think, any planning which gave us this.

Now, we turn to the next development—the revolution in sanitation. This development also I would like to divide into successive stages, going over them very rapidly.

The sanitation revolution began about the end of the 18th century. The first steps in it were such things as vaccination, which came in the 1770's, and isolation—the discovery, for example, that diseases such as plague and so forth could be curtailed by isolation of the sick—but, above all, the discovery that smallpox could be controlled by vaccination. And by the year 1800 there were people who were frenziedly working in Europe to vaccinate Europe.

I remember in my doctorate dissertation I did research in the Archives in Milan and I came across a Dr. Sacco, who spent his whole life apparently 20 hours a day, year after year, trying to vaccinate people in northern Italy faster than people were being born in northern Italy. At that time Napoleon was the king of Italy, after 1805. Every year Sacco sent in a report and in the report he divided up Napoleon's northern Italy into departments. He took the number of people born and the number he had vaccinated in each department; and in any department where he hadn't vaccinated at least as many as were born, he had a word of apology and explanation as to why he couldn't do it—insufficient funds, insufficient time, insufficient assistance, and so forth. Well, this is what I mean by the first stage of this revolution in sanitation—the vaccination-isolation stage.

Well, approximately 60 or 70 years later we got the second stage in the sanitation revolution; that is, the stage that we might call the antiseptic stage. We associate it with the work of Pasteur and Lord Lister, which showed very clearly that most disease is due to microbes, and by controlling the microbe you can control the disease. This was, of course, a tremendous step forward.

Now, again, later in our own century we have had tremendous revolutionary developments in sanitation and in general medicine associated with the antibiotics, chemistry, surgical techniques, artificial valves in hearts, and all kinds of such things. The result of this is that by the revolution in sanitation we have drastically reduced the death rate, leading to a birth increase in population.

That is a perfectly satisfactory thing, because if we increase the population as a result of item six, we have the food to feed them as the result of item four, and we have tasks for them to do as the result of item five. In other words, they follow along once again in a sequence which makes sense and which is helpful to any country or civilization which wishes to absorb it.

Now we come to the demographic explosion. The demographic explosion results from the revolution in sanitation, and I would like to look at table 2 at this point to show you.

Table 2. The Demographic Cycle

	Stage A	Stage B	Stage C	Stage D
Birth rate	High	High	Falling	Low
Death rate	High	Falling	Low	Rising
Numbers	Stable	Rising	Stable	Falling
Age distribution	Many young (below 18)	Many in prime (18-45)	Many middle-aged (over 30)	Many old (over 50)

PART 2

Demographers frequently divide changes in population into four successive stages which they call the demographic cycle. And those authorities in population here will bear with me if I simplify too much. The first stage is stage A. It has four characteristics—a high birth rate; a high death rate; as a result of stable population, in which the population numbers remain approximately the same; and in that population numbers remain approximately the same; and in that population an age distribution in which there are many people who are young. In fact, half of the population would be perhaps considerably less than 18 years of age. Now, the high birth rate means that you have many being born, but the high death rate means that at least a fifth of them, possibly a third of them, die in the first 2 years of their life. That means, of course, that those who survive are a pretty rugged bunch. They have met all the germs, or almost all the germs, and conquered them; and they may live to a ripe old age. That, we call stage A.

Now, what happens is, apparently, that something in the society leads to a falling death rate. In most societies, as we look back over history, the falling death rate was caused originally, it would seem, by an increased output of food, conquering the problem of malnutrition. But at the same time the increased output of food allows more devotion to sanitation and health, more research in medicine, more thought about these matters, and so forth. Thus you begin to conquer the death rate for other reasons than the overcoming of malnutrition, namely, by the overcoming of diseases. Thus you get a falling death rate while the birth rate is still high, which will give you obviously a rising number of people, the third characteristic.

In that stage B you will have many people in the prime of life. By "many" I mean at least half of the population. A society which is in stage B is a society which, demographically speaking, is at its most healthy and most vigorous and most powerful stage, because many men, the majority of men, are in their productive years, and the majority of women are in their fertile years. Therefore you have a society which can remedy disasters to population, which can remedy disasters in production, by more activity of women, more activity of men, and more activity of the two together. Now, that system, stage B, is followed by stage C, in which the birth rate begins to fall, the death rate remains low, and as a result you begin once again to approach a stable population, in which the population in numbers is not drastically increasing any more; the rate of increase is slowing up.

In that society you will have many middle-aged people. I am ashamed of myself for calling people over 30 middle-aged, particularly as last Saturday I had my 47th birthday myself, which makes me, you see, well over middle age. But what I mean here is that in this stage C, with a falling birth rate, low death rate, and stable numbers, you have at least half of your population over the age of 30 and possibly even over the age of 35.

Now, these three stages, A, B, and C, are based largely upon observation of what has happened. Stage D is hypothetical, because I don't know of any culture where we can say for sure that stage D has happened. But it would seem that if you had A, B, and C and the process continues, you will reach D. In D you would have many old people, because of the decline in the death rate, perhaps half the population over 45 years of age, you are going to have a low birth rate, but you are also going to have a rising death rate, because where we have conquered the diseases of youth, we have not yet conquered the diseases of old age, such as cardiac disease, cancer, and other diseases associated with old age. Thus in stage D you will get a situation where the population presumably would be falling. In our Western civilization this cycle has been experienced, at least through the first three stages, and we will presume that the fourth is about due to come up, if it hasn't already begun to knock at the door. In table 3, the letters A, B, C, and D refer to the four stages of the demographic cycle. The table shows which stage would be found at the dates listed on the left in the four geographic areas mentioned at the top.

From the table it is clear that the demographic cycle is not simultaneous everywhere. On the contrary, it began in Western Europe and has spread outward to other areas. As you can see all four areas that I have here—three in Europe and one in Asia—by "Asia" meaning the buffer fringe—all four areas were presumably in stage A in the year 1700. But Western Europe came out of it and got into stage B, passed into C, and I suppose that by the year 2000 will be in D. Central Europe is a little bit later in the phases. So they don't get to stage B until 1850 and they don't get to stage C until 1950, and so forth. They were a little bit late. Eastern Europe is even later.

For example, in 1938 in Bulgaria the death rate of infant mortality in the first year of life, was over 20 percent—something which would be regarded as absolutely unacceptable in Western Europe or central Europe in the year 1938. And thus we have that in Eastern Europe the cycle appears a little later, so that by the year 2000 they are still presumably in C. But in the buffer fringe, in Ceylon, India, and areas such as that, we find that the whole cycle is considerably later, so that by the end of this century they would still be in stage B. Now, stage B, I call the demographic explosion.

To indicate the demographic explosion I have a dotted line in table 3, which we might call the explosive line. It gets later and later as we move further away from Western Europe. And as a result population pressure occurs later as we go outward from Western Europe. So we have an Anglo-French pressure spreading outward about 1850. We have a Germanic-Italian pressure in central Europe about the beginning of this century and continuing into the 20th century. We have a Slavic pressure at the present time. And the presumption, I imagine, would be that in 50 or more years from now we will have an Asiatic pressure. Thus the pressure moves outward. All right. That is what I call the demographic explosion.

Now, to get back to table 1, the last point in the development of our Western experience has been this revolution in transportation and communication. You are perfectly familiar with it. About 1750 or so we got canals and stagecoaches and turnpikes, macadamized roads, where Mr. Macadam told us how to make a road. And then going on, about 1830 we got the steam engine and about 1900 we got automobiles and then airplanes and all the rest of it. I will not have to go into those. It's perfectly obvious. The telegraph came in with the railroads. Electronic communications came along with the airplane, and so forth. Let's now look at the buffer fringe.

When you turn to the buffer fringe, the order in which things happened is entirely different. Where this order (Western World) was almost the way you would have desired it if you had planned it, nothing could be more disastrous than this order (buffer fringe). Once again in the buffer fringe let me start with the situation before Western civilization came in contact with it. In Western civilization at the beginning you had the self-sufficient manor, isolated. In Asia you did not have that. In Asia you had a peasant society in which there was superimposed upon the peasant a very large ruling group, which I frequently call "the quartet," made up of government officials and their bureaucracies, military personnel—armies—bankers and financiers, and, lastly, landlords. And this group of the ruling class cooperated together. They cooperated together to exploit those who were producing food.

Furthermore, the system by which food was being produced here was a system, especially in China, that put tremendous pressure on the soil, and it didn't possess that reserve which at the beginning of our system was to be found in the fallow year. At the beginning of our system one-third of the land was always untilled under the fallow system. But in the buffer fringe, particularly in China, the land is tilled generally every year. Instead of trying to replace the nutritive elements in the soil by a fallow or even by a leguminous crop, which they do to some extent, they replace the nutritive elements in the soil with human excrement spread upon the ground. But this puts them to the margin where to make their agricultural system produce more requires a major revolutionary change.

But they didn't get that. Instead, they got Western weapons, because when we came in, we came in with weapons and it was because of weapons that we were able to come in. We said to China: "We wish to come in." For 50 or 60 or more years they said "No." Finally the British in the opium wars of 1842 and in other struggles crashed open the door to China with our weapons. When Perry went to Japan, just a little over a century ago, he appeared there with black ships and with guns; and the Japanese, although they did not wish to do so, were forced to open their doors.

Now, seeing that, the upper ruling groups wanted our weapons. They began to buy our weapons. But the weapons which we gave them, even when they became what I call amateur weapons to us, were really specialist weapons to them, because a rifle or a revolver, which in 1880 was cheap in America, was still too expensive for a peasant in most of Asia. He didn't have the margin. On the other hand, the government could buy it. So the first event which occurred there intensified the authoritarian character of their society. Furthermore, it intensified the ability of the ruling group to exploit and take from the peasant larger fractions of what he was producing. Bankers were offering credit to peasants, very reluctantly, at 40 percent interest per year. The tax collectors were demanding more and more from the peasant because of the weapons which they wished to buy, and so forth.

Now, in this system the peasants still managed to survive until the commercial crisis came along, which destroyed their ability to survive. This is a very difficult problem. Let me try to explain it. The ruling group in Asia, particularly in eastern Asia, but above all in China, were taking from the peasant at the end of the 19th century so much of what the peasant produced that there wasn't enough left for him for subsistence. In other words, he was forced below the subsistence level by the contributions he had to make to the ruling quartet. How did he manage to survive? Because obviously he did. He managed to survive by handicraft. In their system agricultural peasantry were idle much of the year. They had two seasons of the year when they were very busy, but for about 5 months or even 6 months of the year they were largely idle. We call this "agrarian underemployment" which is still very noticeable in the buffer fringe.

Now, in this period of so much underemployment the peasants made basketry out of the withes, hats out of straw, leatherwork, and various other things; and these things they sold to the cities, to the ruling group. And in return they got credit back on the food that they had to give to this group. Thus the peasants were able at the end of the 19th century to bring themselves above the subsistence level by selling handicraft products to the cities. This was destroyed when Europe came into Asia with mass-production industrial goods, which the ruling class preferred to the peasant handicraft products that they had been buying. Apparently the ruling group, while still demanding the same amount and even more from the peasantry, now ceased to buy the craft products of the peasantry and, instead, were buying the products of the industrial cities of Europe. And this put the peasantry below the subsistence level.

What did they do about it? Not a thing, because the ruling group had the weapons. But then something happened. The pressure of our system upon Asia gradually impelled the ruling group to arm their peasantry. Above all, the fact that Japan adopted our system fairly successfully meant that if Japan were going to be stopped in exploiting the rest of the buffer fringe, she must be resisted with mass armies. Mass armies could be obtained only if the ruling group armed their own peasantry. But once they armed their own peasantry, then they couldn't keep them down below the subsistence level. It was this which destroyed the ruling group—that they armed the peasantry to resist Japan, and their peasants used this weapon against the ruling group. This is really the key to what has happened in China in the last 60 years, and is threatening in other areas.

Now, the commercial crisis, which I have carried down to a much later date, was followed by the transportation revolution. One of the first things that Asia began to demand was railroads and telegraphs. By 1880 they were building railroads and telegraph systems. One other thing I should point out.

The commercial crisis was made much more intense in all of Asia by the fact that when Westerners came in with guns, they made the native governments sign agreements not to raise their import tariff over 5 percent and in one case 8 percent. Japan didn't get free from that tariff until the 20th century.

In China and in the Ottoman Empire they didn't get rid of it until well in the 20th century. And this 5 percent tariff made it impossible for them to keep European industrial goods out and preserve the handicraft of their own peasantry. Well, now, the transportation and communication revolution requires capital. Where are they going to get it? There is no development ahead of it which would provide it. It requires labor. Where are they going to get that? Their economic system, their agricultural system, is already producing hardly enough. Well, the way they got these skilled technologists, where they got these inventions, where they got the capital was, of course, from Europe, generally by borrowing it and building railroads and so forth. But they were not paying for it themselves.

The next thing which occurred is sanitation and medicine. I must say this good word for the British: When the British went into China, went into India, or wherever they went, they did not at once try to clean the place up. That was a good thing. When Americans go in, we start DDT-ing and delousing everyone in sight. We do it to protect our own people; but by doing it we are reducing the death rate in those areas and thus we are forcing them into the demographic revolution before they have the food to sustain it. So the sanitation and medical revolutions arrive. Then comes the demographic revolution. That is followed by their attempts to industrialize. They feel they must industrialize to resist the pressure of the West, to resist the pressure of their own areas which have industrialized, like Japan, or perhaps even to resist the pressure of the bloc that we're not talking about today, the Soviet bloc. And if they are going to industrialize, again, how can they do it?

One way it can be done is by borrowing from Europe, which is now no longer feasible and becomes less and less feasible. Furthermore, it represents a continuation, an increase, of colonialism, and they wish to get away from colonialism. Instead, they wish, if possible, to avoid borrowing. So the way in which it must be done, it would seem, would be to squeeze more out of their own peasantry. That is exactly what is being done in Soviet Russia. Soviet Russia is industrializing by increasing the pressure on their own peasantry when they really haven't got the agricultural revolution.

Now, to this point I have been describing what has happened. In Asia, in the buffer fringe, and in the Soviet bloc as well, they have not yet got seven and they have not yet got eight and I doubt very much if they will ever get eight.

But the whole thing creates a tremendously dangerous situation. And before I stop, as I reach the end of my time, I would like to point out this:

When I speak of the agricultural revolution in Asia, what can they do? Well, they could adopt the second stage in our agricultural revolution, that is, the leguminous-rotation system, which would be a big help. But they probably cannot adopt the American stages which should go right along with that — the farm machinery stage, the fertilizer and chemical stages, and the gasoline power stage — because these things are much too expensive for them and represent buying things, such as chemicals, gasoline, and so forth, which they don't have. Notice a very drastic difference between American agriculture and European agriculture. To put it briefly, it is this: In Europe they have a limited supply of land and in Asia they have a limited supply of land and a surplus of labor. In America we have always historically had a plentiful supply of land and a lack of labor. Therefore our agricultural development has worked toward increasing the output per man-hour. In Europe and in Asia they must work in the direction of increased output per acre or per unit of ground.

These are absolutely antithetical things, it seems to me. Our output per acre is notoriously poor compared, for instance, to Europe's; but our output per man-hour is fantastically high. Therefore for us to go to the people of Asia and say: "You need the agricultural revolution — that means you need tractors, you need DDT, you need chemical fertilizers. All of these things is offering them something which they do not need or want. What they need are much simpler things, and I will end up with a story which illustrates it.

An American from our State Department, I believe, went to Afghanistan to work on some kind of a farm program. Since he had come from Iowa and knew good farming when he saw it, good American farming, he was utterly horrified at the Afghan farming, because it was so poor. So he wrote back to America and he wanted certain things, notably hoes.

He couldn't get hoes. The answer came: "We have no hoes, but we have lots of tractors." But tractors to these people are worthless. So he wrote to his 4-H Club in Iowa and said, "I need hoes." They got 300 of them together and shipped them to him. In his own little garden he increased output per unit of ground so fantastically that all of the neighbors began to say, "How do you do this?" He said, "Simply with a hoe."

In Europe you could increase output simply by plowing 6 inches deeper, because in most of Europe they plough only the upper few inches. That is exhausted, but down a few few inches further is fertile soil which hasn't been used for centuries.

All right. We'll stop now. I have gone over my time.

GENERAL DISCUSSION

COLONEL COOPER: Gentlemen, Dr. Quigley is ready for questions.

QUESTION: Sir, if I may be so impertinent as to say this, your stylized presentation that you made, as compared to the increase of knowledge, may change the time cycle as shown on your chart. I am leading to the knowledge you seem to have of the efforts in birth control and their effect on this demographic explosion. Will this increased knowledge change and compress the time cycle so that it can be done in appreciably less time than in past history.

DR. QUIGLEY: Being a historian and thus acquainted with the past rather than a fortune teller who can look into the future, I really cannot answer that question. It is true that many of these nations are trying—India and others, particularly Japan—to use birth control methods in order to reduce the impact of the demographic explosion. But that will alleviate, I think rather than change the order of things; and it will still leave many other problems of a major character, namely, for example, where do they get capital? They still have to get it out of their agricultural system.

So you can by such things as birth control and many other techniques alleviate this problem. I don't think, though I don't know this, that you can make any major rearrangement of the sequence. I hope you can. I don't want to be pessimistic. I think there is a solution for Asia. Last year, when I talked on this, I made a point which I neglected to make today. That is that in Asia they have a choice right now between using the method which the Russians are using, that is, to take it out of the hides of the peasantry, or adopt some new method, which is not the American method. The American way of life is not exportable to these people, it seems to me, because of this sequence of the arrangement. They have in Asia today the example of China, which is copying the Russian method, and the example of India, which is fumbling around trying to find the third way. And I think this is the most critical problem of that whole area: Will China or will India, by conclusively demonstrating that it is superior, lead to a kind of panic to adopt and follow their procedures? If China wins out, I think we will be in a very serious situation with the whole buffer fringe that may go to the Communist bloc simply because they have to adopt the Communist method if it works.

QUESTION: On this chart of the demographic cycle I was interested in Asia, where you said the demographic explosion is yet to come. Is this a sort of second cycle? Was that earlier invasion of Europe by the Mongol hordes an expression of another demographic explosion in earlier years?

DR. QUIGLEY: No. These things don't happen over the weekend. They don't even happen in a year's time. The demographic explosion in Asia has definitely already started, but it is going to get worse. But I simply divided this up into 50-year periods, and I don't want to put it at 1950, because the real impact is in the future. So I made it the year 2000. But the one that has begun now is the same one which will hit in a real blow some time in the future.

QUESTION: Is this a repeat cycle from the old cycle of the hordes that came over to Europe?

DR. QUIGLEY: No. They were forced out not by a rise in population, but by the drying up of Asia. In other words, when the desert areas of Asia dried, the Desert of Gobi became larger, and that forced pastoral peoples outward. They either went down into China, as the Huns did in the year 300, or they came westward toward Europe. That was climate rather than population.

QUESTION: Do you foresee any possibility of these buffer states to have enough room to increase productivity on existing land as they come to the agricultural revolution ahead of the Industrial Revolution and therefore provide the capital and manpower to do the job in the future?

DR. QUIGLEY: I feel pretty strongly that they must get the agricultural revolution before the Industrial Revolution if they are going to do it in a non-Communist way.

Now, the situation is diverse. In China there isn't available land. In India there is a large quantity of available land. In the Near East, in the Arabic countries, there really isn't much land. But there are ways in which they can increase it, because there are many of those areas, for example, the Islamic countries, which have rather low food productivity now, but which had much higher food productivity 2,000 years ago. Simply copying what the Romans found when they went there would be a very helpful thing. The people of Israel are trying to do that, as you know, in Neguib and the southern desert-and other places. So the problem differs from area to area. On the whole, except for India and Ceylon, I wouldn't say that there's much spare land, but that does not mean that the problem is insoluble.

QUESTION: In your chart that you put on the screen, the development sequence of the Western group as against the buffer fringe seemed to be somewhat different in terms of timing. Could you relate the principal development of those two together in terms of approximate times? I realize that the last two in the buffer fringe—

DR. QUIGLEY: You mean I didn't date the ones in the buffer fringe?

QUESTION: Yes. I was trying to tie the two together.

DR. QUIGLEY: Well, the reason I didn't date them was because they are all in the last 150 years. In other words, the Empress of China went in to open up China in 1794, Perry went to Japan in 1854, and so forth. So it's all the last 150 years or at least the last 200 years for the developments in the buffer fringe. And when you look at that diagram, please be aware that this is a rigid, much oversimplified thing. If I have to talk about it in only 50 or 60 minutes, I have to oversimplify it.

QUESTION: You stated that stage D of the demographic cycle was theoretically based on extrapolations from the previous stages. Don't we have a preview of that in Ireland? From what I have read about it, they have a low birth rate and—

DR. QUIGLEY: Yes. In other words, Western Europe seems already to be approaching this. You may remember that the French General Staff has been worried for more than 50 years, going back to 1910 or even earlier, over the fact that the birth rate in France was falling while the birth rate in Germany didn't seem to be falling. So there were bound to be many more Germans in the future and many fewer Frenchmen. It is quite true that in the extreme western edges of Western Europe we already see it. We don't see it just in Ireland. It's also true in Brittany, and it's probably true in places like Galicia and Spain. Why it is true on the western edges I don't know. But you can observe the beginnings of it there.

QUESTION: You say on the one hand that the American way of life is not exportable. At the same time we as a Nation seem to be encouraging our private capital to go abroad, to make investments in these foreign countries, these underdeveloped countries. Presumably the export of our capital, our dollars, carries with it some strings which could tend to impose on these countries some measure of the American way of life. Are these two situations compatible, or fundamentally is it possible that the export of our capital may not be as wise as it sounds?

DR. QUIGLEY: This once again is the result of oversimplification. American capital can go abroad, but it isn't really used in the American way. To give you an example: If American capital goes abroad and goes into mining or goes into industry, the whole ways in which it is used are not the ways it is used here. For example, in the mines, let us say, of southern Africa you bring the natives on a 3-, or 4-, or 5-year contract, lock them up in a compound, feed them, and take entire care of them. That's the method adopted by Cecil Rhodes some 50 or 60 years ago, you see. That isn't the American way of doing mining, even though, they are using American capital, as they must use capital if they are going to industrialize. Or again in other parts of the buffer fringe you will get a great deal of part-time labor. Even where people come to work in industry, as in India, they do not leave the farm. They are still peasants. They take off in the harvest season. They take off in the planting season. They come back to work. You never know whether you have them or not. So the whole labor problem, the whole technology problem, and many other things are quite different from what they are in America. And when I say that the American way of life isn't exportable, what I mean is that when we go abroad, let's look at what is there, see what their problems are, see what solutions are feasible in terms of what is available, and do not go out there, as so many Americas do, saying: "We've got to make nice little Americans out of them"; getting out at the 5-o'clock whistle and rushing home to look at TV or something like that. That's what I meant really by that.

QUESTION: You mentioned that the overthrow of the ruling group in China was a result of the mass arming of the peasants, as opposed to what is taking place in western Asia. Do you have in mind primarily our military aid programs? If so, are we in fact contributing to the creation of revolution rather than maintaining stability, as intended by these programs?

DR. QUIGLEY: No. I was referring to something earlier than this. You notice that in the buffer fringe sequence the first one here is weapons. I was referring rather to the fact that the Chinese Government armed its own peasantry not with a modern, specialized weapon so much as they did with the earlier amateur weapons, simply the rifle. Now, if a government begins to get the modern, specialized weapons, then it will again be in a position to oppress its own people and thus adopt the Russian system, which is that the Russian ruling group, with specialized weapons, can force the peasantry to give up most of what they produce, to pay a 60 percent or larger turnover tax on the consumer goods they buy, and so forth. Now, this process of giving weapons into the hands of the lower classes, which leads to the overthrow of the upper class, was true in the Far East. It was true in much of the Malay area. It has not yet been true in India. There are very peculiar reasons there — Gandhi and so forth. It certainly has not been true in the Near East, where the Arab governments still have the weapons and the Arab peasants do not have them and cannot get them. And when the government finally does get armored cars and tanks and these other things, some of which they do have, I don't see how the peasant will be able to resist them if he is able to get, let us say, a revolver. It depends on the guerrilla thing. The ability of the guerrillas in southeast Asia and Morocco to withstand modern specialized weapons is to me most reassuring in terms of the future of democracy, although it may seem to most of you as military men a very bad situation, because as military men you would prefer a situation where the military could impose their will upon the people. But I, as a defender of liberty, prefer a situation where the ordinary individual can tell any government, "I won't." "No" is a beautiful word except when it's from the lips of a beautiful woman.

COLONEL COOPER: Dr. Quigley, I will not attempt to pull a Tom Crystal act here. I'd just like to say that you have shown a great depth of knowledge of your subject, which has been presented in a most excellent manner. Thank you very much.

CHANGING COGNITIVE SYSTEMS AS A UNIFYING TECHNIQUE IN AMERICAN STUDIES

Address given in November 1966 at The American Studies Association

There is no known transcript of this address, thus we are dependent on Carroll Quigley's re-creation in a three-page letter to GU professor T. Leonard Mikules.

———————

GEORGETOWN UNIVERSITY
WASHINGTON, D.D. 20007

DEPARTMENT OF HISTORY   12 March 1967

Mr. T. Leonard Mikules
11 Catherdal Street
Annapolis, Maryland

Dear Leonard,

I should apologize for my delay in answering your note of 26 January, but since you are well acquainted with the academic rat-race of oral and other examinations in which we live at this time of year, I shall not try to justify my delay. You asked for a copy of the speech I gave at the Local chapter of the American Studies Association in November. Unfortunately, I do not ever write out such lectures and thus have no copy, but I shall give you the gist of it, because there should be a record of it for my own files as well.

The title was "Changing cognitive systems as a unifying technique in American Studies". I sought to show that historical changes in the cognitive systems of Americans would provide a helpful method for unifying the study of American history, literature and philosophy, which is the aim of the association. My interest in the subject arose from a life-long study of cognitive systems of men turnout history. .

A cognitive system could be defined thus: every people, in order to think about its experiences and to communicate about them, must structure these experiences. At a minimum this process means that the culture imposes on its experiences a system of categories and a system of values for these categories. Thus a system of cognition consists of categorization and valuation applied to experience. Since experience is existential in the sense that it is dynamic and unique, with each event occurring at a specific point in time, space, abstraction, social and personal, context, and can be understood in interior consciousness and communicated to others only if it is classified into some kind of classification, such a cognitive system is necessary if man is to be human in the sense that he is both aware and communicative with others. Yet, because that cognitive system is subjective and conventional (within the social and linguistic system which created it), it becomes the framework within which, the people of that society experience life and it is a screening barrier, which prevents them from experiencing those things for which no provision exists within their cognitive system. At times this means that a cognitive system, becomes a barrier to those experiences which are necessary to the very basic needs of humans, and the members of the society abandon their society's cognitive system, leaving it as an untenanted culture, as the Christians, and others did with Classical culture in the period from AD 200 to 950, when a totally new cognitive (based on hierarchy and quite different values) replaced the dualistic and paralysed cognitive system of Classicism. In turn, the Western cognitive system became ossified about 1300, and was unable to continue on in its growth, along the lines of Western life as embodied in the intrinsic nature of the Christian revelation, and turned back to the Classical example, whose inability to deal with the basic human problems had been fully revealed a thousand years before. (The mark of this return is to be seen in such events as the turn to Roman law, the refusal to go on to philosophic nominalism from moderate realism the failure, to escape from the inhibiting influence of two valued Greek logic which made it impossible to introduce motion and change into the Western vision of reality and thus led to the struggle with Galileo and, above all, with Darwin, and the introduction of duality and absolutism, into the medieval pluralist relativism).

A cognitive system structures reality and thus limits human experience <u>within that culture</u>, so that the members of that culture cannot become aware, think about, or communicate about what is excluded. On the whole, individuals socialized in a culture do not deal with actuality at all but deal with their society's cognitive system's structuring of actuality. This process is established in any individual chiefly through adopting the language of his culture, since any language has an unstated assumed cognitive implied in it. For example, European languages, by organizing action into past-present-future in the verb system makes time and this structuring of time part of the process by which those language-users structure experience. On the other hand, Bantu-speakers use verb systems based on completed and uncompleted action. We now structure time into two (Greek 2-valued logic again), past and future, with is the present simply the dimensionless division between these two, but the Bantu structures time with a broad extended duration of the present, a fairly long past, but an almost dimensionless future. As a result, the future-preference of our value-system (under which we are prepared to make almost any present sacrifice for the sake of some hypothetical future benefits; this is at the base of our religious system and from it came the base for saving and capital-accumulation in our economic system) is not compatible with the present preference of the Bantu, or the average American urban negro, so that our social and economic way of life cannot be exported to either of them.

In a similar way, we divide the single continuum of color in the rainbow into 6 divisions with green and blue as separate colors, and we, from our background in a temperate well-watered climate see a beautiful scene as a contrast of greens and blues, travelling thousands of miles to see a view which consists of four bands of these: a foreground of green, probably the nearer shore of a lake; band of blue, water; beyond that (which in a picture will be higher) a band of green (probably the farther shore, of the lake) and, above that, the blue sky. Thus a beautiful scene to us is four bands of alternating green and blue, but to an African (or a Navahoe) this would be dull, since it would be all one color, and his idea of beauty consists of contrasts in the longer-wave end of the spectrum (red-orange-yellow-brown) where he divides up the spectrum into smaller and mora numerous divisions than we do.

In a similar way, we divide the continuum of states of water into five (ice, snow, slush, water, steam), while the Esquimo divides snow alone into about 52 divisions based on what it is adapted to in his cultural usage. Thus when he looks at snow he does not see what we see, just as we in DC. do not see the same thing as the man in Stowe, Vermont, sees, when we look at snow, although we do see the same word for it.

The dimensions to which a society's cognitive system is applied are numerous and include, as well as those mentioned, space, nature, human nature (such as body and soul or body-emotions-reason, etc.), security and many others. In the middle ages we divided the individual life cycle into only two parts (Greek two-valued logic again): child and adult, with the division about 3 years. Today the most important stage is adolescence, which the middle ages did not recognise at all. (See Philippe Aries' paperback "Centuries of Childhood"). Today we have at least 8 or 9 stages, like many African tribes where these are institutionalized often with crises or initiation ceremonies as transition points.

The study of these changes would provide a unifying principle for American studies, especially if we recognize that our increasingly complex social structure is creating different cognitive systems for the various classes. Shifts both in structuring time and space (such as shifts from the agricultural year and the farmer's day, both based on the sun, to our abstract division of time for urban, commercial, future-preference living (a change which the rural negro cannot make with facility, especially, with his African background), and the shift from human experience to relations with objects or abstractions from the older emphasis on relations with nature and the recent emphasis on inter-personal relations (again, a movement toward an African form of life pattern) among our young people. In this process both nature and weather have bean driven farther from immediate human experience, and the effort to recapture those has become one of the chief aims of the new leisure.

The Vision which we once had of the American class structure has changed steadily, most recently from a ladder to a kind of planetary system centered on govern power.

Most of our literature from about 1900 to about 1940 was an attack on the middle-class cognitive system (future preference, endlessly expandible material demand, external, material status symbols, psychic anxiety, etc), but since 1940 most of our literature has: been simply a verbalization, outside our cognitive system, and outside of middle-class values, as protest against these and as a rejection of all the cognitive structure which makes thought and communication possible within our society. This began with the praise of violence in social Darwinism and works such as Sorel's Reflections on Violence. It culminated in the theatre of the Absurd and the meaningless poetry and painting of today, which reject meaning by rejecting all context.

This rather chaotic flood of ideas, some of which are undoubtedly obscure because they are two briefly stated, will give you some idea of the value of the study of changing cognitive systems in American studies, I

could sum up these uses in five headings:
1. As a unifying method for American studies, since all would have to analyze in terms of experience, categories, and symbols,
2. as a method for studying social change by studying the process by which individuals are socialized in American society in various times, including the use of such underused sources as educational history, history of the family, the role of literature as both a refection of life and a substitute for living, and the verbalization or philosophy, as well as providing a new approach to innovation in American life, especially the process by which each generation rejects at least part of its parents' outlook,
3. as a technique for getting behind all cognitive systems to the actuality of human experience,
4. as a technique for obtaining originality in scholarly works, since the- "originality" of most of these does not rest in any new discoveries but in expressing in new cognitive terms old actualities,
5. as a valuable technique for dealing with American social problems, such as poverty, racial issues, or war and peace, most of which are rooted in epistemological failures.

Please excuse the haste and errors of this letter, I have no stenographic help and I work poorly on a machine. To reduce errors I'll send you a Xerox copy.

Best wishes to you and to Roberta; I am glad that you are enjoying semi-retirement.

Very truly,

Carroll

ROUND TABLE REVIEW: THE NAKED CAPITALIST

Taken from: *Dialogue: A Journal of Mormon Thought*
(Vol. 6, Num. 3/4-Autumn-Winter 1971), pp. 99-116

Participants:
   William E. Fort, Jr.
   Louis C. Midgley
   Carroll Quigley
   W. Cleon Skousen

Dialogue departs from its usual review format in the following exchange of points of view on W. Cleon Skousen's latest book, *The Naked Capitalist* (Salt Lake City, Utah: published by the author, 1970. 144 pp., $2.00), a review-essay of Dr. Carroll Quigley's book, *Tragedy and Hope* (New York: Macmillan, 1966). Originally we asked Professor Louis C. Midgley of Brigham Young University to review Skousen's book for *Dialogue*. Shortly after receiving Midgley's review we received an unsolicited review from Professor William E. Fort, Jr., also of Brigham Young University, which took an approach opposite that of Midgley. Since much of the controversy surrounding Skousen's book centered on the interpretation of Quigley's book, we thought it might be interesting to get a response from Quigley to Skousen's book and Midgley's review. In a further attempt at a dialogue we invited Skousen to reply to Midgley and Quigley and, finally, invited Midgley to write a rejoinder to Skousen. All in all, it is a lively exchange and one we hope our readers enjoy.

THE NAKED CAPITALIST

William E. Fort, Jr.

Dr. Carroll Quigley's book *Tragedy and Hope* might have escaped the attention of anyone but a few scholars except for its careful dissection by W. Cleon Skousen. Skousen possesses unique qualities for this work. His keen, analytical mind has been sharpened by legal training and by sixteen years of service with the F.B.I. In addition, he was a distinguished Chief of Police in Salt Lake City for four years and was editorial director of the law enforcement magazine *Law and Order*. He has been a professor for seven years at Brigham Young University.

Professor Skousen's keen eye detected passages, sandwiched between lengthy discourses in Dr. Quigley's book, that reflected a fascinating pattern of information, fitting neatly into many things he had learned in his years of intelligence work. He knew, for example, that certain very wealthy and powerful persons, both within this country and abroad, are and have been doing things in support of the Communist conspiracy throughout the world. Dr. Bella Dodd, a former member of the national committee of the U.S. Communist Party, told Skousen several years ago that she first became aware of some superleadership right after World War II, when the U.S. Communist Party had difficulty in getting instructions from Moscow on several vital matters requiring immediate attention. The American Communist hierarchy was told that any time they had an emergency of this kind they should contact any one of three designated persons at the Waldorf Towers. Dr. Dodd noted that whenever the Party obtained instructions from any of these three men, Moscow always ratified them. What puzzled Dr. Dodd was the fact that not one of these contacts was a Russian or a Communist. In fact, all three were extremely wealthy capitalists! Dr. Dodd said, "I would certainly like to find out who is really running things. I think the Communist Conspiracy is merely a branch of a much bigger conspiracy!"

The portions gleaned by Professor Skousen from Dr. Quigley's book relate to the secret powers operating behind the scenes to destroy our constitutional republic and our traditional freedom and to establish a one-world, socialist government. Dr. Quigley speaks as an insider of some twenty years standing. He approves wholeheartedly of the secret machinations of those who would destroy our nation and place the world under a socialist dictatorship. He sneers at those American patriots who are fighting Communism, stating that they have missed the right target—the secret group of insiders who would rule the world. He feels that it would be tragedy for the free-enterprise, constitutional Americans to win. On the contrary he believes that our real hope lies in the victory of the secret operators. Hence the title of his book, *Tragedy and Hope*.

Dr. Quigley, however, believes that the real battle is finished and that his side has won. In effect, he believes that it is all over but the shouting and that it is now next to impossible to reverse the process. He traces the secret movement over the years, naming names and places. Some of the names will come as a shock to many Americans. The secret moves will shock them further.

Professor Skousen does an outstanding job of bringing together and crystallizing the important facts of Dr. Quigley's book. *The Naked Capitalist* is a difficult book to put down. Skousen's commentary is enlightening. The complete index and sub-index make it easy to trace the activities of men and organizations.

The Naked Capitalist will answer many questions concerning the strange things that have been going on in the world and in this country for many years. Those who do not have the patience to tackle Dr. Quigley's 1300 page book directly should by all means read Professor Skousen's 144 page commentary. This book is a must for those interested in what is taking place behind the scenes.

THE CULT OF CONSPIRACY

Louis C. Midgley

The Naked Capitalist is intended to expose a massive, top-secret, Capitalist super-conspiracy. Communism and socialism, we are told, are merely some of the fruit of this Gigantic International Monolithic Network of Total Global Power. Skousen now believes that it is the Capitalists who have been secretly "running the world" for many years, forming "a conspiratorial control center higher and stronger than either Moscow or Peiping." *The Naked Capitalist* is intended to strip bare this "Global Establishment" which secretly plans, plots, and conspires to rule the world. Now you have perhaps always thought that the hard-working, money-making Capitalists were the Good Guys in Skousen's demonology. Nothing could be further from the truth. He believes that "globalism," "internationalism," "one-worldism," and ruthless centralized dictatorship are what the Capitalist demons have in mind. They only use communism to achieve these goals.

The "global planners" who are at the center of the Capitalist conspiracy are identified by Skousen as the "leaders of the world's secret center of international banking," the "super-rich," the "super capitalists." The "leaders of London and Wall Street" are chiefs of "the Anglo-American secret society" who are behind communism and everything else. Skousen puts bankers at the top of the list of conspirators: the Rothschilds, Barings, Lazards, Paul Warburg, J. P. Morgan. But also included are the following: John Foster and Alan Dulles, the Rockefellers, Cecil Rhodes, Arnold Toynbee, Walter Lippman, Albert Einstein, George F. Kennan, Douglas Dillon, Dean Ache-son, Henry Kissinger, Henry Cabot Lodge, Arthur Burns, George Ball, Ellsworth Bunker, Paul Hoffman, McGeorge Bundy, the Kennedy family, Dwight Eisenhower, John Dewey, and many others. By any standards, this is quite a list.

The Capitalists, he now tells us, are "the world's secret power structure" and they merely form, use and manipulate communism and socialism and many other things for their own evil purposes. He knows that this thesis is not likely to be believed. "If I had said it, people may have found it too fantastic to believe," Skousen wrote in a letter that accompanied copies of the book that he gave to B.Y.U. faculty members. He claims, however, that he has actually discovered "someone on the inside [of the supposed Capitalist conspiracy] who is willing to tell the story." "I have," he writes, "waited thirty years for someone on the inside of the modern political power structure to talk. At last somebody has." Skousen is referring to Carroll Quigley, a professor of history at Georgetown University. Roughly forty full pages of *The Naked Capitalist* consist of direct quotations from Quigley's *Tragedy and Hope: A History of the World in Our Time*.

But does Quigley really say what Skousen claims he says? The answer is both yes and no. The answer is yes, if you mean: "Are the long passages that Skousen quotes actually in Quigley's book?" Quigley does discuss the role of financial capitalism in recent history as well as various "networks" of Capitalist influence and power. But the answer is an emphatic and final no, if you mean: "Does Quigley think he is revealing or has he revealed a Great Super-Secret Capitalist Conspiracy behind communism?" This is, of course, the crucial point.

Much of what Skousen claims to have found in Quigley's book is simply not there. There are numerous places in *The Naked Capitalist* in which Skousen (1) asserts something about Quigley but then inadvertently reveals that he completely misunderstands Quigley's remarks; (2) simply invents fantastic ideas and attributes them to Quigley; or (3) makes inferences from Quigley's book that go far beyond the bounds of honest commentary. By way of illustration, I will examine a small sampling of these many passages.

1. According to Skousen, "When Dr. Quigley decided to write his 1300-page book called *Tragedy and Hope*, he knew he was deliberately exposing one of the best-kept secrets in the world. As one of the elite insiders, he knew the scope of this power complex and he knew that its leaders hope to eventually attain total global control (p. 4, italics added). Skousen cites no evidence whatsoever to support his suppositions about what Quigley knew. He fastens on one passage (Quigley, p. 950) and infers the totally unwarranted conclusion that Quigley was an "elite 'insider'" on a global conspiracy of Capitalists who are behind communism. Quigley uses the term "insider" merely to describe his role as historian with access to primary source material.

2. Skousen writes: "Obviously, disclosing the existence of a mammoth power network which is trying to take over the world could not help

but arouse the vigorous resistance of the millions of people who are its intended victims. So why did Quigley write his book? His answer appears in a number of places but is especially forceful and clear on pages 979-980. He says in effect, that it is now "too late for the little people to turn back the tide" (p. 4). The truth is that on pages 979-980 Quigley says nothing at all about the purpose of his book. The passage in question is merely a negative account of the isolationist impulse found between 1945-55 in which some favorite nostrums of Skousen are lampooned.

3. Skousen claims that "all through his book, Dr. Quigley assures us that we can trust these benevolent, well-meaning men who are secretly operating behind the scenes. THEY are the hope of the world. All who resist them represent tragedy. Hence the title of the book" (p. 5). If Quigley does something "all through his book," as Skousen claims, it should be easy to give some examples—well, one passage at least. All Skousen presents are his own inferences, for which there is no textual support. If the reader is interested in what Quigley had in mind by the title *Tragedy and Hope*, he should consult pages 1310ff., for it is there that Quigley explains that the tragedy is the threat of war and the hope is that we will come to practice Christian love.

4. After mentioning the imagery in Revelations 13:15-17, Skousen tells us that "Dr. Quigley assures us that this type of global power structure is on the verge of becoming a total reality. He points out that during the past two centuries when the peoples of the world were gradually winning their political freedom from the dynastic monarchies, the major banking families of Europe and America were actually reversing the trend by setting up new dynasties of political control through formation of international financial combines" (p. 7). While it is true that Quigley talks about international bankers and their activities, nowhere does he call their activities a "global power structure." This is Skousen's invention. Nor does Quigley connect the activities of bankers with secret combinations or anything mentioned in Scripture. The assertions that follow the words "Quigley assures us" and "he points out" are merely surmises and conclusions drawn by Skousen and then attributed to Quigley to give them some authority.

5. Skousen thinks it is the Super-Capitalist bankers who are behind all of this and who are chief enemies of the "free-enterprise, property-oriented, open society..." (p. 24). But why would these "super-capitalists," who have the most to gain from free-enterprise, try to

destroy it and replace it with socialism? "Dr. Qpigley provides the answer to this question but it is so startling that at first it seems virtually inconceivable. It becomes rational only as his scattered references to it are collected and digested point by point. In a nutshell, Dr. Quigley has undertaken to expose what every insider like himself has known all along — that the world hierarchy of the dynastic super-rich is out to take over tire planet, doing it with Socialistic legislation where possible, but having no reluctance to use Communist revolution where necessary" (p. 25). But where does Quigley say these things? Quigley is supposedly Skousen's one and only "insider" who has "talked" — his star witness. Quigley does not support in any way Skousen's conspiracy thesis; he has a thesis of his own, but it is not the one Skousen claims to have found in Quigley's book.

6. "As we shall observe shortly," Skousen writes, "Dr. Quigley is sometimes reluctant to admit the full ramifications of his ugly thesis when the shocking and often revolting implications of it spill out on the blood-stained pages of recent history" (p. 25). This is a confused way of granting that Quigley's book does not provide support of Skousen's thesis. But, says Skousen, this "strange contradiction ... should offer no difficulty to the reader once he understands what is happening." Of course, once you accept Skousen's views, it is apparently very easy to interpret anything. But I had the impression that Quigley was the "insider" who had told all and therefore provided the proof that needs no interpretation. However, once we look at Quigley's book, we find that nothing in it makes Skousen-type sense unless it is interpreted in a special way — unless the reader "understands what is happening." It is Skousen who tells us "what is happening" and not Quigley. He is arguing with his own (and only) witness. A confession hardly needs a key so that we can interpret it. And a wild set of inferences hardly constitutes a confession.

7. Skousen writes: "Dr. Quigley bluntly confesses that the International Bankers who had set out to remake the world were perfectly confident that they could use their money to acquire the cooperation and eventual control of the Communist-Socialist conspiratorial groups" (p. 38, italics added). Where does Quigley "bluntly confess" such things? The truth is that Skousen is reporting what he believes the international bankers are up to and then falsely attributing his own invention to Quigley.

8. According to Skousen: "It may seem somewhat contradictory that the very people whom Marx identified as the epitome of 'Capitalism'should

be conspiring with the followers of Marx to overthrow traditional Capitalism and replace it with Socialism. But the record supports the Quigley contention that this is precisely what has been happening" (p. 38, italics added). Where did Quigley contend any such thing? What "record" supports such a contention? These are again wholly unwarranted inferences.

9. Skousen refers to "Dr. Quigley's admission that the remaking of the world by the super-rich was to be along the socialist lines taught at those British institutions which look upon global socialism as the hope of the world" (p. 39, italics added). Where does Quigley admit such a thing? Here is Quigley's statement: "The chief aims of this elaborate, semi-secret organization [the Round Table Groups financed by bankers, as Quigley has earlier shown] were largely commendable: to coordinate the international activities and outlooks of the English-speaking world into one (which would largely, it is true, be that of the London group); to work to maintain peace; to help backward, colonial, and underdeveloped areas to advance toward stability, law and order, and prosperity ALONG LINES SOMEWHAT SIMILAR TO THOSE TAUGHT AT OXFORD AND THE UNIVERSITY OF LONDON (ESPECIALLY THE SCHOOL OF ECONOMICS AND THE SCHOOLS OF AFRICAN AND ORIENTAL STUDIES)" (Quigley, p. 954; quoted by Skousen, p. 39). Skousen reads the last few lines as an open admission that some super-rich types were conspiring to remake the world "along socialist lines." I cannot find anything in the passage which infers that anything would be done "along socialist lines." I have the impression that Skousen uses expressions like "along socialist lines" when Quigley and most everyone else would say "under control by wealthy capitalists."

10. According to Skousen, "One of the singular and amazing things about Dr. Quigley's book is his willingness to frankly and unashamedly confess [sic] some of the most serious acts of subversion by his comrades-in-arms and then think nothing of turning around and flatly denying that they would have had a hand in such a foul and dirty business as betraying people like the Chinese to Communism" (p. 47, italics added). Quigley does say that "there is no evidence of which I am aware of any explicit plot or conspiracy to direct American policy in a direction favorable either to the Soviet Union or to international communism" (p. 947, quoted by Skousen, p. 45). Where are the frank and unashamed admissions? The "comrades-in-arms" remark is gratuitous.

11. According to Skousen, "Dr. Quigley's disclosure that the Council on Foreign Relations and the Institute of Pacific Relations were responsible for what turned out to be a paroxysm of world-wide political subversion, is no more shocking titan his bold declaration that the global collectivists of the London-Wall Street Axis were equally successful in attacking the whole foundation of American culture..." (p. 57, italics added). Quigley does discuss the activities and financial backing of the Council on Foreign Relations and the Institute of Pacific Relations, but he does not thereby disclose that they were responsible for any political subversion (either world-wide or national). Nor does he make a bold declaration about global collectivists being "successful in attacking the whole foundation of American culture." These are entirely the conclusions and opinions of Skousen and they find no support whatever in Quigley's book.

12. Skousen constantly attempts to demonstrate that financial capitalism both directs and supports communism. He asserts, for example, that "Quigley says" that "the secret Establishment powers" are attempting "to gradually move [sic] humanity toward a global collectivist society" (p. 87). There is, however, nothing in *Tragedy and Hope* that links financial capitalism with the goal of "a global collectivist society" or communism or socialism or dictatorship. Quigley notes that the two organizations "were much concerned with freedom of expression for minorities and the rule of law for all"; they "constantly thought in terms of Anglo-American solidarity, of political partition and federation..." (Quigley, p. 954). Exactly what is wrong with such goals? Quigley shows how a few "Communist sympathizers" and fellow travelers infiltrated the CFR and IPR in the 1930's. This is not a new revelation. Quigley also observes that groups such as IPR and CFR constitute the "power structure which the Radical Right in the United States has been attacking for years in the belief that they were attacking the Communists" (956). Quigley calls these efforts of the Radical Right "misdirected attacks." They are so for several reasons, the chief one being that the bankers and their various organizations—what Quigley calls facetiously "the English and American Establishments"—are not Communist or subversive at all and never have been, though some of die groups supported by bankers were once infiltrated by a few sympathizers and fellow travelers. (See Quigley, p. 956).

The story Quigley tells is good enough. Why then expand it into a lurid tale of global conspiracy and subversion when it is not even a story of a secret conspiracy at all, but merely a reasonable account of the role of one group within the complex of American and world politics? It is by a strange magic that Quigley's account of the role of certain international bankers and their friends in England and the United States becomes transformed in Skousen's mind into a top-secret, Super-capitalist, Super-conspiracy of a global nature. Quigley makes it clear that banking interests and the groups they support are (1) not secret (only semi-secret like most financial, governmental and university affairs generally), (2) not a subversive or criminal conspiracy, (3) not global, only international in the sense that some ties were maintained between bankers and intellectuals in England and the United States), and (4) not really monstrous, sinister, or demonic (but more nearly meddling, naive, idealistic and vain—all rather typical faults of both intellectuals and the wealthy).

13. According to Skousen, "Every once in a while, the network lets down its guard long enough for us to get a slight but alarming peep into the inner parts of the mammoth machine winch Dr. Quigley believes is now too big to stop. When one contemplates the interlocking global ramifications which this power structure has developed, it is little wonder that Dr. Quigley feels so tremendously confident about its ultimate and irrevocable victory" (p. 107; italics added). Here again we see Skousen at work asserting what Quigley believes and feels. Skousen supports neither of these assertions with textual evidence. Nowhere in his book does Quigley say or imply the things that Skousen attributes to him.

14. The evidence and argument of *The Naked Capitalist* is a weak reed, but the book still has a good deal of emotional appeal and persuasive power. The message is cleverly staged and artfully developed. Skousen begins with a tale about a conversation with Bella Dodd, a former Communist. This is a nice touch. The reader is made to see Skousen as one familiar with security matters and with important people. The purported conversation with Dodd, for which there is no proof, points the reader to the main idea of the book—that there is "a conspiratorial control center higher and stronger than either Moscow or Peiping." Skousen's "credentials" are thus implied—his FBI background, his knowledge of the state of mind of J. Edgar Hoover, and of subversive actions in government, and finally his sensational discovery of who has been behind everything. Before the average reader ever gets to read a word of Quigley he already knows what Quigley will say and is left with

no doubts at all that Quigley is a front rank, high-up member of a top-secret, malevolent conspiracy.

But the Quigley that Skousen has invented (or rather appropriated from the John Birch Society) is not the real Quigley at all. Skousen's picture of Quigley as an elite member of a criminal conspiracy who is now willing to tell the inside story is unprincipled fabrication and a clear piece of deceit. Unless Skousen had planted in the reader's mind his fantasy about Quigley writing a book "to expose world-wide conspiracy and disclose many of its most secret operations" (p. 4), it would never occur to a reader of *Tragedy and Hope* that Quigley was anything but the author of a textbook on recent world history in which some account is offered of the political activities of financial capitalism.

Suppose that one accepts the tale of super-conspiracy as told by Skousen, what is one to do about it? Once we know about the Establishment, what then? Skousen feels that it is now possible "to mobilize a formidable wave of hard-core resistance to the whole super-structure of world-wide conspiracy" (p. 117). Remember, the world-wide conspiracy he is talking about is financial capitalism. "The future task is political in nature. Essentially, it is a matter of methodically and deliberately uniting the vast resources of political power at the grass roots level and 'throwing the rascals out'" (p. 117). He also claims that "it is essential that one of the national political parties be renovated and reconstructed as a base of operations..." (p. 120). "This situation [the collectivization process] is likely to continue," Skousen tells us "until a sufficient number of Americans become angrily aroused and rise from the grass roots to seize control of one or both of the major parties" (p. 57). Notice the operative words "angrily aroused," "rise," "seize control."

After the "political puppets of the international network" of financial capital are eliminated and replaced and "the political climate has been improved we have a tremendous amount of restructuring to do" (p. 118, italics added). What will we restructure? "The conspiratorial enemy's power base must be eliminated" (p. 118, italics added). The power base of the bankers and their henchmen is, of course, their property and wealth; Skousen wants it eliminated. The economic order must be reconstructed, for "the whole monolithic, inter-locking power structure of international finance is in flagrant violation of the general welfare of the people..." (p. 118). In the name of the people, we should eliminate the power base (that is, the wealth) or finance capital. "This mammoth concentration of economic power is in direct opposition to the traditional American precept that, unless it has been stated otherwise, all power of every sort must remain DISPERSED among the people. Therefore, laws must be passed so that the nightmarish monstrosity of credit and money power which has been rapidly gravitating into a few conspiring hands, can be dismantled" (p. 118, italics added). These sentences seem to be a call for the government to expropriate the wealth of the rich. Skousen's program is (1) to angrily arouse people to the point where they will rise and seize control of a political party, (2) to take over the government, (3) to use its power to eliminate the wealthy, (4) to dismantle credit and money power, and (5) to disperse power to the people. This radical political program is surprisingly close to the rhetoric of the New Left.

Skousen specifies some goals which can be attained, he believes, after expropriation of the wealth and hence the power base of finance capital. (1) This step "would allow us to liberate our captive press, radio and TV facilities so that the people could be told what is going on." (2) "It would facilitate the liberation of the captive public school system..." (3) "It would also facilitate the liberation of certain religious bodies, universities, and other powerful, opinion-molding channels which have been bought-over and corrupted by the fabulous wealth of the network's billion-dollar, tax-exempt foundations." (4) "The Federal Reserve system and the United Nations must go" (pp. 118-19; italics added). What does the word "liberate" mean in this context? It certainly seems to imply wresting control from someone. Does it also imply turning control over to someone else? To whom exactly? And who would do this liberating? The government, perhaps?

I believe that Skousen started his career with the goal of saving the rich from big government, but has found that the rich don't want his help — the rich he now discovers control big government and, in fact, are rich partly because of big government. Now he wants to attack the rich and especially their power base, their wealth. But he is not the first to have it in for Capitalists and to want to save the people from their rich masters. This is exactly the program of various forms of socialism and communism. It is difficult to miss the parallels between Skousen's program and much of the rhetoric of the New Left. But there are other instructive parallels. In Germany, where they also once came to believe that they were oppressed by conspiratorial bankers who also manipulated the Communists, the program was called National Socialism. Under this program the rich would be eliminated and power given back to the people (or so they said), the schools would be liberated so that the truth could be taught about die evil bankers, international ties would be eliminated, churches would be used for national propaganda and other purposes. Skousen also wants a political party to come to power with the express goal of eliminating the wealth and power of the rich (what better name for such a policy than socialism?) and this key process is to be accomplished by national governmental action — an appropriate descriptive title for his program would be National Socialism.

There are a hose of writers, mostly on the left, who have been arguing that political power is in the hands of a wealthy power elite. There is, for example, currently a split among political scientists and sociologists between those who argue that some kind of power elite run things and those who maintain that most everyone has some access to power through democratic processes of decision making. I am surprised that Skousen has apparently never heard about a power elite (or the influence of money in politics or of a military-industrial complex) before he read Quigley. There is a very large literature on these topics. Skousen could have found plenty to chew on in, for example, Ferdinand Lundberg, *The Rich and the Super-Rich: A Study in the Power of Money Today* (New York: Lyle Stuart, 1968).

Has Cleon Skousen simply invented the utterly false, paranoid view of politics and history advanced in *The Naked Capitalist*? Carroll Quigley informs me that for over two years the John Birch Society and other radicals have been busy distorting the contents of his *Tragedy and Hope* in order to support their own paranoid fantasy about a super-conspiracy behind the multitude of evils in the world today. Skousen has bought without question the dogma of the Birchers and other radicals. He is now busy using his rhetorical powers to charm and flatter Church members into accepting the dogmas of his conspiracy cult. He has made an accommodation between the gospel of Jesus Christ and, of all things, a vain and wholly absurd worldly ideology. The immediate result of Skousen's activity is a kind of radical cult within the Church. He and his friends make every effort to teach their radical political dogmas as if they were truths of the gospel of Jesus Christ.

Recently the Saints have been plagued by those who pass around outlandish nonsense as authentic prophecies of John Taylor, and by others who want to mobilize the Saints into Neighborhood Emergency Teams. The Church has had to settle accounts with both groups. The effect of *The Naked Capitalist* is likewise to direct the attention of the Saints away from the gospel and to form a cult. *The Naked Capitalist* sets brother against brother. It divides the Saints into angry, hostile camps, as is evidenced by its impact on students at Brigham Young University, where it is now being used by certain religion teachers as a compendium to the Scriptures. Such a radical and false ideology, no matter how cleverly packaged and rationalized, does not teach us to love our neighbors or forgive others; it does not open us to the sanctifying effects of the Spirit. There is nothing edifying in its bleak message. Skousen's grim tale of evil conspiracy is not the gospel. Nor is the gospel consistent with the idea that the Saints should be preparing for an aggressive, hostile onslaught against some Enemy Super-

Conspiracy. There is no reason for us to put our faith—not even a little of our faith—in some worldly ideology or some radical political program of man.

The Lord has warned the Saints to avoid secret combinations (see Ether 8:19, 22-6); we are not told to start our own secret combination to counter the evils we see or think we see in the world. We are not to follow the pattern set by this world; our politics should be of an entirely different kind; our Kingdom is not of this world. We are not commissioned to win this world for the Lord by joining some seedy and unseemly political mass movement like that offered by the New Left or the Radical Right. No conspiracy, not even a Skousen-type Super-Conspiracy, can possibly frustrate the Kingdom of God; the Saints need not fear the corruption of this world if they keep their eyes and hearts on the Master.

Brigham Young gave us some good advice as to how we as partakers in the Lord's priesthood should deal with political questions: "Let no Religious test be required or the Holy influence and Power of the Priesthood be brought to bear in any Political question. If the inherent merits of all such matters will not furnish argument sufficient for all necessary purposes, then let them go; for it is better that the whole Political fabric, corrupt as we know it to be, should totter and go to destruction, than for our Saints to be offended." Brigham Young warned us not to permit the trivial matter of this world's politics to influence us in the least and added: "and never, no never! no never!! again drag Priesthood into Political gentile warfare." (Letter, July 20, 1849.) In spite of such prophetic warning the conspiracy cult thrives.

QUIGLEY'S RESPONSE

Carroll Quigley

Thank you for the opportunity to read *The Naked Capitalist* and Midg-ley's review of it. I think his review is very perceptive, and there is very little I can add to it.

Midgley is correct in his basic statement that Skousen has simply taken extended passages from my book, in violation of copyright, and put them together in terms of his own assumptions and preconceptions to make a picture very different from my own. Skousen is apparently a political agitator; I am an historian. My book merely tried to give an account of what happened in the world in the early part of the 20th century. I did a good deal of independent research on it, much of it in places which did not attract Skousen's attention at all (such as French economic history, and economic history in general). The book was published five years ago. On the whole, except perhaps for my section on Red China, it has stood the challenge of later information fairly well. The chapter on "Germany From Kaiser to Hitler" has just been re-published by Houghton Mifflin in a book entitled *Why Hitler?*

Midgley has pointed out the chief distortions of my materials in Skousen's book. My picture of "Financial capitalism" said that it was prevalent in the period 1880-1933. Skousen quotes these dates in several places (p. 14), yet he insists that these organizations are still running everything. I said clearly that they were very powerful, but also said that they could not control the situation completely and were unable to prevent things they disliked, such as income and inheritance taxes. Moreover, I thought I had made it clear that the control of bankers was replaced by that of self-financing or government-financed corporations, many of them in the West and South-west, in oil or in aero-space, and I saw a quite different alignment of American politics since 1950 (pp. 1245-1247). Skousen implies that financial capitalism was not only omnipotent but immoral, both of which I denied.

Most notably, Skousen asks in his foreword: "Why do some of the richest people in the world support communism and socialism?" He says that I give the answer. I never anywhere said that financial capitalism or any of its subsidiaries sought to "support communism." On the contrary, I said two things which Skousen consistently ignores: (1) that bankers sought to influence all shades of American political opinion across the board from Right to Left (p. 945); and (2) that Wall Street support of Communist groups was based on three grounds, one of which was to "have a final veto on their publicity and possibly on their actions, if they ever went radical" (p. 938). Morgan's pipeline to die Liberals (the Straights) was no more liberal than his pipeline to the Communists (the Lamonts) was communist. Skousen simply assumes that anyone who tries to infiltrate the communists or contributes funds to them must be a sympathizer, but, as he must know, the FBI has been doing this for years, as the CIA has been doing it all across the political spectrum on American campuses in recent years.

I must say that I was surprised at the picture of myself which I found in Skousen. Midgley is correct in his statement that I never claimed to be an "insider" of the Eastern Establishment, as Skousen seems to believe I was; I simply said that I knew some of these people, and generally liked them, although I objected to some of their policies. It seems to me that Skousen is unable to understand their point of view, simply because he upholds what I would regard as "the Radical Right" view that "exclusive uniformity" is the basis on which our society should be based. My own view is that our whole Western tradition rests, despite frequent aberrations, on what I call "inclusive diversity." These are the last two words of my book, and they are its chief message, which seems to me to be one of the chief aspects of the Christian way of life: that diverse peoples with diverse beliefs must live together and work together in a single community, It seems to me that the Wall Street power group sincerely held this belief; that is why they made Harvard and other institutions they influenced so "liberal." They felt strongly that communists and the Soviet Union and other diverse peoples were in this world together and had to live and let live in order to co-exist. It seems to me that this is what Skousen cannot accept. His political position seems to me to be perilously close to the "exclusive uniformity" which I see in Nazism and in the Radical Right in this country. In fact, his position has echoes of the original Nazi 25 point program.

Midgley says that Skousen was triggered into writing *The Naked Capitalist* by my critical remarks on the Radical Right. I agree with him. If you will look at my book (pages 146-147), you will see that the Round Table Group, under the influence of Lionel Curtis, held basically Christian beliefs. These were sincere. But they bungled them greatly in application. Perhaps it was intellectual arrogance to expect to "build the Kingdom of God here upon this earth," and they certainly failed disastrously. No one knows this better than I do. But I still cannot condemn them, and I cannot see that the American Radical Right has anything better to offer. I think the Round Table effort failed because they tried to work through government, rather than through each person's individual effort in his private life.

SKOUSEN'S REPLY

W. Cleon Skousen

In *The Naked Capitalist* I simply quoted extensive passages from Quigley which described the amazing extent to which a secret financial network gained control over major nations throughout the world. Quigley was very clear and precise in the way he presented his material, and I felt it was a most important contribution. It is regrettable that he now feels compelled to retreat to a more obscure position.

Quigley is unhappy with me for saying that he wrote his book as an "insider." Yet after affirming the existence of this vast, secret power structure of the super-rich he writes: "I know of the operations of this network because I have studied it for twenty years, and was permitted for two years, in the early 1960's, to examine its papers and secret record. I have no aversion to it or to most of its aims and have, for much of my life, been close to it and many of its instruments." Is there any other historian who has been given access to the secret records of the international bankers' establishment? I know of none. Nor do I know of any historian who has been close enough to the "instruments" of the Establishment to reveal so many facts concerning its inside operations.

One of the most astonishing points raised in Quigley's critique was his statement that, "I never anywhere said that financial capitalism sought to support communism." Actually, this is something he stressed very strongly in his book. "Our concern at the moment is with the links between Wall Street and the Left, especially the Communists...."; he goes on to describe how J. P. Morgan's partner, Thomas Lamont, and his family became the "sponsors and financial angels to almost a score of the extreme Left organizations, including the Communist Party itself." He cites other instances, one of which is the Institute of Pacific Relations (pp. 946ff.). He says, "The influence of the Communists in IPR is well established, but the patronage of Wall Street is less well known." He then provides an extremely interesting account of the relationship between Wall Street leaders and their heavily financed forces of subversion which operated in the IPR during that period. Of course, Congressional hearings thoroughly supported my position. So did the Attorney General's investigation in the Amerasia Case. Why is Quigley now attempting to deny his former position?

Both in his book and his critique, Quigley exhibits a very strange attitude toward those who have views which differ from his own. He is very disturbed by the "petty bourgeoisie" in America who have "middle-class values" and are therefore opposed to what I believe is the socialized, one-world society which is being imposed upon them. Obviously Quigley is talking about those who oppose what he believes in. But why must he identify them with the Nazis? Smearing is a tactic used by those who have run out of substantive arguments. Quigley does the same thing in his response to *The Naked Capitalist*. He says my position "has echoes of the original Nazi 25 point program." In what way? He never gets around to telling us.

I have concluded to attribute Midgley's treatment of my book to an adventure in speed reading. Certainly he is a better scholar than the contents of this critique would indicate. He must have written his comments under tremendous pressure and at a time when his sketchy scanning of my book caused him to suffer a trauma of emotional inflammation. I would have preferred to respond to a critique of scholarly, penetrating analysis. That might have been useful to both of us, and I would have welcomed it.

My greatest disappointment in Midgley is his obvious lack of intellectual curiosity. In his anxiety to get out his polemical shotgun and win the debate, he completely missed some rather exciting issues which are presented in

The Naked Capitalist. Some of these have come into prominence just since this book was published. An example of this has been the rather sensational repudiation of the 1968 Republican platform by President Nixon, which my book anticipated. Another has been the submitting of two bills in Congress to retire the privately owned stock of the Federal Reserve System, which coincides with the recommendations in *The Naked Capitalist*. This book also predicted the new China policy with Kissinger carrying the ball for the power network which initiated the policy. Midgley appears to have missed all of this along with a dozen other issues of equal importance.

In the opening portion of his review, Midgley pokes fun at Skousen's "demonology" which is supposed to "strip bare the 'Global Establishment' who secretly plan, plot and subversively conspire to rule the world." As part of his fun, Midgley says, "Since die Capitalist Super-conspiracy is partly an affair of bankers, Skousen heads the list of conspirators with their names: The Rothschilds, Barings, Lazards, Paul Warburg, J.P. Morgan...." This illustrates the superficiality of his reading. This series of names is not my list at all. It is Quigley's. How did Midgley miss this?

Midgley goes on to say: "Skousen has striven to find a link between capitalism and communism." This is not true. The link between wealthy Capitalists and the Communists has been one of the startling facts growing out of government investigations for forty years or more. The great value of Quigley's book is that he verifies with names and organizations what government investigators and private researchers have been saying all along. He further clarifies the reason for the Wall Street-Left Wing link by telling how the heirs to some of the multi-billion dollar fortunes of the world became converted to John Ruskin's version of socialist collectivism. We are dealing with fabulously wealthy men who are out to restructure the world along Plato's pattern of socialist collectivism. Surely Midgley must have read Plato sufficiently to appreciate what a tightly stratified class structure John Ruskin was advocating.

Midgley lists fourteen points which he failed to find in Quigley's book even though I cited the pages where he could find them:

1. Midgley says he could find nothing to indicate Quigley was writing as an "insider." This one we have already covered.

2 & 13. Midgley objected to my deduction that Quigley probably felt safe in telling the Establishment story because of Quigley's feeling that it was now too late for ordinary Americans to organize and turn back the tide. Rather than quibble I will simply refer the reader to pages 979-80 of Quigley's book.

3. What is the meaning behind the title, *Tragedy and Hope*? I have already demonstrated that Quigley sees tragedy in returning to the fundamentals of

the founding fathers. He sees hope in a one-world amalgamation of the United States and the Soviet Union. He calls it "inclusive diversity." In his critique of *The Naked Capitalist* Quigley provides a definition for this strange term. He says it means "that diverse people with diverse beliefs must live together and work together in a single community." Pushing universities toward the liberal Left, accommodating Communists, promoting and financing their clandestine operations, all this is to bring us to what Quigley thinks the Wall Street power group sincerely wanted — a "single community" where people would be required to "live together and work together." All of this smacks of compulsion, the loss of Constitutional freedoms and deceptive, police state tactics.

4. Midgley calls my reference to a prophecy in the Book of Revelation (13:15-17) merely "some imagery." This is John's prophecy that just prior to the Second Coming (which he describes immediately afterwards) there will be a great "beast" rise to power which will create an economic monopoly in which "no man might buy or sell" without its mark. Moroni talks about a similar "secret combination" in the latter days (Ether 8:23). Midgley can disparage such prophecies if he wishes, but it seems to me that what he dismisses as merely "some imagery" is taking on tire flesh and bone of ominous reality.

5. Midgley denies that there is anything in Quigley's book to indicate there is an international financial combine which is pushing the world into a collectivized society. To come to this conclusion, Midgley had to ignore at least half of the "forty pages" which I quoted from Quigley.

6 & 10. Midgley says I cannot quote Quigley as my star witness and then criticize him for trying to cover up the consequences of the conspiracy which the Establishment has been financing. But why not, if it is true?

7. This item deals with the purposes of the Wall Street cabal in financing Left-Wing collectivist groups and has already been answered.

8 & 9. Midgley says it is "totally false" for me to suggest that Quigley believes that the Establishment is moving toward the collectivist Left in order to replace traditional capitalism with a world-wide socialist society. He says Quigley presents no such picture in *Tragedy and Hope*. This leads me to suspect that perhaps Midgley has not read Plato after all. Maybe he had no idea what Quigley was talking about when he traced the ideological gestation of the secret society to John Ruskin's Platonically inspired dream of a one-world socialist society.

11. Midgley wants to know where Quigley makes any bold declaration that the London-Wall Street network was involved in attacking the foundation of the American culture. Communists have as their basic objective not only the political conquest of America but the total destruction of its Judaic-Christian culture. I see no difficulty whatever in establishing that Quigley has been well

aware of the attack the Establishment has been making on tire foundations of the American culture.

12. This item raises the complaint that there is nothing in Quigley's book to show that tire Eastern Establishment is supporting the Communists and pushing toward a globalist union. As we have shown, Quigley specifically verified this point in his review when he carefully defined their goal as "inclusive diversity"—a single society where Americans and Communists must live and work together.

14. Midgley declares that since *The Naked Capitalist* is so lacking in supportive evidence, it must be written off as more "clever" than "cogent." This determination is something I am perfectly willing to leave to the intelligence of the readers.

Finally, Midgley was disturbed by my suggestion that the people take back from government the illegal authority it has expropriated to itself. Although I specifically stated that this should be achieved through established political procedures, Midgley equates me with those he calls the "hysterical radicals." When I suggested that the international bankers' network be deprived of the power they exercise through the Federal Reserve system, Midgley could not visualize anything in this suggestion but a mass appropriation of their wealth by government. This was purely an assumption. He concluded that Skousen has joined the "New Left." The rest of my suggestions were offered in this same spirit, but were translated by Midgley into ominous political monsters ranging all the way from revolutionary communism to Fascist Nazi dictatorship.

My reference to the power elite among the Capitalists led Midgley to expostulate, "I am quite surprised that Skousen has apparently never heard about a power elite ... before he read Quigley." In my book I mentioned that I had known about the secret power structure for over thirty years but had been waiting for someone on the inside to tell us why these wealthy Capitalists would feel there was some advantage in supporting the Communists and Socialists. Once Quigley explained the background and influence of John Ruskin and spelled out the ramifications of the "secret society," it began to make sense. At least to most people. Midgley is one of the exceptions. He suggests that those who believe in the conspiracy must be "cultists." So far as I know, this would include all of the living prophets and all of their immediate predecessors. I doubt whether Midgley would really want to take on anything as formidable as that.

MIDGLEY'S REJOINDER

Louis Midgley

I had rather hoped that Skousen, upon discovering that his Quigley thesis was false, would have had the courage to admit his error, recall his book, disband his cult, stop his radical political agitation, and perhaps even apologize to Carroll Quigley, whose book he has so badly misrepresented and mistreated. Aside from whatever assistance my review could be to the many decent, concerned Saints who have bought the book, I saw the review as a call to repentance to Skousen. I tried to present my objections in a scholarly, forceful but still kindly way. Now it appears that Skousen is not prepared to face up to the fact that his book rests on falsehood. Instead, he has chosen to dissemble and pretend that he has published the truth.

Skousen's reply plays down the more sensationalistic and lurid aspects of his own thesis and, wherever possible, diverts attention to other "exciting issues." The new toned-down version sometimes contradicts the original. For example, I chided him for not knowing much earlier that wealthy people, including bankers, have power and for having waited thirty long years for someone to "let the secret out." He brushed this objection aside by insisting that he mentions that he had always known about the secret power structure, but had merely been waiting for someone on the inside to tell us why these wealthy Capitalists were doing what they were doing. This contradicts the version actually found on page 4 of his book and the letter he initially sent with the book. There he wrote: "Our main problem has been to discover precisely WHO [his emphasis] was behind some of the insane things which have been happening."

The reader who carefully compares my fourteen objections with his responses will find that he has failed in every case to answer them. However, I must draw special attention to some features of his reply.

1. Skousen charges me with having challenged the accuracy of the long quotations he has taken from Quigley. That was not my point at all. All those thousands of words are quoted accurately, as far as I know. What I complained about were the inferences, summaries and conclusions about Quigley that are fallacious, inaccurate, and unsupported by textual evidence.

2. Quigley tells us that the title of his book points to the tragedy of war and the hope that mankind will turn from hatred to Christian love and thereby learn to live with others with whom we differ (see pp. 1310ff.). Unless we begin to manifest love, he maintains, we will destroy ourselves in senseless war. This is what he means by the phrase "inclusive diversity." Therefore he can say "that diverse peoples with diverse beliefs must live together in a single community." Skousen has pounced on the harmless word "must," inferring from it that Quigley wants "compulsion, the loss of Constitutional freedoms and deceptive police state tactics," collectivism, globalism, and "one-world amalgamation of

the United States and the Soviet Union." All these tenable things are inferred from the harmless little word Quigley used to express his belief in the necessity of loving our neighbors.

3. The only "evidence" Skousen offers to show that the wealthy men he so despises are in favor of globalism, socialism, communism, collectivism, etc., is that Quigley says that John Ruskin lectured to bankers at Oxford in 1870. Skousen then quotes someone to show that Ruskin read Plato and that Plato was a mean totalitarian (pp. 26ff). From this he concludes that bankers are totalitarians who plot to bring about communism, socialism and a host of other evils. There is something seriously wrong with the argument that contemporary bankers and other wealthy men support communism and other evils simply because someone has written that Ruskin once read Plato.

4. Skousen ends his reply by arguing that by rejecting his cult of conspiracy I am placing myself in opposition to "all the living prophets and all of their immediate predecessors." As a matter of fact, I do believe that there are numerous, often competing conspiracies in this world. And I am in complete accord with the frequent prophetic judgments brought against the vain and hurtful nonsense of this world. I know the truth of the prophetic warnings against various kinds of radical political activities, including communism and birchism. But there has never been one word from our prophets warning us of Skousen's myth of a bankers' conspiracy. Instead, the prophets tell us that we have nothing to fear from the wicked in this world if we hold fast to the iron rod of the gospel. But that involves not following Skousen-type programs, which fight the worldly wicked with their own tool—hate—rather than return love for the evil that abounds in this world. Obviously, I have placed myself in opposition to such "living prophets" as Robert Welch and many other such pariahs, but that is another matter. Perhaps Skousen accepts such men as "living prophets"; in any case he has certainly attempted to affect an accommodation between their strange message and the gospel of Jesus Christ.

Thousands of Brigham Young University students are currently being indoctrinated in the "gospel" of *The Naked Capitalist* by Skousen and a handful of his disciples who teach "religion" classes. Students and faculty who do not accept the Skousen-type "gospel" are written off as apostates and enemies of the Church. This is a mean game. Wherever Skousen and his disciples are able to spread their cult we see hostile camps, disunity in die Church and loss of conviction in the gospel of Jesus Christ.

DISSENT: DO WE NEED IT?

Address given on August 24, 1970, at The National War College and later published in Perspectives in Defense Management (January 1971), pp. 21-30.

Perspectives in Defense Management
January 1971, pp. 21-30
This article was edited for publication here with the author's approval from a transcript of his presentation to the Industrial College of the Armed Forces on 24 August 1970

DISSENT: DO WE NEED IT?

By: Carroll Quigley

I will not attempt this morning to deal with the whole subject of dissent in the United States. Instead, I propose to deal with it from a single point of view — my own, of course — and to call your attention to some widely held ideas which I regard as erroneous.

First of all, allegiance and dissent, it seems to me, are opposite sides of the same coin. We cannot have organized society without allegiance. A society cannot continue to exist without loyalty. But, I would further add, a society cannot continue to exist that is incapable of reforming itself, and the prerequisite to reform is dissent.

Allegiance is absolutely vital. But so is dissent. To me, allegiance means devotion to symbols and organizational structures, both of which are necessary in any society. Dissent, it seems to me, is the opposite side of the coin. It implies a critical approach to the symbols and to organizational structures of society.

I don't think either allegiance or dissent has anything to do, necessarily, with loyalty and disloyalty. A dissenter can be loyal and usually is. Conversely, a person who has allegiance might be fundamentally disloyal. I'm sure that must be confusing, so let me explain.

I said allegiance is devotion to an organizational structure and symbols. But in any society, any community of people, organizational structures and at least the meaning of symbols inevitably change as a result of critical re-examination of the services they actually perform for the community. Because the community must be preserved, no matter what changes take place in organizational structures or symbols.

Loyalty and disloyalty, I would say, focus on the community itself, rather than on its symbols and structure—the community as an ongoing group of people working together for their basic way of life. Allegiance is more superficial and is never an end in itself. It is important only to the degree that it supports the things which a community must have, such as political stability and, above all, security.

My examination of history shows that communities can live securely through severe political instability and turmoil. In fact, communities have sometimes reached the pinnacle of their political and military power during the most turbulent periods of their history. France, for example, has never experienced more internal violence, instability, and ideological conflict than during the years immediately following the great revolution of 1789—the very years in which her armies overran all the major countries of Europe and Napoleon carved out the largest dominion that Europe had seen since the days of the Roman Empire.

But, in the 19th century, allegiance and dissent had a somewhat different meaning. We had then, for the first time in our history, political communities in which everyone was a member and every subject was an active citizen. For that reason, we expected everyone not only to be loyal but to give allegiance.

Fortunately, in the 19th century we also permitted dissent. The connection between universal political participation, the citizen Army, and democracy—essentially 19th century institutions—is very close. I think in the future we may move away from all of these. Almost certainly we will move away from the mass citizen-Army, and I think we will also, to some extent, move away from democracy. I think we will increasingly come not to expect allegiance from certain segments of the population, perhaps substantial segments.

Now in the 19th century, we tended to think of allegiance, loyalty, and dissent with reference to the governmental system. Allegiance and loyalty were owed to the government; dissent was a threat to the government. In other words, the insecurity and instability that we were concerned with were the kind that might undermine or overthrow the government.

Today I do not think that is the issue. I do not think we have to contend with dissent or even disloyalty capable of overthrowing the United States Government. The danger comes rather from the capability, which almost any dissenting group has, of sabotaging the complicated organizational and operational systems through which our society functions—the telephone system, for example. As you know, we are likely to have a critical fuel problem next winter. We might pull through without too much difficulty if everyone cooperates, but a few determined saboteurs could make a lot of trouble. The reason for this is that we have built up all these complicated, interlocking, and bureaucratic organizational structures which are highly vulnerable to disruption by people who are disloyal to the system, or even by dissenters who merely want to see it reformed.

Notice another distinction that I am making here. Dissent is something inside a person; it is ideas, feeling, attitudes. What a person does is something else. Take urban violence. That is action, something that people do. But what concerns me about dissent is why these people resort to violence. What makes people who are normally decent, restrained, and well-behaved suddenly flare up and throw rocks through windows, burn office records, pour blood on draft files, and generally behave like savages? What causes dissent to lead to violent action?

This violence, let me repeat, does not necessarily lead to revolution, a threat to the government. I don't believe that violent dissent today is at all likely to lead to a takeover of the Government by dissenting groups or even to a demand for drastic changes in our society. But sabotage and violence by dissenting groups can make life very difficult for a large part of our population. In other words, we have the paradoxical situation in which the government is sound and strong while we, people in general, are insecure and vulnerable. Here in Washington, as you know, many people are afraid to go downtown at night. So the theaters are half-empty and even the restaurants are in trouble. All because the anger and despair resulting from social ills has overflowed into violent action which disrupts normal processes of living without really threatening the political structure itself.

No society can stand still. Its institutions must constantly adjust and evolve, and periodically undergo reform, because the needs they are supposed to serve are themselves constantly changing. And institutions cannot grow and reform unless the people whose needs they fail to serve, or serve badly, can make their dissatisfaction felt in short, unless they can actively dissent from things as they are. If dissent is stifled and denied redress, it builds up like a head of steam. Many people assume that dissent and the demand for reform are the first step toward revolution. They are mistaken. My study of history shows pretty generally that revolutions do not come from dissent. They come from a failure to reform, which leads to breakdown. It is quite true that misguided reforms which fail to attack real problems may also result in breakdown. But dissent, and reform responding to dissent, do not lead to revolution. They lead away from it.

There are two kinds of dissent, just as there are two kinds of allegiance: intellectual and emotional. They are quite different. Much of our concern lately, in the government and on the campuses, has been with intellectual dissent. We worry about alien ideologies and revolutionary philosophies, like anarchism. Now I will not say this is a waste of time. But I do believe that far too much time has been spent on it. Intellectual dissent is not the real problem today, particularly in the United States. The real problem today is emotional dissent.

The two are not the same thing—they may well be opposites. People's emotional makeup—the values, needs, and ideas about which they feel strongly and emotionally are often quite different from their intellectual makeup, their rational idea systems. The values that they profess and hold to intellectually may have little to do with their more basic needs, those which inflame their emotions, often without their really knowing why.

Now, action—what people do—usually results from their emotional rather than their intellectual makeup, from their strongly felt but sometimes only dimly understood needs. Afterwards, they justify what they did in terms of an explicit ideology, through the process of rationalization.

I am going to put a diagram on the blackboard here of what I think a human being might look like. And instead of saying man has a body and a soul (which is dualistic thinking) I am going to take a tripartite approach body, emotions, and reason. Reason is concerned with thinking, so I'll put a "T" here. That is the realm of ideology. The emotions are "F"—concerned with feeling. That is associated with what I call outlook, which is people's value systems, the basis on which they classify things and experiences as good or bad.

Incidentally, this affects other kinds of classification, too. You see someone coming down the street, and you classify this person male or female. That is, you did until recently. That makes you laugh, but it is not a trivial matter. When people no longer wish to be obviously male or female, but wish to be obviously neither, clearly there are rather deep-seated emotions involved. These people are expressing attitudes, in a spirit of defiance, which are alien to my generation but which we cannot afford to ignore because a substantial group of the society seems to be turning in that direction. We will have to look behind the strange behavior and try to determine what are the attitudes and needs that cause it.

Then we have the body, which provides the means for action. Talk comes from ideology but action comes from outlook. In one of my earlier lectures here, on Russia and Communist ideology, I argued that what the Russian people do is largely a result of the Russian outlook, rooted deep in their history, going back long before 1917. Russia also has an ideology, Marxism, which was imported from Western Europe. This ideology is not at all suited to their outlook, formed from their ancient traditions, and it certainly doesn't jibe with the character and aims of their revolution. But because the leaders of their revolution were Marxist, they had to rationalize it in terms of the Marxist ideology, which was intellectually quite difficult and doesn't make much sense even to some Marxists.

Action is what matters. A society is fully justified in putting restraints on action. I think it is also justified in putting some restraint on talk because talk can excite people to action. But I do not think a society is justified in putting restraints on what people think or feel. Action is what matters.

Therefore, feelings, which are the cause of action, need to be understood. Ideology is much less important because it usually leads only to talk, not action. People who talk the most violently are seldom the ones who commit violence. My observation has been, particularly among students, that those who commit the violence are the docile types whom you would not expect to even knock over a glass of water at dinner. They are the ones who get themselves arrested for throwing bricks at policemen or calling them fascist pigs. The reason they behave in this way, I believe, is related to the fact that they are habitually unassertive and docile. In a certain kind of exciting situation, they suddenly feel a compulsion to assert that they are somebody, that they can do something, that they can make people notice them.

How do people come to this? The explanation, it seems to me, must lie in their whole past, their whole experience up to that moment. We cannot know this in detail, of course. We can only say that what a person does is the consequence of everything that happened to him, especially while he was growing up.

But for our society as a whole, I think we can say that there is a tendency for people to act in certain ways on the basis of their class origin. Let me put up another diagram here, showing the American class structure and the kinds of outlook and feelings that are typical of the various classes.

America is a middle-class society. The dominant group is the middle class; its values and ideology dominate our society. I would say, moreover, that the feelings of the American people, by and large, are middle class. Now what I mean by "middle class" is a whole series of things. For example, middle-class people have future preference. They are prepared to make all kinds of sacrifices in the present for the sake of a hypothetical future benefit. You are willing to spend 10 months of study here because you think this will help you in the future. We call that future preference.

Not everybody has future preference. There are whole societies which do not have it. Most people in black Africa have present preference. They are mainly concerned with the present moment. Students who rebel against middle-class parents do so not merely by letting their hair grow, by dressing like their girl friends, who in turn dress like them, and so on, but more fundamentally by abandoning future preference and adopting present preference. They live from moment to moment in what we call an existential way.

Middle-class people are extremely insecure. They do not seek their security through the development of a stable, mature personality, sufficiently strong and autonomous to cope with life's problems. Young people today, and indeed an increasing proportion of the American people, tend to stereotype patterns of behavior with which they react to particular types of situations in particular settings—at home, at work, at school. In effect, they try to have a role, like a costume, for each situation. They may have a wide assortment of these roles, which they can play very skillfully, but they lack the integrated, independent personality that would enable them to deal confidently and serenely with any problem that confronts them. They are basically insecure.

To a large extent, too, the American middle class has sought security in material possessions. This is the root of the acquisitive society. The middle-class family wants a nice house with a large lawn, which takes all Saturday afternoon to mow, and a couple of automobiles—these are the visible symbols of success. And when they get them, they want more; they are insatiable. Their material demands are infinitely expandable. They finish off the basement into a rumpus room; then they build a swimming pool; then they buy a motor boat; then they get a cottage down on the bay so they won't have to come back and forth. This goes on and on and on.

This is the American way of life. Many societies have a different way. Certain classes in our society have a different way. But our society is still mostly middle class. And increasingly it has become divided into two segments: middle class proper and lower middle class. The lower middle class is petty bourgeois. These people seek their security in status; status in an organizational structure. They try to find a place for themselves in an organization which has a hierarchy in which they can count on moving up automatically simply by surviving.

Some people still think that most Americans are active, assertive, aggressive, self-reliant people who need no help from anyone, especially the Government, and achieve success as individuals by competing freely with each other. That may have been true 100 years ago. It isn't true today. Today more and more of us are petty bourgeois who snuggle down in a hierarchical bureaucracy where advancement is assured merely by keeping the body warm and not breaking the rules; it doesn't matter whether it is education or the Armed Services or a big corporation or the Government. Notice that high school teachers are universally opposed to merit pay. They are paid on the basis of their degrees and years of teaching experience. Or consider the professor. He gets his Ph. D. by writing a large dissertation on a small subject, and he hopes to God he never meets anyone else who knows anything about that subject. If he does, they don't talk about it; they talk about the weather or baseball.

So our society is becoming more and more a society of white-collar clerks on many levels, including full professors. They live for retirement and find their security through status in structures. In addition, we still have some of the old middle class who are making a lot of money, mainly in entrepreneurial activities.

Up at the top is also another small group, the aristocrats or quasi-aristocrats. These are the people who made it so long ago — a generation or two or three — that their position in society is almost guaranteed. They don't worry about what people think; they don't worry about appearances. They may live in a rundown house and drive an old dilapidated car and wear seedy clothes. Eleanor Roosevelt was one of them. Do you young people remember her? She never worried about what anyone thought; she never cared how she was dressed; she paid no attention to style. These are the aristocrats. They have past preference because their own or their families' achievements in the past are the source of their inner security. They are thus able to deal with the present and the future confidently, without feeling that they must prove something to themselves or others.

I confess to some liking and respect for this group, probably because, as a New Englander, I have been exposed to a fair number of them. In my class at college, for example, there was a boy named Robert Saltonstall. Everybody respected him because he had integrity, he was dependable, he was unselfish. Aristocrats are not much concerned with themselves They don't try to impress anyone. Often they are do-gooders, the sincere kind. If they have money, they often concern themselves with the arts, social welfare, reform, betterment, volunteer work. Many have been big in politics — the Roosevelts, the Rockefellers, the Kennedys. They are the complete antithesis, in every way, of the petty bourgeoisie down here, who, of course, hate them intensely.

Below the petty bourgeoisie are the blue-collar workers. They have present preference. They don't worry about the stock market or the arts or making a killing in real estate or helping others. Their overriding interest is in spectator sports. Every game in the football season, every day of the World Series, every night of the fights — they are glued to the TV. They don't try to impress anybody. They don't dress up. They don't go out much.

In the old days, many of these workers were true craftsmen. They served their apprenticeships, learned their trade well, worked hard, took great pride in their work, whether as a plumber, a painter, a carpenter, a mechanic, or whatever. Today, with assembly line mass-production techniques, no individual worker can be held responsible for his work. If the front wheels fall off the 1969 Fords, you can't pin it on any worker. Conversely, no worker can take much personal pride in a car whose wheels don't fall off. So in recent years the blue-collar class has been becoming more and more petty bourgeois. They're after status and more pay and less responsibility.

Generally, the petty bourgeoisie hate the workers. One reason is that many of the petty bourgeoisie do not really have status security—bank clerks and insurance agents, for instance. People who are really clerks in the lower levels of the white-collar class do not have the security or the labor union protection or, in many cases, the annual income of the blue-collar class. I know bricklayers who are making $15,000 to $18,000 a year. I don't know of any bank clerk who makes that much.

Now there are still a lot of blue-collars who work only when they feel like it. They don't really want the money that much. They'd rather enjoy themselves. Present preference, you see. Instead of salting it away for the kids or for retirement, they knock off work a couple of days in the week and go to the beach or just sit around and drink beer and talk to the neighbors and watch the fights on TV.

At the very bottom, we have what Marx called the lumpenproletariat. The Marxists hated them because they were the oppressed working people who were too stupid to realize they were oppressed. They had no revolutionary spirit, no self-discipline. The middle and lower middle classes are self-disciplined—you have to give them that. You cannot have future preference without self-discipline. Future preference means that, for the sake of some future benefit, you have restrained yourself from indulging your present inclinations. You restrict intercourse with your wife because you are worried about 9 months from now.

The people at the bottom don't think ahead even 9 weeks or 9 days from now. This is the culture of poverty, in the ghettos and the rural slums of Appalachia and the South and the Southwest. It includes blacks, and whites, and Puerto Ricans, and Chicanos, and many other ethnics. These people live in shattered neighborhoods and shattered families and shattered cultures. Oscar Lewis and many other writers have described them in detail.

There are two other groups, the religious and the intellectual. Now, a person who studies or reads books or talks learnedly isn't necessarily an intellectual. An intellectual is essentially a person who believes that truth exists in this world and that, if we work hard, we can discover it. A scientist, or a research historian, who has such a belief would belong to this group. I would put myself there. We study the natural universe or human nature or human societies, observe what they do or have done in the past, and learn more and more about why they do what they do. The religious, on the other hand, believe that truth exists in some other world, not this one. Furthermore, they are pretty sure they have already discovered it.

Dissent is found in all of these class groupings, and it is different in each one. There are dissenters among the aristocrats. That's one reason why the petty bourgeoisie hate them: they think they are Communists, spending foundation money to finance subversive projects and undermine the American way of life. The people in the lower middle class object to anyone or anything different. Anyone who is different is a threat. Many of them are WASP's (White Anglo-Saxon Protestants) but there are a good many Irish, Italians, and other nationalities, too. To them, intellectuals are dangerous; aristocrats are dangerous; workers are dangerous; the ghetto poor are dangerous; even religious people, like Father Berrigan, are dangerous.

The dissent that we find in the aristocratic class is the dissent of people who are troubled by our social problems and who feel that they should devote their lives to remedying them. Formerly they might try to improve society by founding a symphony orchestra or a university or a foundation to finance sending blacks to college. (A black today can get into Harvard and have his way paid even if he has much poorer grades than your son or my son, who probably couldn't get in and certainly couldn't have his way paid.) This group at the top has influence far out of proportion to their numbers.

Many religious people, too, are dissenters. Hardly any of them are Communists or congenital revolutionaries. Mostly they are emotionally hung up on the oppression of the Negro, or the bureaucratization of the government, or the militarization of our society, or other problems which they consider offensive in the sight of God. The intellectual is a dissenter for somewhat similar reasons, except that his dissent grows out of his immediate concern for what is going on in this world. Pollution, poverty, war, and other evils he denounces as offensive to reason, equity, morality, or, in many cases, simply to the ideal of an efficient and orderly society.

I put the intellectuals and the religious on the sides of my diagram, incidentally, to show that people can enter these groups from any level of the structure. For the other groups, the movement is generally up or down into the immediately adjacent group.

There is a change underway, however. Our society used to be a ladder on which people generally climbed upward. More and more now we are going to a planetary structure, in which the great dominant lower middle class, the class that determines our prevailing values and organizational structures in education, government, and most of society, are providing recruits for the other groups — sideways, up, and even down, although the movement downward is relatively small.

As the workers become increasingly petty bourgeois and as middle-class bureaucratic and organizational structures increasingly govern all aspects of our society, our society is increasingly taking on the characteristics of the lower middle class, although the poverty culture is also growing. The working class is not growing. Increasingly we are doing things with engineers sitting at consoles, rather than with workers screwing nuts on wheels. The workers are a diminishing, segment of society, contrary to Marx's prediction that the proletariat would grow and grow.

I have argued elsewhere that many people today are frustrated because we are surrounded by organizational structures and artifacts. Only the petty bourgeoisie can find security and emotional satisfaction in an organizational structure, and only a middle-class person can find them in artifacts, things that men have made, such as houses, yachts, and swimming pools. But human beings who are growing up crave sensation and experience. They want contact with other people, moment-to-moment, intimate contact. I've discovered, however, that the intimacy really isn't there. Young people touch each other, often in an almost ritual way; they sleep together, eat together, have sex together. But I don't see the intimacy. There is a lot of action, of course, but not so much more than in the old days, I believe, because now there is a great deal more talk than action.

This group, the lower middle class, it seems to me, holds the key to the future. I think probably they will win out. If they do, they will resolutely defend our organizational structures and artifacts. They will cling to the automobile, for instance; they will not permit us to adopt more efficient methods of moving people around. They will defend the system very much as it is and, if necessary, they will use all the force they can command. Eventually they will stop dissent altogether, whether from the intellectuals, the religious, the poor, the people who run the foundations, the Ivy League colleges, all the rest. The colleges are already becoming bureaucratized, anyway. I can't see the big universities or the foundations as a strong progressive force. The people who run Harvard and the Ford Foundation look more and more like lower-middle-class bureaucrats who pose no threat to the established order because they are prepared to do anything to defend the system.

In a book of mine, *Tragedy and Hope*, I conclude with two words, "inclusive diversity." The whole book leads up to those two words. It seems to me that the American way of life and the traditions of Western civilization are summed up in this phrase. In recent years, perhaps for much longer, this tradition has been losing ground to the opposing principle, exclusive uniformity — the coalescing of highly uniform groups which exclude people who are different — we build suburbs for middle-class people to get them away from the workers and the poor who are left in the cities. We strengthen segregation in education.

The people who want to halt this trend, the people who want to take people in buses from the ghetto out into the suburbs so they can go to school with middle-class children, the people who wish to end school segregation are the liberals in these groups on the sides and the top: intellectuals, religious, aristocrats. In American politics, the Republican Party has tended to be in the center; the Democratic Party, on the fringes, including the bottom fringes. Notice that the workers are now abandoning the Democratic Party. They are abandoning it because they are becoming lower middle class. The fringes—the intellectuals, the aristocrats, religious people, workers, and the poor—the great coalition that supported the New Deal—this coalition is breaking up.

Now, why do children and adolescents rebel? They rebel because they are brought up in middle-class families with bourgeois values and priorities—future preference and self-discipline (you can't go out tonight, you have to study; you can't have the car this weekend because your grades are slipping)—which demand achievement in a system built around organizational structures and artifacts. They rebel against those things because young people cannot get emotional satisfaction from structures and artifacts. Young people are searching for satisfaction through contact with each other and with nature. That's why they sleep out in the rain and in the cold in groups.

I remember when I was doing some research at Harvard and had to walk across the Boston Commons just about every day, and it rained for 3 weeks. There were hundreds of kids lying there in extreme discomfort who could have been at home sleeping on innerspring mattresses in air-conditioned comfort. Why? Because they wanted to feel something. They had renounced the values of their parents. This was a way of asserting their identity, of dramatizing the fact that they were not merely an extension of their parents' lives. They refused to behave in the way their middle-class parents considered proper or to strive for the goals their parents equated with successful achievement.

This is dissent; dissent from middle-class values and it may take a variety of forms. They may adopt almost any kind of ideology—Zen Buddhism, the Black Muslim movement, Marxism, anarchism—the ideologies do not matter. The stated goals of their agitations and demonstrations and violence do not matter. If they agitate against the draft and you abolished the draft tomorrow, they would still agitate.

There was a young girl on our campus, Catholic, very pious, with a couple of brothers who were priests, one of the best-behaved students we had. She took part in the demonstration at the Pentagon, and the next week she told me about it. She was a rather colorless girl, really, but now she was all excited. She exclaimed, "There we were, all together; marching up the hill, all together!" She belonged, she was with other young people, and they were going somewhere, doing something, and the rest of the world was noticing them. Suppose, as they were marching up the hill, the Pentagon had disappeared, poof! Probably she would have been quiet for a few weeks. But then she'd have found something else that needed to be changed, because she had to satisfy her own inner need to feel, to assert herself as a person, to do something.

Dissent that expresses itself in sabotage and violence comes largely from the children of these two middle-class groups. Now they have aligned themselves with the culture of poverty, with the blacks, with the Black Panthers and similar radical groups. Are they ideologically committed to these groups? I don't think so. They are simply trying to be different from their parents, to live from moment-to-moment: present preference, not future preference. They don't want to accumulate artifacts. They want no place in the establishment.

Dissent against the establishment—its structures and its artifacts—is not necessarily disloyalty. But if it becomes nihilistic, anarchistic, and destructive simply because of the emotional inadequacies of the individual dissenters, then it can become dangerous, not to the government but in terms of the physical damage they can do to our vulnerable operating systems. And in the process, they may also injure some of the very things they value most, such as the prospects for real improvement in the condition of the worst disadvantaged of our society, the blacks and the poor.

QUESTION: Do you envision any real intermingling between the aristocrats and other groups?

DR. QUIGLEY:
Actually, there are few aristocrats and it is not easy to reach them. If they meet you, they behave democratically, but they don't say, "Here is my phone number. Call me up."

But they have been a significant element in the politics of many countries, including this one, particularly in the last generation or so. And most people are not really familiar with them because, while they can be found in many places, they are unobtrusive. There is an aristocrat who lives in Georgetown. He has a house there with a dome, a small version of Monticello. A descendant of Martha Washington, he spends all his time working for the improvement of Georgetown. But he doesn't want his name in the paper.

So people don't notice aristocrats or they don't understand them. There are some parts of the country where it is hard to find them—Reno, Nevada, for example. They are scattered around mostly in places where there are older families, some of them very impoverished now but nevertheless people who command great respect in their community. A book called *Deep South* describes Natchez, Mississippi; it tells about a family there which has no money, and yet nothing is done in that town without consulting with them.

If you are asking me, "Will the rebels against the middle class work with the aristocrats?" they already do to some extent. As you know, they rush out and work for the Kennedys or anyone else they believe to be devoted to a cause beyond their own personal interests. This is the kind of an image a politician has to create in order to get their support.

QUESTION: Do the dissenters typically join established groups, or do they form their own?

DR. QUIGLEY:
Of course they tend to be suspicious of established groups. The religious dissenters may take up religious reform along with political and social causes. The girl I mentioned, who wanted to blow down the Pentaeton, also insisted that Catholic services on Sundays at the university be turned into a real hippie Mass in which she played the guitar. Generally, it would be difficult to align large groups of dissenters because they would disagree on so many things.

QUESTION: Are all the dissenters young people rebelling against the values of their middle-class parents?

DR. QUIGLEY:
No, not all. One group, for example, are the intellectuals who originally founded the Bulletin of the Atomic Scientists to work for control of the atomic bomb. They are almost religious in some of the positions they take.

QUESTION: Do the workers' children not rebel against their parents in the same way as middle-class children?

DR. QUIGLEY:
No, they don't. For one thing; they don't have the economic base. The children of the middle class are rebelling and their parents are picking up the tab. A couple of years ago I met a girl hanging around Du Pont Circle who was getting $150 a month from her parents to stay away from home. Workers' children don't do that. In a real working family, the kids graduate from high school and never go on to college; they have to get a job and support themselves. They may marry pretty quickly. In the old days, the aristocrats and the workers married young

and had many children, while the middle classes postponed marriage and had few children because they looked to the future; they had no more children than they could properly educate. Intellectuals often had many children because they were less concerned about the future and figured they could send their kids to college on scholarships. I would say that the dissenters on the fringes may be of any age, but the dissenters from the middle class are more likely to be adolescents or of college age.

Of course, college students may be 30 years old or even older. Career preparation in the middle class is now pushing up to age 30. A middle-class child who wants to become a medical doctor specializing in some field (which is virtually essential) will not be an income-earning individual until he is 30. And his parents must be willing to finance all that, which means they will also finance his dissent.

QUESTION: Ex-HEW Secretary John Gardner is trying to form a coalition of people of all kinds to work for reform. Do you think this will be successful?

DR. QUIGLEY:
I don't know. John Gardner is a bureaucrat from the eastern establishment as, indeed, Dean Rusk was. Whether this will be successful I don't know. I would be a little dubious. But I think he is on the right track. We have got to induce young people to put their nervous energies and their desire for self-assertion and action into practical reform on a piecemeal basis. But this is very difficult. You have no idea of the pressures that we who are on the firing line in the universities have been under in the last few years, trying to hold back the explosion, trying to persuade students that it is possible to reform but it has to be done on a piecemeal basis above all, that it is necessary first to know the facts of the problem.

They say, "The Congress is corrupt." I ask them, "What do you know about the Congress? Do you know your own Congressman's name?" Usually they don't. It's almost a reflex with them, like seeing a fascist pig in a policeman. To them, all Congressmen are crooks. I tell them they must spend a lot of time learning the American political system and how it functions, and then work within the system. But most of them just won't buy that. They insist the system is totally corrupt. I insist that the system, the establishment, whatever you call it, is so balanced by diverse forces that very slight pressures can produce perceptible results.

For example, I've talked about the lower middle class as the backbone of fascism in the future. I think this may happen. The party members of the Nazi

Party in Germany were consistently lower middle class. I think that the right-wing movements in this country are pretty generally in this group. But, on the other hand, I believe we could make the United States much more stable if the whole middle class could simply get together on a program that would benefit all of them.

Why, for instance, should the middle class as consumers and buyers of automobiles be prepared to defend Ford or General Motors? A piece in the paper yesterday said that the Number 1 complaint of Americans today is about their automobiles. Why should middle-class people let themselves be taxed to death for all kinds of things they don't need for the benefit of corporations which can't even manage themselves efficiently?

In other words, if we can be saved, our salvation may lie in some coalition of diverse elements. But I do insist that we must study the situation, see what's wrong, think it through.

What are the alternatives? Above all, we can't do it with utopianism and nihilism. Utopianism is the belief that nothing is worth doing at all unless it can be done perfectly. This is sheer nonsense. There never was a time when everything was perfect and there never will be. The nihilist says everything must be destroyed first and then rebuilt from the ground up. This is not only nonsense; it is suicide.

QUESTION: Some writers have suggested that the much maligned bourgeois values saving for the future, home ownership, educating your kids, strict standards of morality have given this country the internal stability and the moral stamina which enabled us to win two world wars, maybe others. Would you comment on this?

DR. QUIGLEY:

I would just as soon not go into who won the wars. Most of the wars we get into, the other side seems to win. They told us Japan and Germany were defeated, but they seem to me to be doing awfully well. But I don't think you can have any society without self-discipline, individual responsibility, some kind of property that you can call your own, some basis for identity, some system of moral values. Only emotional people cry, "Down with the middle classes," or any other class. I think that we can design a better society, and we still have about the best society that's around. The fact that we are discontented with its imperfections is not a bad thing in itself, but it is no justification to destroy it. And if we are to have a society in the future which is strong and healthy and stable, it will be based to a very considerable extent on the virtues that you're talking about. But it cannot be based upon a rigid loyalty to structures.

QUESTION: How much support do you believe the dissenters in this country are getting from the Communists?

DR. QUIGLEY:
I'm sure the Communists are supporting the dissenters. But the Communists are of no importance. The Communist Party in this country was destroyed. Read Shannon's history. It is extremely likely that by 1960 one of the chief sources of funds for the Communist Party in this country was the FBI spies who had joined it. And the chief financial support of the Communists from about 1920 to about 1950 was Wall Street. Why? I do not know. If you're interested, look up the story of The Institute of Pacific Relations; it was financed by Lee Higginson & Company of Boston, Frederick Vanderbilt Field of New York, and other big money interests.

When these people cut off this money, about 1949, the Communists were pretty much finished. Their only other source of money was Moscow, and Moscow has never been generous with funds for local Communist Parties, which they believe should support themselves. According to an FBI estimate, I believe, the Communists in this country are down to about 15,000 members. Take Angela Davis. She is emotionally alienated from our society, and for good reasons, but this has little to do with communism, even if she is a member of the Party. This is why I say ideology is not really important in dissent. People become Communists not because they like the ideology, but because they wish to demonstrate their opposition, just as young people let their hair grow and won't polish their shoes or wear neckties.

QUESTION: In your diagram, you have no place for the youth movement as such — the yippies, the hippies, and so on, as a class. They seem to be increasing in numbers. Are they growing into a class which ultimately we will have to support?

DR. QUIGLEY:
Not a social class as I would define it. This is one of the most controversial questions in sociology: What is a social class? I construe social classes here in terms of outlook, the values and priorities that are held neurologically rather than intellectually. I don't regard the various youth cults and groups as a social class. They are not coalescing because I don't think there's any program or even value system that they can agree on. Some people think that, because they're

rebelling against middle-class values, they agree on their own values. They don't. Some of them, for example, believe in having sex every hour of the day; others, that they should give up sex completely — in both cases, because they're against middle-class values.

Anyway, most of them are not doing much, at least from my observation. In fact, it's the neuters who are not sexually identified who are the real troublemakers, the neuters — increasingly female neuters, I notice — egging other people on. I think most of them will eventually find a place in society. At my university, the students range from the extreme left — proclaimed Communists — to the extreme right — outright reactionaries, including some neo-Nazis.

What a college administrator must do, if things polarize, is to try to get the split, the line of cleavage, as far to the left as possible. If he acts precipitately — bringing in the police, for example — he is sunk because the whole middle group will go against the police. Then the split will be toward the right or down the middle.

What he must do is to try to isolate the left. To do that, you have to give them their head to some extent. If you do, they will probably splinter, with only a few dozen real troublemakers on the fringe. What you must avoid above all is a split in the university community that puts a large group on the side of the violent dissenters. That happens when the authorities act too soon and too strongly.

THE MYTHOLOGY OF AMERICAN DEMOCRACY

Perspectives in Defense Management, Winter 1972-1973

This article was edited for publication here with the author's approval from a transcript of his presentation to the Industrial College of the Armed Forces on August 17, 1972.

An unromantic historian argues that the great traditions of American democracy tell us little about how the system has actually worked and evolved.

I could easily make this talk a self-praising, Fourth of July oration, vintage 1880. But that's not what you want and that's not what I am qualified to give you.

I am going to give you an historical view of the American democratic tradition with analytical overtones showing how democracy has changed over the course of our history. The United States is a democracy. I think there is no doubt of that—but the American democratic tradition is largely a myth.

First, a few definitions. I define democracy as majority rule and minority rights. Of these the second is more important than the first. There are many despotisms which have majority rule. Hitler held plebiscites in which he obtained over 92 percent of the vote, and most of the people who were qualified to vote did vote. I think that in China today a majority of the people support the government, but China is certainly not a democracy.

The essential half of this definition then, is the second half, minority rights. What that means is that a minority has those rights which enable it to work within the system and to build itself up to be a majority and replace the governing majority. Moderate deviations from majority rule do not usually undermine democracy. In fact, absolute democracy does not really exist at the nation-state level. For example, a modest poll tax as a qualification for voting would be an infringement on the principle of majority rule but restrictions on the suffrage would have to go pretty far before they really abrogated democracy. On the other hand relatively slight restrictions on minority rights—the freedoms of speech, assembly, and other rights—would rapidly erode democracy.

Another basic point. Democracy is not the highest political value. Speeches about democracy and the democratic tradition might lead you to think this is the most perfect political system ever devised. That just isn't true. There are other political values which are more important and urgent—security, for example. And I would suggest that political stability and political responsibility are also more important.

In fact, I would define a good government as a responsible government. In every society there is a structure of power. A government is responsible when its political processes reflect that power structure, thus ensuring that the power structure will never be able to overthrow the government. If a society in fact could be ruled by a minority because that elite had power to rule and the political system reflected that situation by giving governing power to that elite, then, it seems to me, we would have a responsible government even though it was not democratic.

Some of you are looking puzzled. Why do we have democracy in this country? I'll give you a blunt and simple answer, which means, of course, that it's not the whole truth. We have democracy because around 1880 the distribution of weapons in this society was such that no minority could make a majority obey. If you have a society in which weapons are cheap, so that almost anyone can obtain them, and are easy to use—what I call amateur weapons—then you have democracy. But if the opposite is true, weapons extremely expensive and very difficult to use—the medieval knight, for example, with his castle, the supreme weapons of the year 1100—in such a system, with expensive and difficult-to-use weapons, you could not possibly have majority rule. But in 1880 for $100 you could get the two best weapons in the world, a Winchester rifle and a Colt revolver; so almost anyone could buy them. With weapons like these in the hands of ordinary people, no minority could make the majority obey a despotic government.

Now there are some features of democracy that many people really do not understand. It is said, for example, that our officials are elected by the voters, and the one that gets the most votes is elected. I suggest that this is misleading. The outcome of an election is not determined by those who vote, but by those who don't vote. Since 1945 or so, we have had pretty close elections, with not much more than half of the people voting. In the 1968 election about 80 million voted, and about 50 million qualified to vote did not. The outcome was determined by the 50 million who didn't vote. If you could have got 2 percent of the nonvoters to the polls to vote for your candidate, you could have elected him. And that has been true of most of our recent elections. It's the ones who don't vote who determine the outcome.

Something else we tend to overlook is that the nomination process is much more important than the election process. I startle a lot of my colleagues who think they know England pretty well by asking them how candidates for election are nominated in England. They don't have conventions or primary elections. So the important thing is who names the candidates. In any democratic country, if you could name the candidates of all parties, you wouldn't care who voted or how, because your man would be elected. So the nominations are more important than the elections.

A third point is one I often make in talking with students who are discouraged about their inability to influence the political process. I say this is nonsense. There never was a time when it was easier for ordinary people to influence political affairs than today. One reason, of course, is that big mass of nonvoters. If you can simply get 2 or 3 percent of them to the polls—and that shouldn't be too difficult—then you can elect your candidate, whoever he is.

There are three key factors in elections—money, organization, enthusiasm. If you have two of them you can win. Students may not have much money, but they can organize—apparently McGovern has an organization—and they are enthusiastic. Gene McCarthy went pretty far on enthusiasm alone four years ago, even though he didn't have an organization or much money.

THAT ANGLO-SAXON HERITAGE

Now let's look at some democratic traditions. Most people say that our democratic traditions began in England. This is totally a myth. England was in no sense a democratic country in 1775, when we declared our independence. It remained an undemocratic country until well into the 20th century. Candidates were not nominated by the people, and members of parliament were not even paid until 1911.

Furthermore, England had an oligarchic political structure. It did reform itself radically in the 1820's and became one of the best governments in the world by shifting to what I would call an aristocratic structure, that is, one with a sense of responsibility to the public welfare. But they didn't have a democratic system. An ordinary person couldn't get a secondary education at all until after 1902, and higher education didn't become widely available until after 1945 and the reforms of the last quarter of a century.

Furthermore, both in England and in our country—this is part of our undemocratic heritage from England—access to justice is strictly limited. Until 30 years ago England had a rigidly stratified society, the only one in Europe where you could tell a person's social class the minute he opened his mouth. The upper classes had a different accent. Today, with the BBC and more popular education, speaking accents are blending, as opportunities for changing status are opening upward. But access to law, to the courts, to justice, as well as to education, were strictly limited, and for he most part still are in the English-speaking world.

When somebody infringes your rights, it's usually too expensive for you to defend them. This is true even in income-tax disputes. And it hit me, for example, in the matter of copyright. A fellow published a book a couple of years ago, in which 30 of its 121 pages came right out of a book I had published. I cannot sue him for infringement of copyright because I can't afford it. And he's made so much money out of his book, that he could fight me right up to the Supreme Court, and he might even win. But I don't have the $150,000 it takes to flight a case to the Supreme Court.

So, the American democratic tradition was born here, not in England, and its antecedents go back to non-English sources—for example, the Judaeo-Christian tradition.

THE CONSTITUTION AND THE POWERS

Next, the Constitution. It is not democratic but republican, a different thing. That means only that we don't have a king. It protects minority rights chiefly in the first ten amendments. Before they were added, it provided very little protection for minority rights. It did provide for jury trial, but as I have shown, access to the courts was a class privilege.

These first ten amendments were the basis of minority rights in the Constitution. But they were accompanied by many weaknesses, which have remained throughout our history. It is important that we realize this, because our safety, our lives, and our happiness depend upon our constitutional forms of government.

The Constitution established three branches of government—executive, legislative, and judicial—but any governing system has more than three parts. For instance, the taxing power was split up. Two other powers are especially important: the administrative power and the incorporating power. These are vital in any government. They are not allotted to anyone in the Constitution, certainly not to the Federal Government.

By the incorporating power I mean the right of a government to say that a group of people will be regarded in law as a person with the right to hold property and to sue and be sued in the courts. That power is left with the States.

The administrative power is that discretionary power which is absolutely essential to government. It is best represented, I think, in a policeman controlling traffic at a busy intersection. He starts and stops the traffic according to his judgment of what is best to keep traffic flowing smoothly and safely. That is the administrative power. It is one of the original powers of government. It involves such things as protecting the health and sanitation of any community by such means as requiring vaccination. In constitutional law we call it the police power but that does not mean the policeman's power. It means discretionary power.

For almost 100 years after the Civil War there was a struggle among the three branches of the Government for control of the administrative power. Now we have independent administrative and regulatory agencies which are subject to the courts or to the executive branch or to the congressional branch. In many cases they have become autonomous. For instance, one of the things they did, without guidance from any of the three main branches until very late, was to introduce all the inequities of the English-speaking judicial and legal system into the procedures of administration.

The Constitution made no provision for breaking a deadlock among the three branches. It was assumed that in such a case whatever action was at issue should not be done — in other words, anything worth doing will be supported by all branches of the government. If they don't agree, it's better not to do it. The basic assumption was, of course, that no disasters would result from paralysis in government, because we were secure from sudden and overwhelming attack from abroad. Domestic paralysis we could live with. And as long as we were protected by our two oceans and the British Navy, and later by our own armed forces, we were able to muddle through. Since the advent of nuclear weapons, the situation is different, and the problem of how to ensure prompt action in a crisis, has been a continuing constitutional issue.

One of the most essential parts of our political system is our political parties, which grew up wholly outside the Constitution and the legal system as the links between the three branches of our government. You have been reading about the dispute over delegates for the Republican National Convention. For a long time about a quarter of the Republican delegates did not represent the voters at all because they came from purely Democratic States in the South. Today the non-Republican States do not have so large a block of delegates. McKinley's nomination in 1896 was arranged ahead of time in Thomasville, Georgia, the preceding winter by Mark Hanna's buying up the Southern delegates to the Republican Convention of 1896. The Southern delegates were paid $200 plus rail fare and hotel bills to vote for McKinley. Anyway, the party system has evolved to make up for one of the major deficiencies of the Constitution, the lack of provisions to translate the citizen's vote into a government responsive to the popular will.

Another extraconstitutional development is judicial supremacy. This was simply asserted and exercised by the judiciary, which determines whether legislation is constitutional and makes rulings which the executive branch is supposed to carry out. But in adopting this principle, we have simply taken over the undemocratic feature of the English system, which requires the citizen to defend his rights in courts of law. Today people who are penniless do enjoy that right because they can get the American Civil Liberties Union, or some foundation, or somebody else, to finance their litigation. But an ordinary middle-class person of limited means is denied that right. Both of these institutional developments, political parties and judicial supremacy, are outside the Constitution. Both of them are largely irresponsible. They are not responsible to the people.

THE STAGES OF POLITICAL GROWTH

Let me quickly review the history of American democracy in terms of how candidates are nominated. There were five stages in that historical evolution. In the first, beginning in 1789 and for more than 40 years thereafter, candidates were named by the legislators. This method was called the legislative caucus. Up to the early 1840's there was a steady extension of democracy by changes in the State voting laws, culminating in the Rhode Island reforms of 1842, resulting from Dorr's rebellion, extending the suffrage to the ordinary man. By 1843 voting democracy was established more or less in all the States.

The second stage was the era of the spoils system, and it lasted for a little over 40 years, from just before 1840 to just after 1880. The spoils system arose, from the fact that in a system of mass democracy, where most men at least have the right to vote, there must be some way of nominating candidates for office. The method chosen was the nominating convention. This raised the problem of how to finance sending the delegates to the convention.

The solution developed around 1840 was for the party machine of the winning party in an election to reward the party faithful by appointing them to government office. To the victor belong the spoils. These appointees then kick back money to the party kitty, say, a quarter or 10 percent of their salary every year; and these kick-backs provide the funds for the nomination convention and the process of political campaigning. In that new system government officials themselves went as paid delegates to the nominating conventions, and the nominations and getting out the vote in elections were controlled by the party machines. All of these were local in cities or on a State basis. It was a feudalistic power structure.

One of the interesting features of the whole system is the role that polities played in people's lives. In this period, from 1840 to 1880, politics and religion, frequently revivalist religion, were the chief entertainment outlets the American people had. They did not have organized sports or other kinds of entertainment except an occasional traveling company of actors, and, more often, revivalist preachers. So people identified with a political party.

The closest parallel to this in our own time perhaps, is the national hullabaloo in the late thirties and early forties over the contest between the Yankees and the Dodgers in the World Series, when everybody at least in the eastern part of the country and everybody in New York, was rooting for one or for the other, for totally irrational reasons. This was a purely emotional thing. If their team won they were ecstatic, if their team lost they were downcast. Well, that's what politics was like in the era of the spoils system, and it continued until about the mid-1890's.

Here's how the system worked. Professionals, not amateurs, ran the elections. Issues were of little importance. Charisma was not important; in fact, it was a drawback. The parties put up the most colorless dark horse they could find—the less people knew about him the better—and then counted on enthusiasm for the party to get out the votes.

Elections in that period were pretty close, although after 1865, on the whole, the Republicans did better than the Democrats because the South had become a minority area and the Democrats a minority party. But on the whole few people were interested in issues or in candidates, and it was very difficult for a winning candidate to be reelected because once people got to know him they quickly discovered how dull a person he was. That's why he got nominated in the first place. The nominee was by definition the candidate that the local State party machines had nothing against. The local machines had an effective veto, and by the time they finished vetoing everybody who had any importance or was known, the only one left might be a man like James A. Garfield, a completely dark horse. The only alternative was a Civil War general, who did, of course, exercise some attraction. The elections were extremely close, and up to 80 percent of the electorate voted. We have the exact figures for most of this period. The average was 78.5 percent. We have never gone that high since 1896.

This spoils system was, in a sense, a shakedown operation, particularly against business. And as business and finance became stronger, they became increasingly restive under this exploitation by party machines. Take the New York Customs House, which had 1,100 officials who were the very core of the New York election machine, which in turn was the core of the system for the whole country. Those 1,100 officials kicked back a good part of their salaries to the New York State party machine. So they in turn, charged businessmen outrageous tariffs, as much as the traffic would bear. The laws were ignored. The customs officials would tie up a shipment of steel and keep it tied up until the tariff they demanded was paid.

As a consequence, businessmen changed the system in 1880-1883. A great man, William C. Whitney (who later started the modern American Navy as Secretary of the Navy in the Cleveland administration), devised a scheme to cut the very roots out from under the party machines. He established the Civil Service in the Pendleton Act of 1883. This had the effect of cutting off most of the funds on which the party machines depended. So the parties now had to look to big business to finance them.

This led to the third historical stage, the era of big-business domination, from 1884 to 1932. It was radically different from the one preceding. Voting dropped off drastically. In the 1870's political activity had cut across all groups and classes—rich and poor, while and black, Catholic and Protestant. Negroes were more active in politics in the 1870's and 1880's than they have been at any time in the 20th century until very recently. Politics was everybody's game. But once big business got control, voting fell off and hovered around 52 percent, instead of the 78 percent it had been before. The professionals were pushed out and amateurs took over—people who came in for one campaign or two, generally financed by business—men like William McKinley, who was elected President in 1896.

Then, big business discovered it could control the Republican National Convention, because of all those delegates from the Solid South who did not represent voters and who therefore could easily be bought. From 1896 on, as a result, the Republicans dominated the national scene through amateur control of politics, and increasingly restricting political activity among middle class whites to the WASP's. It was in the 1890's that we got the Jim Crow laws and other restrictions which in one way or another ensured that certain minority groups really couldn't expect to make it.

Eventually big business undermined its own dominance by being too greedy—there's no other word for it—in the 1920's. They alienated not only the workers and the farmers and the petit-bourgeois white-collar workers, but much of the middle classes, including most of the merchants and light industry. All that was left, still in control at the top, was high finance (sometimes called Wall Street) and heavy industry—steel, coal, the automobile industry, and so on. By running politics solely for their own benefit they alienated everybody else.

So in 1932 everybody else lined up behind a Democrat. In the once solid mid-West, which for decades had voted Republican year in and year out—except rarely for a third party as in 1892 and in 1924—many people now decided that the Civil War had been over for a long time and it was time to vote Democratic.

Out of this situation came the New Deal, the fourth stage. The New Deal was a system of organized blocs. Formerly organized finance and organized heavy industry had run everything else. Now the New Deal set about organizing all the other interests, especially mass labor in the CIO, the Steel Workers' Organizing Committee (SWOC), and the United Mine Workers, which had been the only really strong labor union before 1930. They organized mass labor; they organized the farmers, they organized others: Most of their money came from merchants. The largest contributor to Franklin Roosevelt's campaign in 1932 was the Strauss family of R. H. Macy. Second largest was Vincent Astor, whose real-estate holdings in New York City had been injured by the depression. Third was Bernard Baruch (who is considered one of the founding fathers of this institution), who was a professional contributor to the Democratic Party.

These were the groups that the New Deal organized. What they wanted to set up was a system of countervailing blocs: finance, heavy industry, light industry, professional groups, labor, farmers, and so forth. They figured that if any party or political group got control of the Government and acted too selfishly, the others would form a coalition and restore the balance.

THREATS TO DEMOCRACY

Well, the New Deal ran its course, and since about 1950 or so we have had plutocratic control. I said before that three things were necessary to win elections: money, enthusiasm, organization. The role of money has increased to the point where it's more and more difficult to offset the lack of it with good organization and enthusiasm. Organization must be super-efficient and enthusiasm has to be sustained and widespread. Because the costs of elections, what with TV air time, air transportation, and all the rest of it, have climbed sky-high. It cost McGovern $6 million just to get the nomination, and God knows what it would take to win the election. The Democrats just don't have it. Do they have organization and enthusiasm? It's hard to tell. I'm afraid the enthusiasm has dwindled to some extent.

Anyway, we now have a plutocratic system, and many politicians see it simply as a matter of buying elections. Here's why. As our economy is now structured, the big corporations — aerospace, oil, and so on — are able to pour out millions to support the candidates they favor. The restrictions on the books are easily evaded, and the politicians in power won't do much about it because they want some, too.

The second reason is that labor unions are now a part of the system. They too want to get on the gravy train, and are no longer concerned with defending the rights of ordinary men or making the political system more democratic. Their outlook is little different from that of the big corporations, because this in effect is what they are. They are enormously rich, they are not democratically run, and they have increasingly taken on the characteristics of great corporations: irresponsibility, anonymity, and undemocratic procedures.

So money is one of the great threats to democracy. A second threat is what Roman law called *persona ficta*, fictitious persons — corporations, labor unions, and similar organizations which have the legal status of persons in the sense that they can buy and sell property, they can sue and be sued in the courts, they are generally anonymous, they are certainly irresponsible, and they are increasingly powerful. The 15th amendment and various court rulings have given corporations all the rights of living persons. This is dangerous because they already have certain rights that real persons don't have, principally immortality. That's the saving grace about even the worst scoundrel: someday he will die, and maybe we can wait that long. We felt that way about, Hitler, and Stalin. Maybe Mao is different; we'll see. But a corporation never dies. It has the first quality of divinity, as the ancient Greeks defined it. They called their gods the immortals, because the only quality they had that set them apart from men was that they never died.

Besides setting limits to corporate immortality, we must put other restraints upon all fictitious persons, including foundations, universities, and all such entities. From 1890 there was competition among the States to lower the restraints on corporations. Originally, when a corporation was set up, its charter specified what it was entitled to do, sell hamburgers to the public or whatever. Today there are no restrictions, no restraints, no reporting. Even the Congress can't find out what are the actual costs, expenditures, and profits of the automobile manufacturers, whose profits are incredibly high and yet they are going to raise their prices even higher.

We've got to make our corporations more responsible.

Another danger to democracy. I have just spent 3½ years studying ancient China, Islam, and Byzantium. What undermined all these civilizations is clearly evident. You see it most clearly in Augustus Caesar. What did his power rest upon? He wore many hats. He had the powers of a tribune, he was chief priest, he was commander in chief, he was consul. There were two consuls, but does anybody know the name of the other one? One of the threats to our constitutional system, it seems to me, is that the President of the United States has many hats.

First he is head of the State. Secondly, he is head of the government. As you know, these are different things. Ambassadors are accredited to the head of the State. This seriously hurt us at the Paris Peace Conference, after World

War I when President Wilson represented the United States. Of the five major powers, four were represented by prime ministers, who are heads of governments. Wilson, who was a head of State had the power of immediate decision, and the English really took advantage of this. They got him to commit himself to certain things and then used them to bargain for other things they wanted. He wanted Latin America more or less out of the League of Nations, so in return for that they got him to promise to reduce the U.S. Navy in the 1922 Naval Conference. The head of the State in most, countries is the king or the president. But our President is both.

Thirdly, he is head of a political party. Look at the problems this creates for Nixon right now. If the bugging of the Democratic National Committee headquarters in the Watergate is ever pinned on the Republican Party, many people will see the President himself as responsible.

Fourthly, he is Commander in Chief. The point came up yesterday in some law court that there has been no declaration of war in Southeast Asia either by Congress, as the Constitution provides, or by a President.

Now, let's look at Augustus Caesar again. Augustus Caesar's real power was in his role as commander in chief. The Latin word is *imperator* which we now translate as emperor. He was emperor because be was commander in chief and for no other reason.

I won't go into any fantasies or scenarios about what could happen. You could think of them yourself. Thank God, in this country—I believe also in Russia—the armed forces do not directly or even significantly interfere in politics as armed forces, as they do for example in Latin American countries, or in the recent attempt by part of the Moroccan Air Force to assassinate the King. This is unthinkable in our country. And what makes it unthinkable has nothing to do with restraints placed upon the military in our government, but with their self-restraint, their sense of obligation to our system. And for that we should be very thankful.

But suppose a Presidential candidate lost the election, decided he wanted to be President anyway, and persuaded the military leaders to support him. To you military types this may seem an absolute fantasy. How could the generals and admirals be sure the rank and file would support such an undertaking. But historically this has happened again and again in almost every civilization, usually in the later stages of decline.

The President is also the head of the administrative system with discretionary and emergency powers.

Another threat to democracy is mass culture. There is an increasingly pervasive belief in the United States that equality of opportunity is not enough; we should also have equality in rewards for performance. Everybody starts the race together and finishes together; everybody wins. You see this in universities which are abolishing all grading, all track systems, all encouragement of excellence. The whole trend both in colleges and in high schools is toward equalization and uniformity.

Our democratic system is not based and cannot be based on uniformity. It must be based on diversity. We need the diverse talents of many people working together because of their shared belief in the necessity and value of our constitutional way of life.

Finally, more and more we have subordinated means and methods to goals. If the end is good, to hell with the legality. You can see this clearly in the Southeast Asia war. It should have been put up to Congress to declare war. You say that's mere legality. But when legality and constitutional restraints go by the board, then you are simply saying that might makes right, and more and more you will rely on force to achieve your goals.

REMEDIES

What to do about this? Well, reduce the influence of money. There are many ways of doing this. I urged 30 years ago public financing of elections. Try in every way possible to reward enthusiasm and dedicated effort, strive to internalize individual controls by built-in restraints. Our Armed Forces have these to a considerable degree. But let's internalize controls also in the business world and in labor unions and in the universities and everywhere else. This involves social restraints and the kind of social relationships in which people attach more importance to the good opinion of their friends and associates than to material gain, power, or success.

We must provide nuclei of pluralistic balancing of forces which can unite to resist despotism by agreement on the widest possible interests. What are those interests? Being human is one, and an important one. We're all people and we're all consumers, so the rights of human beings and of consumers should be the big issues around which the pluralistic grouping and constant reshuffling of power groups should revolve.

We must curtail gross growth. I would distinguish between expansion, which is good, growth, which is neutral, and gross growth, which is damaging. We've got to reduce gross growth by going back to the beginning with new methods of doing things.

Here's an example of what I mean. Consider the related problems of pollution and shortage of energy. We are now going to spend at least $3 billion to ensure delivery of Middle East oil to this country by building supertankers and deep-water harbors to accommodate them. At present we have only one port in the United States that can handle them, near Seattle. They're even talking about spending $47 million, I think, to deepen the tunnel bridge across the Chesapeake Bay so that supertankers can come under it.

There's another solution, the hydrogen engine. Its emissions will be only water vapor. Or we can use the sun's energy directly. Out in New Mexico they get 400 or 500 days of consecutive sunshine. So cover some of these sun-baked surfaces with energy accumulating devices and channel the energy into our electric grid. There was an article on this in Science three weeks ago and a book came out recently on the hydrogen engine.

Now one last point. In the Government there are trigger points. A trigger point I call a point where slight changes, if you press it, will have enormous repercussions. I'll give you one example. Congress operates on the seniority principle. Seniority is an obstacle to responsibility and to democracy. Does that mean we must abolish seniority? Not at all. We can make a very simple change, what I call a trigger point change. Simply provide that any committee at any time by majority vote can bring out legislation on the floor. Who can object to that? Let the committees become responsible instead of authoritarian.

DISCUSSION

QUESTION: Would you elaborate on your statement that we need to reduce our gross growth? I don't understand that term as you use it.

DR. QUIGLEY: Look at it this way. Our society is made up of a series of what I call operational lines, each of which satisfies an area of human needs — military, political, economic, social, emotional, intellectual, religious. At the far end of these lines are resources. Behind resources are the technologies that exploit and use them. Technology is embedded in technological systems; in the military, these would be weapon systems. Behind these systems are the patterns of thought, feeling, and action in the society. Behind them, in turn, are human desires, and behind these are human needs.

Now human needs are socialized into desires. We need food but we desire steak or hamburger and will not eat roast locusts or pickled whale blubber, as a friend of mine had handed to him in Iceland one time. So needs are socialized into desires, desires operate through patterns of culture upon a technological system — business system, military system, some other kind of system — and technology works on resources.

A system is past its prime and in trouble when it increases the satisfaction of needs simply by using more and more and more resources, instead of using the same or fewer resources more efficiently. In short, as our needs and desires increase, we need better technologies and better systems which can satisfy our needs without using more resources. For example, Japan, Italy, and Germany were have-not countries before World War II. They went to war to get more of the world's economic goods for themselves. They were defeated, and lost a lot of their resources. Then we reformed the organizational structure of their economic system, and introduced new technology, and today all three of them are have nations, with the highest standard of living they have ever had, on a smaller resource base.

In short, you have to improve the technology and systems portions of the operational line in order to increase satisfaction of need. The operational or output end of the line should be dominated by the input of needs and desires, but without continually increasing the consumption of resources. Gross growth results when, say, the need for moving around is satisfied by a transportation system which uses the same old technology to produce more and more automobiles, superhighways, concrete parking lots, underground offices (to make room for the parking lots), and so on. That is gross growth.

Expansion occurs when you satisfy more needs with the same resources by improving the operational system which is processing resources into satisfaction of needs. This is not the system we've got today.

QUESTION: Which powers of the President do you believe should be curtailed?

DR. QUIGLEY: I didn't say anything about curtailing his powers. All I want is responsibility. Particularly when responsibility is already fixed in the Constitution, it should be exercised. Specifically, the power to make war is vested in the Congress. If that's where we want it, then let's use it. If we don't, then we should change the Constitution and maybe give the President the power to make war. But he doesn't have it now.

In other words I want to bring the legal situation closer to the actual situation, because I think it's dangerous for the legal situation to deviate noticeably from the actual power structure. That's how you get into wars. A war occurs only when one, if not both sides, misjudges the actual power relationships. As long as the legal situation is what they both agree upon—in other words, it reflects the actual power relationship—then they will act according to the law. We always prefer to act upon the basis of our conception of what the facts are and law is a kind of conceptualization or idealization of the real world—rather than on the basis of an objective view of reality.

So it's important that the ideal and the real not be too far apart when vital decisions are made. When the Japanese attacked Pearl Harbor, or when Hitler attacked Russia, both had perceptions of reality that were dangerously at variance with the real power situation. Their decisions, in other words, were irresponsible.

QUESTION: You expressed concern over our multi-hatted President. What remedies would you suggest to deal with the threat of a President who wears many hats?

DR. QUIGLEY: I think we should start with the Congress. If the President gets away with a lot of things that are or may be unconstitutional, that's the fault of the Congress. The Congress should enforce their responsibilities. They should never go along with a President like Johnson who could go down there and get them to agree to just about anything, because he was a very difficult man to say no to.

Walter Lippmann says the Congress is getting stronger and the executive weaker, but this is the reverse of the truth. The Congress is getting weaker. They let all kinds of things go by, because they're interested in their own vested interests, particularly their committee chairmanships.

The Congress should be more responsible to the people, and the best way to do that is, of course, to have a well-informed electorate. So this goes back to my original proposal to curtail the power of money in elections and increase the power of enthusiasm and organization.

QUESTION: You started to talk about trigger points. Could you give some more illustrations of what you mean?

DR. QUIGLEY: Well, the nomination process is an important one. We have had some improvements in the process over the last 8 years, but in the Democratic Party, at least, there is a tendency to fall for slogans and make changes which don't really get at what is needed. Specifically, I would not favor any nomination process which stipulates how many women or how many blacks or how many young people must be delegates. The important thing is that any black or any young person or any Catholic or any Hottentot who wants to function in the system can do so. So the place to begin, I would say, is the nomination process. There again you have to restrict the power of money.

Then in the election we have to get the nonvoters to vote, make them feel it's important. You have no idea the struggle I had with my students two or three years ago. All they wanted to do was to destroy the system. I told them they were crazy. They simply had no idea how the system worked, what determines which legislation comes to the floor of Congress, how candidates for Congress are nominated, and things like that. They were just against the system. Burn it down, blow it up, destroy it.

Do you know that the McCarthy campaign began in my freshmen class at Georgetown? I didn't realize at the time that Ellen McCarthy was in the class. After I talked to the class that December, she got the whole crowd to go up to New Hampshire for the primary. I'm sure Gene had the same idea. But what I tried to show the kids was that they could influence the process by working in the system. There are all kinds of ways to do it, and above all there are those 50 million people who are nonvoters.

First, however, you have to know how the system actually functions. Today no system functions the way it seems at first glance, and never the way the people who are in it describe it. That is certainly true in the system of higher education in which I operate, where the jobs go to the fellow who has a Ph.D., not to the one who is best qualified!

QUESTION: Would you comment on the relationship of the availability of cheap weapons to the current efforts to control small handguns?

DR. QUIGLEY: Well, I don't think the American people should be disarmed, but on the other hand I think it's perfectly possible to keep track of every gun that is made. We could have a licensing system, with every gun numbered and every time it changes hands it is reported to a central computer. Just make sure that the person who gets the identification actually is who he says he is, and hold him responsible if the gun gets into someone else's hands, unless it is stolen and he promptly reports it.

Of course, the small handguns can't be equated with the cheaper weapons of the 1880's because the latter were really the basic weapons of their day. A citizenry armed with rifles and revolvers at that time was in little danger of succumbing to the military, which didn't have anything much better. That has no relation to today's situation, and that's why I'm worried about the prospect of an all-professional army, which as I said, is a terrible threat to any democratic system. We're going for a professional army for the same reason that the Romans did. They couldn't keep people in the army, away from their homes, for 20 and 25 years if they were just drafted men. So they established a professional army.

Well, pretty soon the soldiers married the girls in the locality and pretty soon barbarians were enlisting, and one day the Romans woke up to discover they didn't, even have a Roman or a Latin-speaking army at all, but an army of barbarian mercenaries. And you've all read about what that army did to Roman society in the early centuries of the Christian era.

I'm not saying this is likely to happen to us—the emergence of a non-American mercenary army, I mean—but high pay and fringe benefits are going to attract a pretty varied assortment of types, and I just don't foresee what it may lead to. And I do know, as a historian, that whenever weapons become difficult to use and expensive to obtain, democracy as a functioning political system is in grave danger. How can we avoid the danger? I believe internal restraints are the only solution, in the long run. And how you build those I don't know.

The crime rate of the largest city in the world, Tokyo, is approximately one seventh of the crime rate of a city like New York. Why? Internal restraints. Those internal restraints are rooted in something that maybe we don't want to buy, in the Japanese family. In the United States, crime rates among, Chinese-Americans are infinitesimal on a percentage basis compared to, say, those among the Irish in the 1860's or the Italians in the 1920's. The reason is that the Irish and Italians were broken up sociologically into atomized, self-centered individuals.

> *A political aspirant in the United States begins by discerning his own interest, and discovering those other interests which may be collected around, and amalgamated with it. He then contrives to find some doctrine of principle which may suit the purposes of this new association, and which he adopts in order to bring forward his party and secure its popularity: just as the imprimatur of the king was in former days printed upon the title-page of a volume, and was thus incorporated with a book to which it in no wise belonged.*
>
> —De Toequeville, *Democracy in America*

PUBLIC AUTHORITY AND THE STATE IN THE WESTERN TRADITION: A THOUSAND YEARS OF GROWTH, A.D. 976-1976

THE OSCAR IDEN LECTURES

The Oscar Iden Lectures are delivered annually at the School of Foreign Service. Their purpose is to illuminate trends and issues in world affairs which are of special consequence to the United States.

The Iden Lectures were established in 1976 through the generosity of Mr. and Mrs. Oscar Iden, SFS '24. Their contribution of an endowment fund to the School provides a permanent basis for funding the lectures. The Idens' generosity to the School has been continuous over the years and it is fitting that their abiding educational interest should take the form of a distinguished lecture series in their name.

In October, 1976, Professor Carroll Quigley delivered the first series of Oscar Iden Lectures entitled "Public Authority and the State in the Western Tradition: A Thousand Years of Growth, 976-1976." The lecture series was an occasion to re-gather around Professor Quigley who had retired from the School of Foreign Service the previous spring after forty years of teaching. The audience was composed chiefly of Professor Quigley's colleagues and former students who were grateful for the chance to be informed once again by his brilliance and eloquence.

About a month after the final lecture, Professor Quigley died suddenly. The lectures which he had intended to prepare for publication had only been partially edited by him. In order to bring his final lectures and *tour d'horizon* to print, we asked his former teaching assistant, Helen Veit, to prepare them. She has assembled the manuscript which is published here, taking care to be faithful to both Professor Quigley's style and to the nature of the occasion itself. Accordingly, the printed lectures are as true and direct a translation and reflection of the lecture series as it has been possible to produce.

This publication is intended primarily for distribution to Professor Quigley's friends and former students. It is being sent with particular appreciation to those who have contributed to the Carroll Quigley Fund which is being established to create an endowed professorship at the School of Foreign Service. To facilitate additional contributions to this Fund, a pledge card is enclosed.

Dean Peter F. Krogh
School of Foreign Service

PART I: "THE STATE OF COMMUNITIES", A.D. 976-1576

For a decade after 1931, my chief intellectual concern was the growth of the European state in the Old Regime, before 1789. I dreamed that at some date in the future, perhaps thirty years in the future, I would write the definitive history of the growth of public authority and the development of the European state. But after 1941 I had to abandon the project because I was too busy with my teaching—which I enjoyed thoroughly—and no longer had access to an adequate library. Above all, I discovered that other historians were becoming so narrowly specialized, and their historical concepts so inadequate, that it was almost impossible to explain to them what had happened in the growth of the state. They lacked the conceptual paradigms, the knowledge of comparative developments, and even the understanding of their own specialties to grasp a subject as broad and of such long duration as the growth of public authority over the last thousand years. Anyone who does not understand the long term development of this subject cannot understand the more limited aspects of it in more recent periods. But modern historians are increasingly specialized in narrow ranges of chronology, geographic area, and aspects of changing events.

Let me give you a few examples of how the lack of adequate paradigms blocks our understanding of the history of our subject.

The area of political action in our society is a circle in which at least four actors may intervene: the government, individuals, communities, and voluntary associations, especially corporations. Yet, for the last century, discussion of political actions, and especially the controversies arising out of such actions, have been carried on in terms of only two actors, the government and the individual. Nineteenth century books often assumed a polarization of the individual versus the state, while many twentieth century books seek to portray the state as the solution of most individuals' problems. Conservatives, from von Hayek to Ayn Rand, now try to curtail government in the excuse that this will give more freedom to individuals, while liberals try to destroy communities with the aim of making all individuals identical, including boys and girls. And since what we get in history is never what any one individual or group is struggling for, but is the resultant of diverse groups struggling, the area of political action will be increasingly reduced to an arena where the individual, detached from any sustaining community, is faced by gigantic and irresponsible corporations.

A second example is derived directly from the field of history. More than fifteen years ago, an old friend of mine, Professor Robert R. Palmer—we were colleagues at Princeton in the History Department in 1936 and 1937—won fame, and fortune from the publication of a large book on the eighteenth century revolutions in Europe and America. The book was loaded with facts, but lacked any real understanding of the subject. Even the title, *The Age of the Democratic Revolution*, was misleading because neither the French Revolution nor the American Revolution was "democratic." Bob Palmer is a very industrious person with a very agile mind, and a ready verbalizer, but he does not know what he means by "revolution" or by "democratic," and he is totally wrong if he believes the eighteenth century revolution, in the United States or the English-speaking world in general, was the same as the eighteenth century revolution in France: in fact, they were the opposite. The French Revolution was a struggle to obtain sovereignty by a government which did not have it. The English-speaking Revolution was an effort by states which had sovereignty to curtail it, divide it up, hamper it, by means of such things as federalism, separation of powers, electoral colleges, and so forth.

My third example of the injuries inflicted on the historiography of the growth of the state is more personal. My doctoral dissertation on the Public Administration of the Napoleonic Kingdom of Italy (Harvard, 1938) was never published because over-specialized experts who read the version revised for publication persisted in rejecting the aspects of the book in which they were not specialists. The only man who read it and had the slightest idea what it was all about was Salvemini, the great historian from the University of Florence, who was a refugee in this country at the time. The book's message could be understood only by an historian who knew the history of Italy, France, and Austria, and was equally familiar with events before the French Revolution and afterwards. But these national and chronological boundaries are exactly the ones recent historians hesitate to cross, for the French were reluctant to admit that the late revolutionary and Napoleonic reforms in French government had been anticipated in Italy, while many Italian historians knew nothing about French government before 1789 and wanted to concentrate only on the Risorgimento after 1814. No one was much interested in my discovery that the French state as it developed under Napoleon was based largely on Italian precedents. For example, while the French state before 1789 had no budgets or accounts, Napoleon's budgets in both France and Italy were strikingly similar to the budgets of the Duchy of Milan in the sixteenth century. Similarly, the unified educational system established by Napoleon in France in 1808 was anticipated in the Kingdom of Piedmont in the 1720's. Such discoveries form part of the history of the growth of the European state, but are not of much interest to the narrow and overspecialized controversies of the last half century. So instead of writing the history of public authority, I got into what was, I suppose, my much stronger activity: the creation of the necessary conceptual paradigms, structures, and frameworks for understanding historical processes.

The basic entity we must understand is the civilization as a whole. Although I tell you I'm going to talk about the last thousand years, 976-1976, Western Civilization, of which we are a part, has been around for a considerably longer time than that. We might say Western Civilization began around 550, but there was no significant structure of public authority until almost 1050, with no state at all over the preceding two centuries, 850-1050. Yet 950 is significant as the point at which our Western Civilization began the first of its three great Ages of Expansion, 970-1270. (The other two were 1440-1590 and 1770-1890). This first age of expansion applies to the core of Western Civilization, the area between the Rhine River and the Loire, the area which formed the core of the Carolingian Empire (687-887). This Empire was the earliest political structure of the new Western Civilization, one of four new civilizations which sprouted from the ruins of Classical Civilization after A.D. 500. These four were Byzantine (330-1453), Islamic (630-1922), Russian (800- ?), and Western (550- ?). Each of them modified the traditions it accepted from the ruins of Classical Civilization and created its own distinctive culture.

Another paradigm I want to establish is a difference between two kinds of civilizations, which means a difference between two kinds of governments in them. Asiatic civilizations, which I call Class B Civilizations, generally do not attempt to deal with individuals or with the problems of individuals; they leave interpersonal relationships to the local or kinship community. Class A Civilizations include Classical Civilization, our own Western Civilization, or the first Chinese or Sinic Civilization, whose dates are 1800 B.C. to 400 A.D. In Class A Civilizations, although the civilization begins as an area of common culture made up of communities, there is a long term trend to destroy and break down those communities.

The way I would like to express this would be—and I used to draw it on the blackboard—by saying that all civilizations start out as aggregations of communities. Those communities are generally of two types, either local, such as parishes, neighborhoods, villages, or manors; or kinship communities, families, clans, and so forth. When a civilization begins with such communities, as ours did in 550, there is no state, and there are no atomized individuals. I will not go into the details of this, but in such communities, there are no written laws; all law is customary. Most controls on behavior are what I call internalized, that is, they are built into your hormones and your neurological responses. You do what is necessary to remain a member of the community, because if you were not a member of the community, you would be nothing. You would not be a man. As you may know if you have ever studied linguistics, the names which many primitive and not-so-primitive peoples have for themselves is their word for man. The communities from which Classical Civilization came were clans, kinship groups; the communities from which Western Civilization came were local villages and manors. Lucky civilizations, such as Chinese Civilization over the past 1500 years, generally have communities which are both kinship and local.

What happens in the course of a Class A Civilization, over a thousand or more years, is that the fundamental communities are broken up and gradually disintegrate into smaller and smaller groups, and may end up simply as what we call nuclear families, a father and a mother, who eventually lose all discipline and control of their children. The result of this process is a state which is not only sovereign but totalitarian, and it is filled with isolated individuals.

Of the four civilizations which came out of Classical Antiquity's wreckage, two, Islamic and Byzantine, clearly are Class B Civilizations, that is, they continued to work for communities. Their governments were governments of limited powers, of which the most important were raising money and recruiting soldiers. The finest example of such an Asiatic Despotism was the Mongolian Empire of Jenghiz Khan about A. D. 1250, but its origins go back to the Persian Empires of the Achaemenids and the Sassanids. Good examples of such a structure are the Chinese Civilization of 220-1949, the Byzantine Empire after 640, and the Islamic sultanates which eventually culminated in the Ottoman Empire. The efforts of the Carolingian Franks to establish a similar empire in Western Civilization collapsed and led to the Dark Age of 860-970.

These eastern political traditions might be called Providential Empire or Providential Monarchy, and they are associated with the idea of a Providential Deity. To us today, who shove religion off into a corner and insist that it must have nothing to do with politics or business or many other things, it may be hard to grasp that one of the most potent things in establishing the structure of the state in any civilization has always been men's ideas of the nature of deity. I will not take time to give you my paradigm for that; I'll simply point out to you something which should be obvious. The deity—God—has many different attributes. He is creator; he is masculine; he is transcendental, that is, he is outside of the world of space and time—that was established by 500 B.C. Eventually, he is one; that is what Muhammad insisted on. And then he is omnipotent, all-powerful. I stop at this point; Providential Empires never got further than this.

The next development in our ideas of deity in Western Civilization was that God is good. That was established by the prophets of the desert by the fifth century B.C. Then came the Christian message, God is love, and by the year 1250 A.D., the scholastic inference that God is pure reason. If God is good, he cannot do everything; he can only do things that are good. And if he can do only good, and cannot do evil, then there is something higher than God: the rules of ethics. Thus the great contribution, even before Christ, to the Western idea of deity, was the idea of Transcendental Ethical Monotheism.

On the other hand, if God is one, omnipotent and providential, which means he interferes in the world, then whatever happens in the world does so because he permitted it. And whatever he permitted, who is any ordinary human being to question it? (If you read the *Book of Job*, you will see that this contradiction comes into the conversation where Job says, "God, you're running the world all wrong. You're letting bad people be elected President..." and so forth.) In Providential Monarchy, deity is heaven. The Chinese word is *tian*, which means heaven; the word in the original Indo-European language was something like *dyess*. From this came *deus* and eventually *Zeus*. It meant *bright, brilliant sky*. This deity is a being of arbitrary and willful omnipotence; the ruler on earth is picked by the deity and is the vicar of Omnipotent Will on earth. This means you must accept whatever happens: it leads, of course, to fatalism, although the people in these societies frequently don't accept that in their actions.

This idea of Providential Deity has a number of results. There is no rule of law; there is only the rule of God's will. This is part of the heresy of the West. When the Crusaders went to capture Jerusalem, and their war cry was, "God wills it!" they should have been rejected. This is not Western, because the Western idea is that God gives man free will, and if men do evil things, they are responsible. In the West, accordingly, you get the rule of law. In Providential Monarchy you get the rule of will. Their slogan became, "one God in heaven; one ruler on earth," which meant that Providential Monarchs frequently tried to conquer the world. I have already said that Jenghiz Khan was the greatest of them. His government, his army, his whole attitude are very much worth studying; his organization was a magnificent machine for world conquest and world rule as the vicar of heaven on earth.

There are no constitutional rules of political succession in a Providential Monarchy. There are no constitutional rules of succession in Islamic Civilization, in Byzantine Civilization or in Russian Civilization—ever. To talk about constitutional law in Russia is to talk nonsense. Alexander the First left a note in his desk saying that he wanted his second son, I believe, to succeed him, and that settled it. That was not an act of constitutional law: it was an act of will. This is still true in Russia today. It is also true in China: China was always a Providential Monarchy. But in the West, where we have the rule of law, where even God is under the rules of ethics, we have a very different situation, and we expect to have constitutional rules of political action, including the rules of political succession.

The Carolingian Empire, whose dates are, let us say, approximately 687-887, was an attempt to impose in the West a Providential Monarchy, which was a heresy, not in terms of the Western beliefs of the time, but in terms of the beliefs intrinsic in the nature of Western thought, including our belief in Christ and in both of the Testaments. While all the books I read are full of praise of Charlemagne, Charlemagne was a willful man, trying to do the impossible by conquering practically the whole world. Fortunately, he failed, and the idea of Providential Deity weakened in the West until after 1400.

The fundamental reason for this Carolingian political failure was the constantly deepening economic depression, which had begun about A.D. 270 and continued for seven centuries. As a result of this depression, it became less and less possible for Charlemagne even to conquer the provinces in his own empire, and totally impossible to rule those provinces. As the depression became worse and worse, transportation broke down, all bridges collapsed. (I have read a magnificent account of someone trying to go from Chartres to Paris in this period. To drive this would take about half an hour, I guess, depending on the traffic. It took him something like eleven days: when he got there, his horse died of exhaustion. And he had to do such things as try to patch holes in bridges by using his shield, so the horse wouldn't fall through, and so forth.) All commerce disappeared; everyone was reduced to living from the piece of land he was on.

Another reason Charlemagne could not conquer great distances was that it became economically impossible to capture any fortified building, because the besiegers could not stay there long enough — they could not take enough men or enough food — to starve out the defenders. And if they carried a very small amount of food, they had to take a smaller number of men, in which case the defenders would come out and chase them away. Elaborate weapons disappeared, including most siege equipment and besieging knowledge: all the significant missile weapons, such as composite bows and crossbows, ceased to be made: and the weaponry of Western Europe was reduced to the mounted spearman and his fortified residence. This military system lacked mobility and could neither protect nor control commerce; it could not impose tolls and was forced back almost entirely to seeking its economic support from rents squeezed from peasant villages. So by the year 900 we had a two class society in Western Europe: peasants who produced food, and a small percentage of fighters, who fought on horseback with shock weapons.

The last Carolingian was removed in 887 for not fighting the Vikings vigorously enough, and for one hundred years there was no ruler. As a result, the area that had been Carolingian Neustria, between the Loire and the Rhine, was reduced to a large number of self-sufficient villages, subject to the private power of mounted spearmen, without any state, monarchy or public authority. This period, and these social conditions, we call a Dark Age. There is nothing wrong with Dark Ages; they are frequently the most productive periods in the history of any civilization. Any of you who have read Lynn White's book on the technological advances of the Dark Ages, such as the plow and harnessing, know that Western Civilization got a great deal from its Dark Age. But, most significantly, out of the Dark Age that followed the collapse of the Carolingian Empire, came the most magnificent thing we have in our society: the recognition that people can have a society without having a state. In other words, this experience wiped away the assumption that is found throughout Classical Antiquity, except among unorthodox and heretical thinkers, that the state and the society are identical, and therefore you can desire nothing more than to be a citizen.

In the fourth century B.C., Aristotle told us that the *polis* is a koinonia or community, that is, an organic structure of dissimilar parts cooperating together for mutual satisfaction of their needs. He said a man cut off from the *polis* is not a man; he just looks like a man. He's like a thumb cut off from a hand. It looks like a thumb, but it's just a piece of meat. When, through war and conquest, the political organization of Classical Civilization expanded from *polis* to imperium, it was still assumed that the empire was a community, although even in Aristotle's day the community was breaking down into competitive groups, parties and cliques. The attempt to persuade everyone that the political unit was a community became more and more unconvincing, although rulers and conservative philosophers continued to insist upon it because it seemed to be the only way to prevent the political organization from disintegrating into an assemblage of atomized and antagonistic individuals. No other communities were approved of, and in many cases no other communities were permitted. Every society has what we might call the orthodox theory of the state for that society, and every society has a suppressed heresy of the state in that society. In Classical Antiquity the orthodoxy was that the state is the community and no one should desire anything else. Everyone's life should be public; everyone should be prepared to give up anything, including his life, for the state, because the state is his community. And if he says he's going to go off and found his own commune, by that statement, he becomes a traitor. One of the first ones to do that was Epicurus, in the fourth century B.C.; Epicurus said all he wanted to do was to sit down in a quiet garden with his friends and talk—and ignore politics. (We are rapidly approaching that in our society today, but we have not yet reached the point where it is regarded as heretical. But we are like Classical Civilization: we are trying to grind down individuals into identical atoms in a mass culture in which all communities are disapproved. And if any community wishes to stand apart, we will go in by force and do anything necessary to make them become the kind of red-blooded Americans we all should want to be.)

During this Dark Age, the Mediterranean Sea became a border zone among three new civilizations, a totally different situation from that in Classical Civilization when it had been the connecting link among the parts of the civilization, so that, for example, the city of Rome could bring its food from Egypt when it could not bring food from Lombardy in Italy. East of Neustria, from the Rhine to beyond the Elbe, Europe became an area of colonization by Western Civilization. But from 976 until after 1200, the most significant boundary of our civilization was to the north, in a great crescent from the Atlantic across the Baltic and Scandinavia to Russia.

From this area—much neglected in our history books, but of vital importance—the Vikings were pouring outward. From 750 to 930 they were pouring outward as raiders, slavers, pirates, men of violence and virility. Then there was a brief lull. From 980, for a hundred years, to about 1080, they were coming out as monarchies, that is organized state structures. I call this *Northern Monarchy*. Northern Monarchies had certain definite characteristics. Where those characteristics came from I do not know; it has not been discussed. They may have come from Byzantium or from some memory of the Carolingians. By A.D. 1000 the Viking bands had reached Newfoundland, Greenland and Iceland in the West, and were ravaging Western Europe and the western Mediterranean as far as Italy, while in the east they established the foundations of the Russian state and attacked Constantinople without success in 941 and 971. They occupied parts of northeastern England from Scandinavia after 856 and held the English throne under Sven Forked Beard and his son Canute in 1013-1035. Viking raiders occupied Normandy in 911 and became a vassal duchy of the king of France; from Normandy they conquered England in 1066 under their Duke William. And in 1018 in southern Italy, Normans of Viking descent, fighting on the side of the pope, met in battle with Varangians of Viking descent, fighting in behalf of the Byzantine Empire.

Northern Monarchy is of very great significance; it created states with powers which to us seem very precocious. For example, it raised a military force and taxes on the basis of assessments on plots of land, which in England are called hides, but which are also found in Russia. They had standing armies of mercenary soldiers. Archaeologists have recently excavated four large camps in Denmark, built about the year 1000 by the king Sven Forked Beard, where his standing army was ready at any moment to embark in ships and go off to fight.

A significant element in the success of Northern Monarchy was its development of battle tactics. This was achieved about 1050 and included at least four elements: a three-stage battle in which a missile barrage, a shock assault, and a cavalry pursuit were used in sequence; a recognition of the significance of tactical logistics, especially by water, before any attack; the use of a reserve force withheld from the action until it could be applied with maximum effect; and the removal of the leader from the front line of battle to a detached position from which he could control the critical moments of transition between the stages of the battle. These tactics were much more sophisticated than the feudal tactics of French Neustria, in which a battle was reduced to the second stage of shock assault by a mass of mounted knights with little organizational structure and with the nominal leader often leading the charge of his undisciplined forces.

The influence of Northern Monarchy and of Norman battle tactics was stronger in England than in France and after 1066 produced a more powerful and better organized government than the Capetian monarchy. It combined three elements: the remaining traditions and institutions of the Anglo-Saxon monarchy; the feudal type of governmental and manorial relations as brought from Normandy in 1066; and the fact that conquest in 1066 gave the king the authority to establish practices which the Capetians could not adopt until after their great disasters in the Hundred Years War in 1345-1360.

In Northern France the situation was quite different, since feudal decentralization was not counterbalanced there by either Northern Monarchy or conquest. One hundred years after the last Carolingian was deposed, a microscopic lord near Paris was permitted by the seven or eight great lords who surrounded him, and who were much more powerful than he, to adopt a royal title. His name was Hugh Capet; the date is 987. Hugh Capet was the first of the Capetian kings of France, and he was allowed to take that title because he was so weak. With the title of king he was also allowed the title of suzerain, which is a feudal lord who has no feudal lord above him. (I will not attempt to describe the feudal system if you don't know it.) But he did not even have the powers of a real suzerain, because the feudal lords who were technically his vassals did not perform military service, did not come to his court to settle disputes, and had very little to do with him. Nevertheless, the power of the religious aura of kingship allowed him gradually to accumulate more and more power.

Now I want to say a few words about the title of king. King is a religious title; it means a ruler who has been consecrated with holy oils by an archbishop in an archepiscopal cathedral, in a ceremony very similar to the sacrament of confirmation. This title of king allowed him to assume certain powers, such as, the king should see that everyone gets justice: he will seek justice on earth with God's blessing. The king should see that everyone gets protection, the king's peace, in other words. To the vassals that meant the Capetians should provide ethical and moral support for their individual and political rights, which was exactly what they wanted. The interesting thing is that in 1792, when Louis XVI was going to the scaffold, he still believed that the obligation he had as king was to support the rights of everyone, including the nobles and the Church. This was the central core of the Old Regime and it cannot be emphasized too much: the king is the source of justice. And as such, he was bound more than anyone else in the society to obey the laws.

With this idea of legal restraints on the king, I want to combine something else which may, perhaps, be difficult. The idea of property in Classical Antiquity is summed up in the word *proprietas*, which means possession of all the innumerable and un-designated rights in an object, maybe with a few specific restraints. In other words, you may have a car that will go 150 miles an hour, but you're not supposed to drive it 150 miles an hour. But you can drive it or not; you can rent it; you can sell it. That is *proprietas*. It is not the medieval idea of property. In the early Middle Ages no one worried about proprietas in the ultimate sense of possession of a title. All anyone cared about was specific rights to do specific things or to obtain specified benefits from an object. For example, some people might have the right to grow crops on a piece of land in ways specified by custom at certain times of the year; while others might have rights to graze animals on it in fixed numbers for fixed periods; a church might have the right to a customary fraction of the crop; and a lord might hold certain rights over it, to hunt on it, to collect fees for having its grain ground into flour in his mill, and so forth. Thus the medieval idea of property was specific rights, and the word we use for it is *dominia*, which is a plural.

The obligation of the Capetian king was to preserve everyone's dominia, and this included his own property, because it was not his, it belonged to the monarchy, to the family. Thus he could not alienate the demesne, as we call it, the landed property of the monarchy. From this emerged two intertwined principles which became the central core of the Old Regime in France until 1789: first, the king was under legal restraints, and secondly, the medieval idea of property as dominia, that is, as bundles of customary individual rights, was entrenched.

After 1000, as their power grew, the Capetians were able to assume certain dimly remembered powers that had been associated with the Carolingians: to coin money; to call out all able-bodied men for military service in an emergency; to insure that all men lived in peace and had justice; to protect the Church and religion; to grant rights of self-government to municipalities; and to regulate commerce, especially exports, so that there would be no shortage of food for the people. Associated with these, especially with the last one, was an aspect of kingship which came to be called la police, that is, not "police power," but the "policy power," what we might call administrative power, a significant element in the modern conception of sovereignty. Its chief idea is that in an emergency or complicated social situation, the ordinary rules may not work and there must be in the society a power of discretion to suspend or modify those rules.

In building up the powers of the monarchy, one of the greatest assets of the Capetians was their ability to make the title King of the French hereditary rather than elective. They were able to do this because they produced sons for eight generations over 341 years, from 987 to 1328, and the early kings were able to have their sons coronated while the fathers were still alive. After 1314-1328, by adoption of the Salic law in royal succession, the dynasty continued under its Valois branch from 1328-1589, providing six hundred years of male succession without a serious dispute. The more powerful feudal lords who surrounded the Capetians did not have as much luck; for one thing, they took too many risks by going off on the Crusades and so forth.

As the families of these vassals died out, their territories reverted to the king as suzerain through the right of escheat, that is, if a territory, a group of dominia, had no heir, it reverted to the king, who could grant it out to someone else. In this way the kings were gradually able to create a superficial territorial unity of France before 1500, but the fiefdoms were usually given as apanages to junior members of the royal family, so this unity was in appearance rather than in fact. In most cases the royal authority was extended as suzerainty rather than sovereignty, and local acquiescence was obtained by leaving the laws, taxes and customs intact. The royal family was less powerful in these apanages than the rulers they were replacing, who had not been under the obligation to be as law-abiding as the king and as subject to the rules of what was right.

In this way there gradually grew up a legalized confusion of extremely limited sovereignty, because in the Middle Ages any customary right one might have over a person or an object, which was beneficial to the holder and had been exercised long enough to be recognized as custom, became a legal right to be protected by judicial action in the proper court. In English law this is called the right of prescription: if you do something for more than twenty-one years, you may gain the right to do it against a private owner of private property. You may notice that every few years Rockefeller Center in New York City is roped off and you are not allowed to walk between the buildings. This is to prevent you from walking there for twenty-one years and gaining a prescriptive right to do so. But in English law the right of prescription cannot be exercised against the state. In France it was; in fact, it was the obligation of the king to protect such rights.

In France, bundles of such rights, or dominia, formed tenures, which came to be known as fiefs in the feudal system, benefices in the ecclesiastical system, and holdings in the manorial system. Each of these gradually developed its own law, courts and judicial procedures. After about 1050 a fourth field of law arose to cover commerce, towns and merchants; the Law Merchant. And finally, as royal government and public authority appeared and grew, a fifth field of royal justice and public law appeared. In all of these, the rule of law and not the rule of will was assumed. (This opened the way to something which is typical of the West: the rule of lawyers and judges. There have been three periods in the history of Western Civilization during which we have been overwhelmed by lawyers and judges, who tell us again and again that we cannot do certain things because they are illegal, even if those things are absolutely essential. The first period would be from 1313 to about 1480; the second was from about 1690 to the French Revolution; which was a revolt against a mass of confused, legalistic rigidity preventing necessary reforms. The third is our own day, when judges and lawyers are running everything and we are obsessed by legalism and litigation.)

Although the kings of France were seeking to extend the royal domain and to extend their authority within the domain from at least 1050, advances were on a piecemeal basis until well along in the Hundred Years War with England (1338-1453). The English attempt to conquer France in that war was hopeless. They could win battles, but they could not control territory. Eventually all they did was go out and plunder, living off the country, killing people, burning villages, seizing rich people and demanding ransoms, and so forth. The English believed that if they punished the French in this way, the people would realize that the king of France would not protect them, and therefore they should turn their allegiance to the king of England. But the English were quite mistaken in this, because the people of western France had expected protection not from the king but from their local lords, and the demonstrations of English brutality made them shift their allegiance from the local lords to the king of France. This reached its peak in Joan of Arc, who in 1429 summoned the whole religious loyalty of France and focused it on the pious, retiring Dauphin; this enabled the French to throw out the English in about 25 years.

That Dauphin, who became Charles VII (1422-1461), was one of the most significant rulers in French history, although he has been relatively neglected by historians, and a recent English biography by M. G. A. Vale (1974) leaves out almost everything of importance. Most books on his reign have tended to concentrate on the superficially exciting events of the first half of it rather than the much more significant administrative acts of the second half, after 1436. Charles, a deeply religious man, sought to get down in writing the customary rules of political life in France with an effective and just royal government at its core. He established a royal army with a regular system of taxation to support it. But he did two other things which are much more important. In 1438, while the war was still going on, he codified the customary relations of the Church of France in the Pragmatic Sanction of Bourges; this recognized the Gallican Church as a largely autonomous society, free from both royal and papal control, electing its own bishops, controlling its own property, and so forth.

And then in 1454, one year after the war ended—this is amazing—the king issued an edict, Montils-le-Tours. I do not find this mentioned in most history books, although it was probably the most important edict of the Old Regime. It ordered each locality to codify its local customs as the law of that district. The decree was re-issued three times by 1505 and was carried out by 1580, when France had 365 different local law codes based largely on dominia. This meant the king had condemned France to what we would call legal or administrative disunity, and it was one of the chief, if not the most important, causes of the Revolution of 1789. Accepted by the kings and applied by the courts, this legal structure so hampered the actions of the government that the monarchy was never able to achieve a fully sovereign state and was in semi-paralysis long before 1789.

France achieved territorial unity by 1500, but this meant only one thing: all France had the same king. Most dominia, including those which arose after 1500, were legally valid, often guaranteed by royal promises. Taxes were different everywhere, because they were collected according to local custom. There were tolls preventing commerce from moving everywhere. There was no unity of the judicial system: at one time there were fourteen supreme courts. Almost every commodity had different units of measurement, which differed from place to place, and also changed in size over time. Thousands of local tolls and fees became dominia, often collected by private interests. This made transportation costs so high that goods made in France often could not compete with foreign-made goods over much of France, and the poor sometimes starved while there was a surplus of grain in neighboring provinces. It was a realm of organized legal confusion, good business for lawyers and judges but very bad for businessmen, with hundreds of different laws, jurisdictions, weights and measures, monetary units, economic regulations, and small monopolistic markets.

This disunified condition led inevitably to the French Revolution, although it took hundreds of years to reach that point. In 1789, no state could survive which had different systems of weights and measurements for every commodity; which had different laws, so that Rousseau could say you changed laws every time you changed your post horse; which had conflicting jurisdictions; which had different tax rates, so in some districts the rich paid nothing in taxes while the poor paid a great deal, while in others the rich paid a great deal, and so forth. It was chaos, because whatever was, was custom, and under the prescriptive rights that custom was dominia, and dominia was the law.

And as a result, in 1789 we find a solution to a problem which, when I was younger than even the students who are here, struck me right in the face: I always had the eyes of a child. I asked; "If the king of France was absolute, as all the books say he was, how could he be bankrupt, unless the country was bankrupt?" But no one claims that France was bankrupt in 1789; France was among the wealthiest countries of Europe. So if the king was absolute, there was no reason why he could not use his absolute power to raise the money he needed from a wealthy economic system like that of France.

That is one of the reasons I studied this subject, and I found that the king of France was not absolute—he was not even sovereign. Indeed, he had reached the peak of his power around 1520 and 1576, when we are ending this lecture, his power was already collapsing into a growing mass of increasingly rigid restraints. I'll give you one example.

The king could not borrow, because he had no collateral. The property of the monarchy was not his, so he could not offer any of the royal possessions as collateral on loans. If he wanted to borrow 100,000 livres and could put up as collateral a necklace or something of the Queen's, which wasn't part of the royal dominia, that would be all right. But he had to borrow millions. For centuries, therefore, since the kings could not alienate properties, they alienated incomes. This means that when they wanted to borrow money, they would say, "I'll never pay back the principal, but I will pay you the interest on it. Here is an income that has just come free, because the family who has been getting it for three hundred years has died out. It yields, let us say 100,000 a year, and at ten percent interest you will give me a million. And if you ever want the principal back, you can always sell an income of 100,000 a year for a million." In this way, by 1789 every income the king had was committed to some expense.

In 1561 the king had to find enormous sums of money. (To save time, I won't explain how he got so badly in debt.) The city of Paris offered to guarantee the loans given to him, but they needed insurance that the interest would be paid, so the Church of France volunteered to pay the interest. This is called *les Rentes sur l'Hôtel de Ville de Paris*, and within 150 years, it made the Church of France stronger and more of a sovereign political entity than the monarchy itself.

PART II: "THE STATE OF ESTATES", A.D. 1576-1776

In my first lecture, I portrayed the sweep of a thousand years that we are concerned with as beginning with a period in 976 when we had no state at all. All power was private power. But we also had no individuals, that is, no isolated individuals. All we had were individuals so deeply embedded in local self-sufficient communities that the power relationships within which they functioned were in their day-to-day activities, and the controls of their behavior were almost totally internalized in their neurological and hormone systems. So they obeyed what seemed to them to be their inner compulsions while they fulfilled their functions in this interwoven community structure, which changed so slowly that even in a long life of sixty or seventy years—and, of course, most people in those days did not live long lives—almost no changes would be noticed by anyone in the patterns embedded inside themselves.

And at the end of the thousand year period, in the year 1976, we no longer have communities, except shattered, broken, crippled, isolated ones. Instead, we have states of monstrous power and frustrated, isolated individuals; and the state and the individuals are working together from opposite sides to destroy what we have left of communities—local, family, or whatever they might be.

Over this long period of a thousand years, the growth of the state, which is our subject, began with the appearance of a state apparatus of a very primitive kind, made up of a king and his assistants, who eventually became a monarch and a bureaucracy. Around this core, there gradually accumulated sufficient activities to make what we would regard as a public authority and, ultimately, a state. The mark of that process can be most clearly indicated, I think, by the development of what we call sovereignty. Without sovereignty, I do not think we could say that a state is much of a state, although we might call it one. There has been a great deal of talk about sovereignty in books—not very much, unfortunately, in history books—but no one has ever bothered to define it. From my study of the growth of the state, I have been able, it seems to me, to put together what sovereignty consists of, historically, in the tradition of our Western Civilization. To me, sovereignty seems to have eight functions or aspects, and I will define them for you in the approximate order in which they appeared.

1. All human needs require that a person live and cooperate with other

people for satisfaction. None of us can satisfy any significant human needs by acting alone in a state of nature. The two fundamental needs men had from the beginning are, first, that the group within which a community is functioning and satisfying the needs of its members must be defended from outside attack. So the first aspect of sovereignty is defense.

2. Secondly, disputes and conflicts within the group must be settled, so that insiders cooperate rather than fight with one another and open themselves to enemy attack. Thus defense against outsiders is first; settling disputes among insiders is second.

3. The third one is very difficult to talk about. Years ago, I gave a whole course on it: the administrative power. The French word for it—and most of my study of public authority was done in the French language and in French public law—is *la police*. It does not mean "police," it rather means "policy," and I suppose it would best be defined as the power to take those discretionary actions which are necessary for the continued existence of the community. In the Middle Ages and in the Dark Age with which I began, one of the chief needs was that the food supply not be interrupted, and by the early eighteenth century, in France, if you said "la police," it meant control of the grain trade. However, in strict legal understanding it meant much more. For example, it meant, "What emergency measures would be taken and who would order them if a plague appeared? The dead must be buried the same day. Everyone must get a swine flu injection." And things of this kind. Notice: it's nothing you can designate. But administrative power is a most significant power, and when I taught the subject, I shocked the students by saying that in my opinion it is almost the most important of the eight aspects of sovereignty, and there is no provision for it whatever in the Constitution of the United States.

When people talked in terms of three branches or aspects of government, they tended to call the administrative power "the headless fourth branch of the government." Around 1930, Lord Hewart, the Lord Chief Justice of England, wrote a book entitled, *The New Despotism: The Headless Fourth Branch of Government*, and yet I could show him that a thousand years before his book, this power, *la police*, had existed as one of the attributes necessary to keep a community or a group of people cooperating and functioning together. I want to emphasize that this power is discretionary. The finest example I can give you is a police officer directing traffic at a busy intersection: he has the power to start and stop the traffic as he sees fit, and can enforce his decisions with the power of the state. This does not obey any of the rules of public authority which the common lawyers of today insist are necessary.

(But I might as well keep my passion on that subject for the third lecture, which will include the period when the efforts to create administrative power in this country were destroyed. The first effort was the establishment of the Interstate Commerce Commission in 1889, but it has since been paralyzed and made impossible in a number of ways, such as the insistence that such commissions must use the procedures of the common law courts, which is nonsense in discretionary power. It's as if you asked a policeman directing traffic down here at the Key Bridge end of M Street to obey common law procedural requirements.)

4. The fourth is quite obvious: the taxing power, mobilizing resources for public purposes. Notice that the French government did not have the taxing power when the French Revolution began in 1789. But I'll get back to that.

5. The fifth is legislative power. This has always been confusing because for many centuries, and certainly in 976, there was no legislative power and yet there were laws and rules. The reason is that in a society dominated by communities, in which personal behavior is regulated largely by internalized controls, the rules are not made by an outsider. You discover the rules by observing how people act. Accordingly, in the early history of Western Civilization, the law was found and not made, and it was a very drastic innovation when we shifted from finding the law to making the law. We have not really made that transition completely in the common law countries even yet: we still say that the judges are finding the law by looking back to previous decisions.

When the royal judges first began to go around England trying cases, they never proclaimed or imposed the law; they gathered together a group of sworn local people and asked, "What do you do in a case like this?" Generally, the jury, as we call them, could give an answer based on local custom, but in some cases they would look puzzled and say, "No one here remembers such a case." Let's say it was arson or something of the kind. Then the judges would say, "In traveling around England trying cases, we have found that the most common rule is this—" and thus they established the common law. The common law in England was the law the royal judges discovered by going around and finding out what the local customary law was, and filling in the gaps with what was common to England. Thus the common law in England was a royal creation, through local custom.

In France, as I showed you last time, the law was the codification of local customs in all their diversity. I will say very little more about the legislative process, but the first examples of writing down the laws were not regarded as making new rules at all: they were simply promulgations of customs. It took centuries before people realized that we did have a legislative process going on and were, in fact, making new rules. That's the fifth aspect, legislation.

6. The sixth aspect we might as well call the executive, the enforcement of law and judicial decisions. It is of relatively little importance in the early history of a civilization. But executive action became increasingly necessary as time went on, communities disintegrated, and peoples' behavior became less subject to internalized controls and more subject to external controls such as force, duress, threats, fines, restitution, or other kinds of outside, external pressure. Today we think almost entirely in terms of law and order. If someone campaigns for the Presidency on a platform of Law and Order, he means that he will intensify the external controls upon behavior of which people do not approve. That is executive power.

The last two aspects of sovereignty are of tremendous importance, and they are, perhaps, the most significant today. And yet they are rarely discussed in connection with sovereignty.

7. The seventh is money control. I pointed out last time that from the beginning, back to 500 B.C., the coinage and control of money was one of the attributes of royalty. Today, of course, it includes much more than just coinage: it means the creation and control of money and credit, and in the English-speaking world these are not a part of sovereignty. They are in private hands, even though they are the most important powers that exist in a society such as ours today.

8. And the last aspect of sovereignty is the incorporating power; the right to say that a group of people is a single legal entity, that is, to create corporations. This did not exist in the English-speaking world until quite recently. It always existed in the Roman Law. One of the distinctive things about the Roman Law was that only the imperium — public authority — and individuals existed. If any other legal groups existed — and by legal, I mean they had the right to own property and to sue and be sued in the courts — then they had to have some kind of a charter from the Imperial power to justify this. With the fall of Rome that power of incorporation ceased entirely, and corporations of the year 970 had no charters of incorporation. There were thousands of them across Europe, many of them ecclesiastical, but other kinds as well. Because of their lack of charters, it was never quite clear, for example, whether each diocese or each parish was a corporation; generally, each monastery or convent was considered to be a corporation.

All right, those are the eight aspects of sovereignty. Once I have defined them in this way, it will be quite clear to you that when I come to the end of tonight's lecture in 1789, very few states in Europe will have all of them. Indeed, when I began the lecture tonight in 1576, almost no states in Europe had all of them. However, if a state had six or so of them, we might say it was a sovereign state or a sovereign entity.

Now, our next problem is this: How was it possible to build up a sovereign entity around the basic administrative core? Unless something of an administrative nature already existed, it could hardly be expected that the attributes of sovereignty could accumulate. Although there were a few exceptions, such as city-states like Venice, which did not have a monarch, the basic core in landed territories was a monarch and his assistants, which I will call a bureaucracy. In accumulating sovereignty, the king and his bureaucrats needed allies outside: they needed money and they needed personnel, that is, a group of people who could read, write, keep records, handle cases of justice in the courts, and keep track of the money in the treasury. These officials would have seals to indicate that they were doing their jobs by authority of the king. (The study of seals is quite interesting. I've been in archives where seals were lying around loose on the floor, and I did want to pick up a couple. One in particular was a beautiful seal of green wax—Henry the Second, I believe it was—but they would let me take only two that were lying there. They were papal bulls of the late medieval period that had somehow been cut off. Papal bulls are only as big as a quarter, and they're lead, with garish yellow and red silk strings attaching them to the document, which break off quite easily.)

The gradual economic expansion and growth of these thousand years, with the resulting social changes, made it possible for the monarchy to find allies. I don't believe I will take the time to write them on the board here, but, at the beginning, all we have are lords and serfs, a two-class society. Then, when the king began to appear with his bureaucracy—and we'll put him outside the classes—the lords separated in the eleventh century as a result of the Investiture struggle into the lords spiritual, that is the clergy, and the lords temporal, what we would call the nobility; with the peasants, we have a three-class system. Eventually, the beginnings of commerce and the growth of towns gave rise to a middle class, the merchants, the burghers—and you would put them in there—so you now have peasants, burghers, nobles, clergy, and above it all, the king with his bureaucracy. You would have those clearly established by the year 1300. Within fifty years, when they reached a great crisis, you have an additional one, city craftsmen in guilds: woodworkers, leather-workers, people of this kind. You might also make a distinction in this period and say that not all landlords were noble; there were lesser landlords, who were not noble. In England they were a vitally important group that is frequently called the gentry. That would be, let us say, around 1400 or 1450, and thus you would have the clergy, the nobles, gentry, burghers, craftsmen, peasants. And then, if you come up past tonight's lecture, into the 19th century, you would find a new kind of bourgeoisie in the city, the industrial bourgeoisie, and this created a new working class in the city, the proletariat, while craftsmen were being pushed aside.

The monarch had to find allies down below, in order to accumulate powers to use when he was resisted. His first alliance was with the clergy, and he was resisted by the nobility. But soon the clergy and nobility allied together, and he was resisted by them jointly. He then found allies in the bourgeoisie, the merchants or the sons of merchants, who could read and write and count, and indeed were much more loyal to the king than any clergy had ever been. In England and other places, the kings found allies among the gentry. In Eastern Europe, the Junkers, younger sons of the landed class, became the prince's officials. Notice that at no time, at least in the period covered by the first two lectures, did the king find any allies worth talking about in what was really the most important group in society, the peasants, who were producing the food for everyone else. One of the discoveries I have made in my ten years of study on this subject has been that it is no use to be in possession of something essential and expect it to be a source of power. If you examine the basic human needs, such as food and I assume, sex, perhaps health, you will never find that those who possess these or provide others with them have been able to obtain enough power to play any role in political action. So we will leave the peasants out of our discussion.

Thus, not all of these groups obtained status and became a focus of political authority. Those that did form the subtitle of the lecture tonight: Estates. The number of Estates in a society is no real sign of the number of social classes. I have given you six social classes that existed in many places, let us say, in 1789. However, I do not know any country with six Estates. In England they had two, the lords temporal and spiritual, and the commons. The commons was made up of gentry from the shires and the bourgeoisie from the municipalities. England, then, had four classes but only two houses. In France you will find they had three Estates: the clergy, the nobility, and the rest, called the Third, which did provide a certain representation for the peasants. But, as you certainly know, the so-called Estates-General did not meet in France for 175 years. After 1614, it was not called to assemble until the king was forced to call it in 1789, and that's what started the French Revolution. It wasn't called because the king did not want more problems than he already had, and he would have had more. If you go farther east in Europe, you will find places where there are four or five Estates, and in the course of history some of these changed: groups were eliminated until the number was reduced.

My next point is extraordinarily complex. I have to make a distinction, which I have already been developing, that as you go eastward across Europe, the situation is quite different. I have already shown you one difference between England and France. But there are two other zones with which we must deal. France goes from the English Channel to the Rhine. Western Germany goes from the Rhine to the Elbe River. Eastern Europe goes from the Elbe River to the Pinsk Marshes or the Pripet River, which is considerably east of Warsaw. It is the natural boundary between Europe and Asia and is very close to the actual boundary today between Russia and Poland. These four zones had totally different experiences, depending on what happened to their Estates, and these experiences were crucial in what happened to monarchical authority and state power. So I think it is perfectly justifiable to call these two hundred years the Age of Estates.

I usually introduced these four zones by comparing them to a ham and cheese sandwich: that is to say, England and Eastern Europe are similar in certain ways, although very different in others, while France and West Germany resemble one another more than they do England or Eastern Europe. We might say it is a ham and cheese sandwich made with one slice of white bread and one slice of rye. The chief comparison I want to make at once is this: England was an area of large estates; Eastern Europe was an area of large estates; but France and West Germany were areas of family-sized farms or peasant proprietorships. These differences of land tenure were based on a number of things: the system of justice, including the kind of law, the group in society which controlled the judges, and the method of studying the law; the history of serfdom; and the fate of towns, guild and other corporative bodies. I will discuss these in more detail in a moment.

Generally, in the period of Estates, government functions were not centralized; they were not uniform; they were assigned to different persons, different groups, different boards, different committees, on an ad hoc basis, without any rational distinctions such as we would accept, and this situation existed, in many cases, even on the low levels of villages or parishes, although peasants and parish priests were very infrequently found on these governing boards.

Well into the period we are concerned with this evening, dynastic monarchy was essentially a personal thing. In the beginnings of Western Civilization, we had feudalism with no monarchy, or no monarchy of any significance. The next period we call feudal monarchy, when allegiance and loyalty were owed to the monarch only by his vassals. Following that, we have the period we are dealing with tonight, dynastic monarchy, in which loyalty and allegiance were due to the dynasty to which the monarch belonged — the Tudors or the Bourbons or the Hohenzollerns — but always on a personal basis. Treason was disloyalty to a person or to the dynasty; it was not disloyalty to the state, to the community, or to the territory in which people lived. However, by the period from 1576 to 1776, loyalty was expected from all people who were active political participants. That would probably be much less than twenty percent of the population, because, as I said, it still included no peasants, who were at least eighty percent of the people in Europe. And there were other groups, too, who were not included.

A general rule you might keep in mind is that the more extensive the power — that is, the greater acreage you had — the less intense it was: extension at the sacrifice of intention. By intention I mean how far down into the society the royal power could go. In the period we are covering tonight, you will find almost no country in Europe in which the royal power interfered with the behavior of peasants. I won't go further with this subject. I could give you a periodization of it, but there's no point in it.

Now we will look at these four zones in more detail.

In England, sovereignty was achieved early. I want to emphasize that England, by 1400, did have what I would call a sovereign state. That state, however, was not in the hands of the king, but instead was controlled by a joint corporation known technically as *Rex in Parliamento*, the king in parliament. And this possessor of sovereignty was, I am quite sure, although I haven't investigated it exhaustively, not just English, but an aspect of Northern Monarchy. You will find, for example, the oldest parliament in the world today — more than a thousand years old — is in Iceland, and others are in such places as Norway and Denmark. This idea of a ruler having the power to do almost anything, if the parliament agrees, is also the basic background of a tremendous political power like that of Gustavus Adolphus in 1630, in the Thirty Years War.

Serfdom ended in England by 1300, simply because the peasants, instead of working on the lord's land a couple of days a week, began to pay him money, say a penny a day. They made an agreement: "You won't have to work for me any more — and I'm just as glad because I'm not going to grow food, I'm going to raise sheep for wool, or something of this kind. So if you owe me two days work a week, give me two pennies a week instead." This ultimately ended serfdom, but it also meant that, through judicial interpretation, the peasants lost their rights in the land they worked, and that land became the large estates of the English aristocracy.

In the Middle Ages, if we go back for a moment to 976, no one owned the land; people had rights of usage in the land. When William the Conqueror, in 1087, sent out his officials for the Domesday survey, they asked, "Of whom is this land held? Who holds it? What people live upon it? What obligations do they have?" But eventually some troublemaker—and, according to Rousseau, he should have been struck dead—asked, "Who owns this land?" That is, who has *proprietas* in this land? The question should never have been asked. They should have continued to ask, "What *dominia* exist in this land, and who owns them?" But when the question, "Who own this land?" was asked in England, the judges—and I will show you why in a moment—answered that the peasants' payment to the lords was rent, and from that they reasoned that the lords must own the land and the peasants had no rights in it.

Clearly, how judges were recruited was of the utmost importance. How did an Englishman become a judge? Did he have to know the law? And if he had to know the law, how did he learn it? The gentry were unpaid members of Parliament; they were also unpaid local magistrates, the Justices of the Peace and so forth. The local Justice of the Peace in England, which was the lowest level of justice throughout this period and into the twentieth century, was not expected to know the law. But royal judges were expected to know the common law, the law that was found. If an English gentleman wanted to learn the law, he did not go to a law school and certainly not to a university, because the common law was not taught in universities. It was taught in four very expensive eating clubs in Westminster, the Inns of Court: the Inner Temple, the Middle Temple, Lincoln's Inn, and Grey's Inn. These were the places where the judges and lawyers who were trying cases in Westminster spent the evenings during the judicial sessions. Not only did they discuss the cases that were going on each day, but men who were regarded as authorities gave discussions afterwards in the lounge in regard to contracts or whatever it might be, and by eating meals there, it was possible to pick up the necessary knowledge of the law. But this was expensive; it required hundreds of guineas, which would be hundreds of dollars in our language. Only the landed oligarchy could afford it, and only people who were lawyers and had passed the bar through this process could become judges. So in much of English history, there was a very small and expensive educational loophole through which people could work their way to positions of power, and the result was that only those men who had affluent parents could become lawyers and judges. And until the end of this lecture, at least until 1776, the only affluent people would be the gentry landlord class. Their eldest son took over their estates; the second son went, perhaps, into the army or the navy, or found a place in the Church, a living, as they called it; and the third son would go to the Inns of Court and try to become a lawyer.

By 1776—and this will conclude my discussion of England, which is very brief, and as you can see, inadequate—there was a landed oligarchy in England.

That landed oligarchy controlled the Parliament: it had taken it away from the king in the civil wars of the seventeenth century. It also controlled the court system and the interpretation of the law. Naturally, when any dispute arose, "What rights does someone have in this piece of land?" they invariably decided in favor of the landlord group and against any other group, above all, any peasants. As a result, England's rural areas became depopulated. In the early eighteenth century, Goldsmith wrote "The Deserted Village." "Sweet Auburn, loveliest village of the plain..."—but there's no one there. Or if you read "Elegy in a Country Churchyard," once again, there's no one around. The whole countryside was deserted by the eighteenth century. The people came to America, or they went to other places, and this eventually gave us the British Empire.

France I will save, because I want to end up with France.

Now let us look at West Germany, where there was a totally different situation. In the western part of Europe they had what in my day at Harvard we called "Ren and Ref," Renaissance and Reformation. But in Germany they had "Ren and Ref and Rec"—the Reception—because they generally adopted the Roman law in the sixteenth century. This meant that if the prince could make Roman law be obeyed, he became sovereign, and he used his power to protect the landholdings of the peasantry, rather than to protect the rights of the nobles or the clergy, although serfdom still existed in Germany in 1800, and only the defeat by Napoleon made them decide to abolish it, in approximately 1808. Furthermore, as a result of the Renaissance, the prince in Western Germany became head of the Church, which was also an imitation of Roman law: the Roman Emperor was the Supreme Pontiff, Pontifex Maximus, the head of all the priests in the Roman religious system.

Most of the princes of Germany were not kings, because they could not adopt the title of king in the Holy Roman Empire without the permission of the Emperor, and the Emperor would not allow that unless he was bribed or was sure he could trust the family of the prince. He could trust the Wittelsbachs, so he allowed them to be kings of Bavaria. But he could not trust the Hohenzollerns, who were Electors of Brandenburg, so when they wanted to take the title of king in 1701, they could do so only in Prussia, which is outside the Holy Roman Empire. And the correct title was not King of Prussia, although that was adopted within 100 years; it was King in Prussia.

In West Germany the Emperor was elective, and so the same thing happened to him as happened to all elected kings and princes: he had to make concessions and go into debt to get the money and votes he needed in order to be elected Emperor. Thus the Empire disintegrated into principalities which the Emperor could not control. The Emperor continued to exist until 1808, when his title was changed by Napoleon from Holy Roman Emperor to Hapsburg Emperor of Austria, but all the rights and powers of the Hapsburgs were the powers of the hundreds of inheritances they had. The most significant of these, of course, were those of the Archdukes of Austria, but they were Kings of Hungary, Kings of Bohemia, and many other things, as you know.

The result of this disintegration and the Reception of Roman law was a large number of small sovereign principalities, some of them so small that we are told you could walk around the circumference of the principality before breakfast. And without spending any time upon it, I want to point out that, in my opinion, the greatest age of European history in the post-medieval period, certainly up to the time of Napoleon, was Western Germany in the late eighteenth century. I think you will see, if you make a list of the great geniuses in the history of Europe, that they are clustered in that period. I will not attempt to do it, but think of the greatest mathematician. Englishmen will always say it was Newton, but it was a German who lived in that period, Gauss. The greatest musician, Beethoven—or, if you dispute it, two or three great musicians. Great philosophers and poets, Herder, Goethe and others. It was a very great period, a period much worth studying.

When the German princes received the Roman law at the time of the Reformation, and also made themselves heads of the Church, they established the following things: the prince was at the top and beneath him, in law, were individuals. Corporations must have a charter. Judges were agents of the prince: he named them, he could fire them, he should pay them. The prince was, in most cases, the head of the Church, although often he was not aggressively orthodox, so there could be Calvinist princes who were heads of the Lutheran Church in their principalities. The Roman or civil law was studied in the universities. The prince controlled the armed forces, and that meant Germany was decentralized into hundreds of principalities. But that does not mean it wasn't a good place.

Now, moving on to the next zone, in Eastern Europe, the rulers did not have the money, and above all, could not find the skilled personnel to keep records, so they couldn't build up a bureaucracy. They did not want to create a bureaucracy out of townspeople, and the towns were few and far between. Furthermore, the towns in Germany were collapsing into a long period of depression beginning in the Renaissance or certainly by 1500. Therefore, in general, the princes of Eastern Europe used the nobility and gentry or their younger sons in their bureaucracy. But they were not paid officials because the princes could not afford to pay them, and, naturally, they were administrators only in their own localities, .where they would administer for their own benefit and not necessarily in the interests of the prince, the ruler.

As a result of this, all the earlier monarchs of Eastern Europe vanished, and generally, the state they represented vanished with them. It's worth pointing this out. Why did the kingdoms of Lithuania and Bohemia, or principalities such as Transylvania, or, above all, the kingdom of Poland disappear? They disappeared because the king or prince found himself facing an Estate made up very largely of landlords, and he could not get the money or the skilled bureaucracy or the other things he needed; he could not even get an army, because he couldn't hire mercenaries without money. As a result, the nobles were able to destroy him; in most cases, they did so by refusing to admit that his family had any hereditary right to the throne. (It is correct that Kingship originally was an elective, not a hereditary title; it was only after years of dispute that hereditary kingship—inherited by fundamental laws of the monarchy—gradually became accepted in Western Europe.) These elective kingships were suicidal, not just for the monarchy, but for the country itself, because the Estates would elect as king only that man, who promised to reduce the royal power the most. We almost had such a competition in the 1976 election. If we had Ford and Reagan running against each other—in a way, I would like to have seen that, except you would have to vote for one or the other, I suppose, and there really is no difference between them—they would be saying, "I will govern less. I will cut taxes. I will cut back big government. I will do all kinds of things to reduce the government if you elect me." This is what the elected monarchs of Eastern Europe did, and eventually they had no powers at all.

At that point occurred the military revolution, which began about 1440 and was well established by 1579. By the military revolution I mean this: The previous weaponry, particularly in Eastern Europe, was mounted nobles on horseback with spears, in other words, what we would call *knights*. But after 1400, these were not successful. Infantrymen with spears, such as the Swiss pikemen, or infantrymen with missile weapons such as arquebusiers—guns—protected by spearmen or obstacles of various kinds, and, above all, artillery became necessary for the control of the nobles inside a country. They were used for this purpose by the kings of France and of England. But they were also necessary to protect the country against outside invaders. And the Estates controlled by landlords in Eastern Europe refused to permit that military revolution. They preferred going down to defeat with an obsolete system of weaponry if they could be certain that they would retain control of the people who lived on their estates: serfdom had begun only about 1300 in Eastern Europe. This is why large estates, abject serfdom, and the domination of a landed group became increasingly prevalent in Eastern Europe. As you know, in Poland the "free veto" meant that nothing could be done if even a single landlord dissented. That is as if we had a parliamentary body whose every decision had to be unanimous. All of this happened because the nobles wanted to stick together in order to get what they could in their own little areas.

These landlords were opposed to cities and to traders in cities. They wanted the trade for themselves, or they wanted foreigners, such as the Dutch, the Swedes, or the Hanseatic League, to come to their estates on the Vistula River, for example, and buy the goods they produced with serf labor, that is, grain, wool, hides, lumber, and things of this kind. As a result, Eastern Europe fell backward into a colonial area. Its trade and its middle class more or less vanished. The cities became insignificant, and trade in the cities was largely taken over by foreigners and aliens, many of whom were Jews: this is the origin of the ghettos and pales of Eastern European cities. Incidentally, this process is not unique in Poland. It is very common in history for a landed group in control of a society to destroy commercial activity and allow it to fall into the hands of aliens, as the Ottoman Empire and the Russians allowed their commerce to be controlled by Frenchmen and Greeks and various others. This is a widely prevalent system.

Another difference between Eastern Europe and the other zones is that corporate bodies ceased to be of much significance. Guilds and towns became unimportant, and these are the two chief secular bodies we would find in Western Europe. Indeed, the Church as a series of corporate bodies also tended to become part of the landlords system, so that a prince or a member of a princely family would be the local bishop or archbishop. In Prussia, for example, Albert of Brandenburg, who was bishop of at least three places and archbishop, I believe, of two, became the Hobenzollern Prince of Prussia. On the other hand, in Western Europe, the guilds and, above all, the towns had great vitality and a life of their own, as well as an independent role in law, in spite of the fact that in a truly sovereign state there would be no corporations without a charter, as I've indicated to you.

Now we will return to France. France is the most interesting case: it did not achieve sovereignty, as I explained to you last time, because the king felt obliged to rule according to law. That meant he had to protect *dominia* and not insist on *proprietas*, but it also meant that he did not have the powers to be an effective king. He had enormous incomes, but, even in total, they were not enough for what was demanded of him. Therefore, instead of collecting the money from all of them into a treasury and then paying out what was necessary, and having some kind of budget or system of accounts, he got people to promise they would do something for him, such as a royal printing or something of the kind, and then he said, "Here is a free income: it is the Octrois, the tolls going into a city. (It might be Rheims, for example, or a number of cities.) I will divert these tolls to you, and that will pay you for being my printer and publishing my ordinances and so forth." Generally, at least sixty to eighty percent of the royal incomes were committed to such purposes, and the only funds available in any particular year were the incomes that came free for some reason. For example, if he gave an income for life, it would come back to him when the person died, or if he gave it for ten years, it would come back at the end of that period.

Since even this was not sufficient to raise money, he had to do other things. As I indicated to you last time, he did not have credit, because he couldn't alienate anything the monarch owned: it wasn't his. Therefore, he did not have credit. But there was another restriction. If he could get credit and borrowed money, the laws against usury were still in force and remained so until the French Revolution. The royal officials got around that in two ways. One was by saying that certain moderate payments on borrowed money were necessary as insurance against loss and were not interest for the use of the money. But that limit, in most cases, was 5 1/2 percent, which was not sufficient because it was easy to get ten percent for money in the seventeenth or the early eighteenth century, and there were occasions when you could certainly get twelve percent. Instead, they devised a system called *les rentes*, the incomes, which worked in this way: "How would you like to buy an income? Here is an income that yields 50,000 a year. That will be the interest, but we won't call it that.

If you give me 100,000, I'll let you have it for a year. That's fifty percent interest. Then at the end of the year, I won't be able to give you back the 100,000, so if you want it back, sell the income to someone else." So *rentes* became claims upon incomes which could be sold almost as we sell stock exchange certificates. They became one of the chief sources of royal income, but the royal bureaucracy built up fantastic burdens of debt in this way.

I won't go into the details of it, but eventually everything they were doing in the financial world was illegal—much worse than Watergate. In order to satisfy the supervisors and accountants, they had to create thousands of forged and fraudulent documents to indicate that they were getting only 5 1/2 percent and that the money was being repaid. They would make a document saying it had been repaid, and then they would make another document saying that someone else had bought it—and that someone else was your brother-in-law, and so no change had been made at all. This is a most fantastic story, and if you're interested, I will recommend a book by a man named Julian Dent, *Crisis in Finance: Crown Financiers and Society in Seventeenth Century France*. It was published in 1973. It is an extraordinary, hair-raising book. The result of this system was that the king of France was over the edge of bankruptcy:

for two hundred years, during all of the period covered by this lecture tonight, his incomes, in gross, were smaller than the interest payments he owed, in gross. And Mr. Dent had to spend years working on this before he was able to discover what was going on.

Because of this, the king could not pay officials. He had to let people take positions in the government and use those positions to get money as fees. If the fees were not adequate, they could take several positions, and then neglect all of them and spend a good deal of time working at something else, as a jeweler perhaps. (The Near East is like this, as you know, today. Everyone in the Near East has five jobs and they appear at each of them briefly, to say, "How is everything today?" And then they go off to another job. And if you put it all together, it barely gets them by.) The king of France discovered that people were willing to pay to get jobs like this, so he began to sell offices that were totally unnecessary. For example, there were inspections to make sure that the quality of textiles was up to the established rules. And every time an official inspected, he examined only one bolt out of a thousand, if that, and then sold you a tag for each of the thousand. Generally, he would come in and say, "Let's go over and have a drink." So they sat in the café and he said, "Now, how many is it that you want?" And the merchant answered, "I have a thousand bolts." "All right, here's a thousand tags, and at fifty cents each, give me five hundred dollars." And they would attach each one to a bolt. Originally there were six inspections. But the king discovered that he could name dozens more inspectors who would pay him money to go around selling inspection stickers, so they might then have eight stickers on each bolt of cloth, and the merchant had to pay for all of them. Now this is only part of an insane situation. This is a totally irrational society, which is obviously crippled in its ability to satisfy basic human needs, and is, I think, almost as obviously explosive, in the sense that a revolution is bound to cane unless drastic changes are made in a hurry.

The king also lost the legislative power, because all the judges owned their seats. A judgeship became almost exactly what a seat on the stock exchange is now. That is, if you had a judicial seat, you imposed fees on cases as a result of your judicial activity, and those fees became your income. The value of the seat was the average annual income capitalized at the rate of interest. So if you made 10,000 a year out of your job, and ten percent was considered a fair return on investment, then you could probably sell the seat for 100,000. Thus the judicial seats became the possession of a new class in society, the noblesse de la robe longue, the nobility of the long robe. This was an hereditary nobility in the sense that the possession of the judicial seat went from father to son. You may remember that Montesquieu, who wrote *L'Esprit des Lois*, had inherited a seat from an uncle, and when his book was such a success, he preferred to be a popular writer, so he sold the seat.

The existence of this independent judicial class meant that the king could not control judicial cases: the judges would decide them against him. And this was the group who decided that the peasants in France owned the land but still owed manorial dues, which continued to exist up to the French Revolution and were not abolished until 4 August 1789. But they were not of great significance; they were simply a nuisance. They did not involve week work or things of that kind; they were paid off in money whose value, because of the inflation, had become so small that the payment was hardly worth collecting. (We could say that the whole history of France is the history of inflation.) As a result, France was all broken up into small holdings into the nineteenth century.

This judicial system also meant that the king could not legislate, because if he issued an ordinance, a decree, or something of the kind, the judges could claim they had never heard of it. In order to have it enforced, the king had to send it to them and say, "Register it." Then they would answer, "We don't like it. We won't register it; we'll send it back." I won't go into the details, but it became a long and involved ritual. The king would send the chancellor to order it written down, and the judges would review it. The king himself would then appear; this was called a *lit de justice*, a bed of justice, because the king was reclining. In a *lit de justice*, the justices admitted that in the presence of the king they became clerks, so they wrote the decree in their books and registered it. But then they wrote on the margin, "Inscribed in the presence of the king—coram rege—and they never enforced it.

Not only did the king have neither the judicial nor the legislative power, he also did not have either the taxing power or the ability to reform the tax system. Since everything was the result of centuries of custom, the taxes were extraordinarily inequitable. That is, people who were not wealthy paid heavy taxes, people who were quite wealthy paid very little—just as we do today, only they were much more excited about it, although it was probably no more inequitable than our system, which is very inequitable, if you know anything about it. The judges refused to allow any new taxes, and above all, they would not allow one thing—I'm making this very simple—the so called *taille tariffé*. A *taille* was a direct tax assessed upon people; *tariffé* is what we call "graduated;" so this is a graduated income tax. Again and again in the eighteenth century, the king tried to register a graduated income tax; and again and again it was refused by the judges. And he went and ordered it, and they inscribed it, but they would not allow it to be collected. They did not prevent it by saying, "We will not enforce it;" they issued an order that any Frenchman who answered any questions about his income would be in contempt of court. That's the kind of Supreme Court we need today!

Thus the king lost the taxing power, the legislative power, the judicial power. Finally, in December 1770, the king realized he was bankrupt. He was engaged in great wars with Britain for control of India, North America, and the world and so forth; in seven years he was going to come to the rescue of the United States in the American Revolution. He had to do something about the court system, so in December 1770 he abolished it and established a new one, in which the judges were named and paid by the king, and the rules were greatly simplified. It wouldn't work. Why? Because he refused to act illegally, and he admitted that those judicial seats he had abolished were private property and therefore he had to pay the judges the value of their seats. And he could not get the money because he could not tax. Furthermore; no one would take cases to the new courts because they said, "Well, we know he has no money. He can't pay the value of the old judicial seats to the judges, so eventually he will have to put them back." And, in 1776, the new king, Louis XVI, put them all back. As a result, when the king called the Estates General in 1789, it was at the insistence of the Parliament, the Supreme Court of Paris.

Now I should mention one last thing, the incorporating power. I said that very few governments at that time had the incorporating power; certainly the king of France and his government did not. France was filled with corporations that had no charters. Some, such as the Cathedral of Rheims, had been there long before there was a king of France, and there were churches, towns, universities, guilds, innumerable ones. Furthermore, the litigation among these corporations was endless, just like today—although we have this in medical science even more than in law today: they keep the thing going forever because it's a source of income. When the Estates General assembled in 1789 and abolished the judicial system of France, there was a case that had been before the courts for more than three hundred years. It was a lawsuit between the second-hand clothing dealers guild and the guild of the tailors of the City of Paris; it had been going on for so long because it was such a juicy plum for the lawyers and the judges. (We're moving in this direction in both medicine and law, and I hope not in higher education, in the United States today.) In 1776, as a step toward gaining the incorporating power, Turgot abolished the guilds. Once again, it couldn't be done. He would have had to pay off all their debts, and they had enormous debts.

When the revolution came, it was a tremendous earthquake. It wiped out just about everything. When I was in Paris in 1937, I found that there were thousands of tons of law books and legal papers of all kinds, and no one had to look at them after the French Revolution because they pulled down the curtain: they said, "What was, is over." And in 1802 they set up a new system of law, a single book, *The Code Napoleon*, that's smaller than an ordinary Bible.

The French Revolution created a fully sovereign state, which had all power. That sovereignty was embodied not in the monarchy, but in the nation, meaning that the residents are no longer subjects, they are citizens, they are participants in this new entity, *la patrie*. These are revolutionary changes. All legal restraints on public action are replaced by acts of sovereignty. The sovereign power in France after the French Revolution can do anything, the only restraint is that it must be done according to the rules of the sovereign power. It did remain a Western Civilization government, under the rule of law, but the law was procedural rules and no longer substantive limits on what could be done. This, to me, is of the utmost importance, because it leads to next week's lecture: the polity was transformed from an interwoven, chaotic, hierarchical system of subjects in communities and corporations to a system that is a naked dualism of supreme state power and individuals. I hope you'll pardon my bad French: "Un État vraiment libré ne doit souffrir dans son sein aucune corporation pas même celles qui vouée à l'enseignement public bien merité de la patrie." I'll translate it: "A state truly free will not suffer within its bosom any corporation, not even those devoted to public education, which is well deserved by the fatherland." In other words, on the 18th of August 1792, the French proclaimed, "There are no groups in our society. If you want to form a group, it must be voluntary, it has no legal existence. If you want it to have a legal existence, you must get a charter."

This is a return to the Roman system. But it raises future problems: it says that men are equal before the law. If men are legally equal and are equal participants in the polity, why should they not be politically equal? And, eventually, why should they not be economically equal? If sovereignty can do anything, and law is merely an act of sovereignty, why should wealth not be divided?

PART III: "THE STATE OF INDIVIDUALS", A.D. 1776-1976

This is the most difficult of the three lectures I'm giving on the history of the thousand years of the growth of public authority. What happened in the last two hundred years is fairly clear to me, but it is not easy to convey it to you, even to those of you who have had courses with me and are familiar with the framework of much of my thinking. One reason for this difficulty, of course, is the complexity of the subject itself, but after all, the preceding eight hundred years were quite as complex as these last two hundred years we will deal with this evening. A much more fundamental reason for the difficulty, though, is this: The reality of the last two hundred years of the history of the history of Western Civilization, including the history of our own country, is not reflected in the general brainwashing you have received, in the political mythology you have been hearing, or in the historiography of the period as it exists today.

I will divide the period from 1776 to 1976 into two parts. The first, to about 1890, was a period of expansion of industrial society; the last eighty years, approximately, have been an age of profound crisis, not only in our own country, but in Western Civilization, which is the unit in which I carry on my thinking on the subject. In order to deal with this period, I have to go back to fundamentals, and particularly to the fundamentals of human values, and to do that, we must have paradigms. The whole thousand years, as I explained in my first lecture, is a shift from a society made up of communities in 976, to a society today, where we have states of monstrous power and atomized individuals. I will use certain definitions: A society is an organization of persons and artifacts—things made by people—and it's an organization to satisfy human needs. It would not exist if it had not come into existence to satisfy human needs. Notice: I do not say human desires. One of the striking things about our society today is the remoteness of our desires from our needs. If you ask anyone what he wants, what he desires, he will give you a list of things which are as remote as can be from human needs. In our society, the process we have been tracing for a thousand years is the growth of the state. As I indicated in the first lecture, a state is not the same thing as a society, although the Greeks and the Romans thought it was. A state is an organization of power on a territorial basis. The link between a society, whether it be made up of communities or individuals, and a state is this: Power rests on the ability to satisfy human needs.

Now I will put on the board something with which former students are familiar. I always call it the levels of culture, the aspects of a society: military, political, economic, social, emotional, religious, and intellectual. Those are your basic human needs. The interesting thing about them is that they are arranged in evolutionary sequence. Millions of years ago, even before men became human, they had a need for defense of the group, because it is perfectly obvious that men cannot live outside of groups. They can satisfy their needs only by cooperating within a group. But I'll go further than that, and return to it again in a moment: Men will not become men unless they grow up in communities. We will come back to that because it is the basis of my lecture tonight.

If you have a group, it must be defended against outsiders; that's military. Before men came out of the trees they had that need. If your needs are to be satisfied within some kind of group, you must have ways of settling disputes and arguments, and reconciling individual problems within the group; that's political. You must have organizational patterns for satisfying material needs, food, clothing, shelter: that's economic.

Then came two which have been largely been destroyed or frustrated in the last thousand years of Western Civilization. Men have social needs. They have a need for other people; they have a need to love and be loved. They have a need to be noticed. Sirhan Sirhan killed Robert Kennedy because no one had ever noticed him and he was determined that, from now on, someone would know he existed. In fact, most of these "motiveless" assassinations are of this type. Someone went up to the top of the University of Texas tower and shot something like seventeen people before they caught him. That was because no one had ever noticed him. People need other people. That's the social need. The basis of social relationships is reciprocity: if you cooperate with others, others will cooperate with you.

The next is emotional need. Men must have emotional experiences. This is obtained in two ways that I can see: moment to moment relationships with other people and moment to moment relationships with nature. Our society has so cluttered up our lives with artifacts — TV sets or automobiles or whatever — and organizational structures that moment to moment relationships with nature are almost impossible. Most people don't even know what the weather outside is like. Someone said recently that until September we had a great drought here in Washington, and four or five people standing there said, "That's ridiculous." We had a shortage of about eight inches of rain. Because people now are in buildings, it doesn't matter to them whether it's raining or not.

The next is the religious. It became fashionable in Western Civilization, particularly in the last hundred years, to be scornful of religion. But it is a fact that human beings have religious needs. They have a need for a feeling of certitude in their minds about things they cannot control and they do not fully understand, and, with humility, they will admit they do not understand. When you destroy people's religious expression, they will establish secularized religions like Marxism.

Then, on the intellectual level: people have intellectual needs. I used to tell students that Marilyn Monroe had profound intellectual needs. And when no one would treat her as an intellect or even as a potential intellect, for obvious reasons, she was starved for intellectual experience. That's why she married a man like Arthur Miller: she thought he was an intellectual. All right, those are human needs. Power is the ability to satisfy those needs. And someone who says that power is organized force, or that power is the outcome of an election, or that power is the ability to cut off our oil supply, has a completely inadequate way of looking at it. My experience and study of the destruction of civilizations and of the collapse of great empires has convinced me that empires and civilizations do not collapse because of deficiencies on the military or the political levels. The Roman army never met an army that was better than it was. But the Roman army could not be sustained when all these things had collapsed and no one cared. No one wanted to serve, no one wanted to pay taxes, no one cared.

The other part of this will require you to put these things together to some extent. Persons, personalities if you wish, can be made only in communities. A community is made up of intimate relationships among diverse types of individuals—a kinship group, a local group, a neighborhood, a village, a large family. Without communities, no infant will be sufficiently socialized. He may grow up to be forty years old, he may have made an extremely good living, he may have engendered half a dozen children, but he is still an infant unless he has been properly socialized and that occurs in the first four or five years of life. In our society today, we have attempted to throw the whole burden of socializing our population upon the school system, to which the individual arrives only at the age of four or five. A few years ago they had big programs to take children to school for a few hours at age two and three and four, but that will not socialize them. The first two years are very important. The way a child is treated in the first two days is of vital importance. He has to be loved, above all he has to be talked to. A state of individuals, such as we have now reached in Western Civilization, will not create persons, and the atomized individuals who make it up will be motivated by desires which do not necessarily reflect needs. Instead of needing other people they need a shot of heroin; instead of some kind of religious conviction, they have to be with the winning team.

Human needs are the basis of power. The state, as I said, is a power structure on a territorial basis, and the state will survive only if it has sufficient ability to satisfy enough of these needs. It is not enough for it to have organized force, and when a politician says, "Elect me President and I will establish law and order," he means organized force or power of other kinds. I won't analyze this level; it's too complex and we don't have time. I will simply say that the object of the political level is to legitimize power: that is, to get people, in their minds, to recognize and accept the actual power relationship in their society.

Next Tuesday a decision will be made as to who will be President of the United States. That will not at all necessarily reflect the actual power relationships in the United States. If all the people who are intellectually frustrated would vote, the result might be quite different. Many of you come to these lectures because you are intellectually frustrated, and you want to be exposed again to my insistent demands that you think about things. For example, we no longer have intellectually satisfying arrangements in our educational system, in our arts, humanities or anything else; instead we have slogans and ideologies. An ideology is a religious or emotional expression; it is not an intellectual expression. So when a society is reaching its end, in the last couple of centuries, you have what I call misplacement of satisfactions. You find your emotional satisfaction in making a lot of money, or in being elected to the White House in 1972, or in proving to the poor, half-naked people of Southeast Asia that you can kill them in large numbers.

The state is a good state if it is sovereign and if it is responsible. It is more or less incidental whether a state is, for example, democratic. If democracy reflects the structure of power in the society, then the state should be democratic. But if the pattern of power in a society is not democratic, then you cannot have a democratic state. This is what happens in Latin America, Africa and places like that, when you have an election and the army doesn't like the man who is elected, so they move in and throw him out. The outcome of the election does not reflect the power situation, in which the dominant thing is organized force. When I say governments have to be responsible, I'm saying the same thing as when I said they have to be legitimate: they have to reflect the power structure of the society. Politics is the area for establishing responsibility by legitimizing power, that is, somehow demonstrating the power structure to people, and it may take a revolution, such as the French Revolution, or it may take a war, like the American Civil War. In the American Civil War, for example, the structure of power in the United States was such—perhaps unfortunately, I don't know—that the South could not leave unless the North was willing. It was that simple. But it took a war to prove it.

I defined sovereignty last time, but I want to run through it for the benefit of those who weren't here. Sovereignty has eight aspects: DEFENSE; JUDICIAL, i.e., settling disputes; ADMINISTRATIVE, i.e., discretionary actions for the public need; TAXATION, i.e., mobilizing resources: this is one of the powers the French government didn't have in 1770; LEGISLATION, i.e., the finding of rules and the establishment of rules through promulgation and statue; EXECUTIVE, i.e., the enforcement of laws and judicial decisions. Then there are two which are of absolute paramount importance today: MONETARY, the creation and control of money and credit—if that is not an aspect of the public sovereignty, then the state is far less than fully sovereign; and lastly the eighth one, THE INCORPORATING POWER, the right to say that an association of people is a fictitious person with the right to hold property and to sue in the courts. Notice: the federal government of the United States today does not have the seventh and eighth but I'll come back to that later.

In the meantime, I'm still on my introduction for this evening, and I want to discuss what happened in the last thousand years. If we go back before 976, when you had communities, the main core of people's life and experience, which controlled their behavior and determined their lives—controls and rewards, I call it—was in the religious, emotional and social levels. They had religious beliefs, they had social and emotional relationships with the people they saw every day. That was the core of their lives. The significant thing is that those controls and rewards were internalized: they were what was acquired very largely in the first four or five years of life. When a child is born, he is not a person[ality], he is a human being. He is utterly potential. When someone becomes a personality, such as you or myself, then he has traits, which were acquired out of his potentialities as the result of experience over numerous years.

This is why they could get along without a state in 976: all the significant controls were internalized. I took the year 976 because, although Western Civilization had come into existence about two hundred years before that, it began to expand in 976. By that I mean they began to produce more goods per person per day per year. You know what I mean by expansion if you took my freshman course: increased output per capita, increased knowledge, increased geographic area for the civilization itself, and increased population. That began in 976, and we'll put an arrow here at the economic level to indicate it. The economic expansion was achieved chiefly by specialization and exchange: instead of each little group's trying to satisfy all its own needs, groups began to concentrate and, for example, produce wool and exchange it for other things. That process of increasing specialization and exchange, which is the basis of expansion in our civilization, I call commercialization. As long as the society is expanding, that process of commercialization will continue as it has for a thousand years in our society, so that today everything is commercialized, politics, religion, education, ideology, belief, the armed services. Practically everything is commercialized; everything has its price.

When this expansion reaches a crisis, you get increasing *politicization*. I won't go into the details of this. It can be explained in detail, as most of you, perhaps, know. *Politicization* means that the expansion is slowing up, and you are no longer attempting to achieve increased output per capita, or increased wealth, or increased satisfactions, or whatever is motivating you, by economic expansion, but you are doing so by mobilizing power. We have seen this going on in our society for almost a century.

And then, as the society continues and does not reform, you get increased militarization. You can certainly see that process in Western Civilization and in the history of the United States. In the last forty years our society has been drastically militarized. It isn't yet as militarized as other societies and other periods have been; we still have a long way to go in this direction. Our civilization has a couple of centuries to go, I would guess. Things are moving faster than they did in any civilization I ever knew before this one, but we probably will have another century or two.

As this process goes on, you get certain other things. I've hinted at a number of them. One is misplacement of satisfactions. You find your satisfactions — your emotional satisfaction, your social satisfaction — not in moment to moment relationships with nature or with other people, but with power, or with wealth, or even with organized force — sadism, in some cases: Go out and murder a lot of people in a war, a just war, naturally.

The second thing that occurs as this goes on is increasing remoteness of desires from needs. I've mentioned this. Then the next thing is an increasing confusion between means and ends. The ends are the human needs, but if I asked people what these needs are, they can hardly tell me. Instead they want the means they have been brainwashed to accept, that they think will satisfy their needs. But it's perfectly obvious that the methods that we have been using are not working. Never was any society in human history as rich and as powerful as Western Civilization and the United States, and it is not a happy society. Just this week, I looked at a book called "The Joyless Economy", by an economist, Tibor Scitovsky, who diagrammed some of these things.

In the final aspect of this process, controls on behavior shift from the intermediate levels of human experience — social, emotional and religious — to the lower, military and political, or to the upper, ideological. They become the externalized controls of a mature society: weapons, bureaucracies, material rewards, or ideology. Customary conformity is replaced by conscious decision-making, and this usually implies a shift from your own conformity to someone else's decision. In its final stages, the civilization becomes a dualism of almost totalitarian imperial power and an amorphous mass culture of atomized individuals.

All of this is for the sake of establishing a few paradigms.

What happened in the last two hundred years? In 1776, Western Civilization was approaching a revolutionary situation. A revolutionary situation is one in which the structure of power — real power — is not reflected in the structure of law, institutions, and conventional arrangements. Law and legal arrangements, including constitutional structures, were not legitimate in much of Western Civilization in 1776. They were not responsible because they did not reflect power. Whether it was the English Parliament, which had a legal right to rule America; or the nightmarish constitution of France, which no longer reflected the structure in French society in any way; or, east of the Rhine, with the enlightened despotisms, the laws of the polity of Europe did not reflect the power structure at all, as Napoleon very soon showed them. This, therefore, is a revolutionary situation.

Let's look a little more closely at these.

In England, the laws of the polity established control of the country in an oligarchy of landowners, the Whig oligarchy. Members of the House of Commons were sent to Parliament by pieces of land, and anyone who owned a piece of land with the right to send a member to Parliament, and could do so whether anyone lived on the piece of land or not. It was not a reflection of the power structure of England to say that pieces of land were powerful. I do not have to demonstrate to you that the legal arrangements by which the British Parliament made the rules to govern life in the United States were equally unrealistic.

I'll leave France for a moment and go east of the Rhine. In Central Europe we had what was called Enlightened Despotism: small principalities ruled by despots who had a legal right to say, "This will happen; that will happen; something else will happen."

In the period from 1776 onward, for about twenty-five years, they tried to establish a more rational life in their principalities, but they couldn't do it. Their system of weights and measures — I won't attempt to describe them to you — were absolute, unholy chaos. They had a different weight or measurement for every commodity and those measurements changed as you went from village to village or from district to district. They also had been changing in size for hundreds of years, because the power of the creditors was so great that, if you owed a bushel of wheat to your landlord, all the landlords together, over generations, could make the bushel a larger measure.

I discussed Eastern Europe adequately in my last lecture. I'll simply point out that in this period Poland disappeared, because the Polish landlord class would rather keep their serfs than be politically independent. They were unwilling to organize a modern army, with modern weapons and modern military training, to defend Poland against outside enemies, such as Prussia, Russia or Austria. As a result, those three got together and divided up Poland in 1795, so Poland no longer existed. Under Napoleon there was a Grand Duchy of Warsaw, but Poland did not exist again until 1919.

In France, as I described to you last week, the polity had reached a condition of total paralysis. The government did not have sovereignty. It did not have the taxing power; it did not have the legislative power; it did not have the incorporating power; it did not have the judicial power; it did not have most of the eight aspects of sovereignty I've mentioned to you. And in 1776 the government became aware of this, when they tried to abolish the guilds and could not do so, because under the law they could not be abolished unless their debts were paid. The government could not pay their debts because it did not have the taxing power. And it didn't have the taxing power because it didn't have the judicial power: if it took someone to court, the judges would say, "No, you have no right to examine his income. You can only ask him what he has been paying for the last couple of hundred years on that piece of property or whatever it is."

The result was the explosion of the French Revolution, which produced, by the time of Napoleon, let's say 1805, the most sovereign state in Europe. Notice: Napoleon was an enlightened despot, the last one in Europe. Anyone who says, as Robert Palmer, for instance, that France was leading the parade in 1789 in terms of government and public authority, just doesn't know what he's talking about. In 1789 France was bringing up the absolute rear as far as public authority and sovereignty were concerned. That is why France gets its enlightened despot so late. He wasn't even a Frenchman; he was an Italian; and he imposed an Italian government on France. Because it was so rational, so powerful, so well-organized, and the new sovereignty was embodied in a new entity, the nation, it had a power which made it possible for Napoleon to conquer almost all of Europe. He was, however, ultimately defeated, as most conquerors of all Europe have been throughout history: William II in 1918, Hitler in 1945, Philip II in the sixteenth century, Henry V of England the early fifteenth century, and so forth.

By 1820, after the Napoleonic system had been replaced, all four of these geographical zones I have mentioned were unstable, but they were much more stable and much more legitimate then they had been in 1776. Now, although I say that in 1820 they were fundamentally not that stable, we know there was political stability in Europe for at least three generations after that date, until at least the 1860's. There was a brief war in 1866 but I won't go into that. The stability of Europe from 1815 to 1855 is something on which we now look with nostalgia. The reasons for this apparent stability had nothing to do with the structure of the state, except the degree to which the structure of the state had become sufficiently rationalized and sovereign through the period of revolution from 1776 to about 1820. With additional events, the situation looked stable, and these additional events produced a new Age of Expansion.

The first of these was the expansion of technology, including the Agricultural and Industrial Revolutions. The Agricultural Revolution of about 1720 and onward made it possible to produce more and more food from land with less and less labour. The Industrial Revolution began about 1750 and was the application of inanimate energy to the production on a large scale. (Incidentally, 1776 is a very significant year, and this is not just because the American Revolution began during it. Watt's patent of the steam engine was in 1776; Adam Smith's Wealth of Nations was published in 1776; the failure of the French to reorganize their political system occurred in 1776, and so forth.) The disruption of communities, the destruction of religion and the frustration of emotions were greatly intensified by the Industrial Revolution: railroads, factories, growth of cities, technological revolution in the countryside and in the growing of food, and so forth.

The appearance of stability in the nineteenth century Age of Expansion was also due to the externalization of rewards and controls. This eventually brought on an acceleration of the main focus of the main focus of the activities of the society downward again to the levels of culture, from the areas of internal controls to the areas of external controls. If you can be bought, with a higher salary, to go to San Diego and give up all your friends and associations, that is an external control. If you can be forced to go there by the draft, that is militarization.

Another thing which became very obvious in the nineteenth century was the increasing role of propaganda for the purpose of changing people's ways of looking at society, and the success of this propaganda helped to create an impression of stability. At the beginning of the lecture, I offended some of you by saying you had been brainwashed. This is not an insult; it's a simple statement of fact. When any infant is born and socialized in a society, even if he is to become a very mature individual, he has been brainwashed. That is, he has been given a structure for categorizing his experience and a system of values applied to that structure of categories. But in our society, in the nineteenth and twentieth centuries, this has now become a propagandist system in which emphasis is put on the future: Think only of the future. This is the ideology against which the young people of the 1950's and 1960's rebelled. Future preference: plan; study hard; save. All the things I used to hear from my maiden aunts: "Wise bees save honey; wise boys save money," and they each secretly gave me a dollar as I was leaving. "A penny saved is a penny earned." " A stitch in time....." Everything that's in "Poor Richard", the Benjamin Franklin propaganda machine.

Another aspect of this nineteenth century propaganda system is the increasing emphasis upon material desires. If you had the material things you wanted—a nice house in the suburbs, a swimming pool, a couple of big cars, a place in the country, a motor boat, a trailer to take it back and forth—you should be happy and satisfied. Now it's endless—a pocket computer, a citizens' band radio, whatever you want.

A third idea we were brainwashed into believing was that the only important thing was individualism. They called it freedom. There is no such thing as freedom. There is something called liberty; it's quite different. I'll not spend much time on this. If you're interested, read Ruggiero's "History of European Liberalism", Oxford University Press, 1927, particularly the first couple of chapters. That's the English translation of an Italian book. Freedom is freedom from restraints. We're always under restraints. The difference between a stable society and an unstable one is that the restraints in an unstable one are external. In a stable society, government ultimately becomes unnecessary; the restraints on people's actions are internal, they're self-disciplined. They are the restraints you have accepted because they make it possible for you to satisfy all your needs to the degree that is good for you.

Another thing that they have brainwashed us into believing in the last 150 years is that quantitative change is superior to any qualitative attributes. In other words, if we can turn out more automobiles this year than last, it doesn't matter if they're half as good. The same is true of everything. We are quantifying everything, and this is why we are trying to put everything on computers. Governments no longer have to make decisions; computers will do it.

Another thing they have succeeded in doing is to give us vicarious satisfactions for many of our frustrations. It is unbelievable to see how the American people are hung up on vicarious experiences: television, movies, mass spectator sports. You have no idea what the small towns of America are like on a Friday night like this, when the local high school football or basketball team is engaged in competition with their neighbor eighteen miles away. And what a gloomy place the chapel or church is Sunday if they lose—it won't matter if it rains. People need exercise; they do not need to watch other people exercise, particularly people who already have had too much exercise. Another vicarious satisfaction is the sexy magazines; this is vicarious sex. To anyone rushing to buy one, I'd like to say, "The real thing is better."

The brainwashing which has been going on for 150 years has also resulted in the replacement of intellectual activities and of religion by ideologies and by science. It is hardly possible to discuss the problems of the historical past without running up against Marxist interpretations. I have nothing against Marx, except that his theories do not explain what happened, and this, to me, is a fatal defect. The very idea that there is some kind of conflict between science and religion is completely mistaken. Science is a method for investigating experience, and religion is something quite different. Religion is the fundamental, necessary internalization of our system of more permanent values.

Another thing they have tried to get us to believe in the last 150 years—and the idea is now dying in front of us—is the myth that the nation, as the repository of sovereignty, can be both a state and a community. This is the great ideological innovation of the French revolution, you see. The nation can be the repository of sovereignty. But suppose weapons in a society are such that it is possible for a government to impose its will over an area a thousand miles across. And suppose that in that thousand mile area there are a number of nations, such as the Bretons, Catalonians, the Welsh, the Lithuanians. These are as much nations as the ones that somehow or other became the embodiments of sovereignty in the nineteenth century. Why did the English, the French, the Castilians, the Hohenzollerns, and others become the repository of sovereignty as nations: (notice: they missed out in the whole Balkan and Danube areas.) They did so because, at that time, weapons made it possible to compel obedience over areas which were approximately the same size as these national groups I have mentioned. As a result, they were able to crush out other nationalisms, such as the Scots, the Welsh, the Irish, the Catalonians—who had a much longer and more cultured history than the Castilians—the Provencals, and many others. In other words, nationalism is an episode in history, and it fit a certain power structure and a certain configuration of human life in our civilization. Now what's happening? They all want autonomy. The Scots think they can get their independence and control oil in the North Sea, and then England will become a colonial area for Edinburgh. And so forth.

In 1820, thus, the state was essentially unstable, in spite of appearances. It was not fully sovereign. For example, it did not have the control of money and credit in most places; it did not have control of corporations in most places. It was not stable because the nation is not a satisfactory community. The very idea that, because everyone who speaks French is in the same nation and, in the nineteenth century, in the same state, they must therefore be in the same community, is just not true. The nation or the state, as we now have it in terms of the structure of power, cannot be a community.

Another thing which may serve to point out the instability of the power system of the state: the individual cannot be made the basic unit of a society, as we have tried to do, or of the state, because the internalization of controls must be the preponderant influence in any stable society. Even in a society in which it appears that all power is in the hands of the government—Soviet Russia, let's say—at least eighty percent of all human behavior is regulated by internalized controls socialized in the people by the way they were treated from the moment they were born. As a result, they have come to accept certain things that allow the Russian state to act as if it can do anything, when it obviously can't and knows it can't. Notice the new Russian budget announced this week: as a result of our pouring our food surpluses into Russia, they are now going to increase the consumption of their expenditures.

Also related to the problem of internalized controls is the shift of weapons in our society. This is a profound problem. I have spent ten years working on it throughout all of history, and I hope eventually to produce a book if I can find a publisher. There will be endless analyses of Chinese history, Byzantine history and Russian history and everything else, and the book is about nine-tenths written. I'd say in the last ten years the shift of weapons in any civilization and, above all, in our civilization, from shock weapons to missile weapons has a dominant influence on the ability to control individuals: individuals cannot be controlled by missile weapons. Notice that if you go back several hundred years to the Middle Ages, all weapons were shock, that is, you came at the enemy with a spear or a sword. Even as late as 1916, in the First World War, you came at the Germans with bayonets after a preliminary barrage with artillery. But we have now shifted almost completely to missile weapons. Missile weapons are weapons that you hurl. You may shoot, you may have bombs dropped from airplanes, you may throw hand grenades: these are missile weapons. The essential difference between a shock weapon and a missile weapon is this: a missile weapon is either fired or it isn't fired. It cannot be half-fired. Once you let it go, it's out of your control. It is a killing weapon. But a shock weapon—a billy club or a bayonet—can be used to any degree you wish. If you say to someone, "Get up and get out of my room," and you pull out a machines gun, or you call in a B-52 bomber, or you pull the pin in a hand grenade,.... But with a bayonet you can persuade him.

In our society, individual behavior can no longer be controlled by any system of weaponry we have. In fact, we do not have enough people, even if we equip them with shock weapons, to control the behavior of that part of the population which does not have internalized controls.

One reason for that, of course, is that the twenty percent who do have internalized controls are concentrated in certain areas. I won't go into the subject of controls. It opens up the whole field of guerrilla resistance, terrorism, and everything else; these cannot be controlled by any system or organized structure or force that exists, at least on the basis of missile weaponry. And, as I said, it would take too many people on the basis of shock weaponry. We have now done what the Romans did when they started to commit suicide: we have shifted from an army of citizens to an army of mercenaries, and those mercenaries are being recruited in our society, as they were in Roman society, from the twenty percent of the population which does not have the internalized controls of the civilization.

The appearance of stability from 1840 to about 1900 was superficial, temporary and destructive in the long run, because, as I have said, you must have communities, and communities and societies must rest upon cooperation and not on competition. Anyone who says that society can be run on the basis of everyone's trying to maximize his own greed is talking total nonsense. All the history of human society shows that it's nonsense. And to teach it in schools, and to go on television and call it the "American way of life" still doesn't make it true. Competition and envy cannot become the basis of any society or any community.

The economic and technological achievements of industrialization in this period were fundamentally mistaken. This could get quite technical; I'll try not to. The economic expansion of industrialization has been based on plundering the natural capital of the globe that was created over millions of years: the plundering of the soils of their fertility; the plundering of the human communities, whether they were our own or someone else's, in Africa or anywhere else; the plundering of the forest. In 1776 the wealth of forest in North America was beyond belief; within 150 years, it has been destroyed and more than ninety percent of it wasted. And it had in it three hundred years of accumulated capital savings and investment of sunlight and the fertility of the soil. (And now that our bread is going to have five times as much fiber by being made out of sawdust, we're going to have to go on plundering the forests to an even larger degree; this, I am sure, is one of the reasons why two days ago President Ford signed the new bill allowing clear cutting in the National Forests. We need that roughage or fiber in our bread, we have taken out all the natural fiber of the wheat, of course, and thrown it away.)

The energy which gave us the Industrial Revolution — coal, oil, natural gas — represented the accumulated savings of four weeks of sunlight that managed somehow to be saved in the earth out of the three billion years of sunshine. That is what the fossil fuels are. This is not income to be spent; this is capital to be saved and invested. But we have already destroyed into entropy — a form of energy which is no longer able to be utilized — eleven or twelve days of that accumulated twenty-eight days of sunlight. And we have wasted it.

The fundamental, all pervasive cause of world instability today is the destruction of communities by the commercialization of all human relationships and the resulting neuroses and psychoses. The technological acceleration of transportation, communication, and weapons systems is now creating power areas wider than existing political structures. We still have at least half a dozen political structures in Europe, but our technology and the power system of Western Civilization today are such that most of Europe should be a single power system. This creates instability.

Medical science and the population explosion have continued to produce more and more people when the supply of food and the supply of jobs are becoming increasingly precarious, not only in the United States, but everywhere, because the whole purpose of using fossil fuels in the corporate structure is to eliminate jobs. "Labor saving," we call it, as if there were something wrong with working. Working is one of the joys of life. And if we created a society in which working is a pain in the neck, then we have created a society which is not fit for human beings. It will be obvious to you that I have enjoyed my work, although at the end of my career I have no conviction that I did any good. Fortunately, I had a marvelous father and a marvelous mother, and we were taught you don't have to win, but you have to give it all you've got. Then it won't matter.

To get back to sovereignty and the structure of the state, another cause of today's instability is that we now have a society in America, in Europe and in much of the world which is totally dominated by the two elements of sovereignty that are not included in the state structure: control of credit and banking and the corporation. These are free of political controls and social responsibility, and they have largely monopolized power in Western Civilization and in American society. They are ruthlessly going forward to eliminate land, labor, entrepreneurial-managerial skills, and everything else the economists once told us were the chief elements of production. The only element of production they are concerned with is the one they can control: capital.

So now everything is capital intensive, including medicine, and it hasn't worked. I'll give you just one example. No one has a more capital intensive medical system than the United States and many of you may be well satisfied with it. I simply want to point out a couple of facts. When a baby boy is born in the United State, his expectation of life is less than in nineteen other countries in the world. And it's that good only because our infant mortality rate is better than our adult mortality rate. In other words, in infant mortality we are about ninth or tenth; these figures date from about 1972, I think. Now let us look at a ten year old boy in the United States today. His expectation of life is less than that in thirty other countries, according to the United Nations statistics. We pay more than the people in any of those thirty countries for a capital intensive medical system devoted to keeping people who are almost dead alive a few more days, instead of making people grow up healthy by teaching them that work is fun, by teaching then that they don't have to be gluttons—in the United States, more than half of our food is wasted, maybe because it isn't that good. Exercise, moderation and so forth—it's all the old stuff we used to get in Sunday school. It just happens to be correct.

Our agricultural system is another cause of instability. It used to be a system in which seed was put into the earth to create food by taking sunlight, rain and the wealth of the soil, but we have replaced it with an agricultural system which is entirely capital intensive. We have eliminated labor and have even eliminated land to a considerable extent, so that we now pour out what we call food, but it's really a chemical synthetic. We have done this by putting a larger and larger amount of chemical fertilizers and pesticides made from fossil fuels into a smaller and smaller amount of soil. To give you one figure: Every bushel of corn we send to the Russians represents one gallon of gasoline, and then they tell us that, by selling our grain to the Russians, we're getting the foreign exchange that will allow us to pay for petroleum at fourteen dollars a barrel. No one has stopped to ask how many gallons were used to grow the grain and send it to the Russians.

In the thirty years from 1940 to 1970, three million American farms were abandoned because the families who worked them could not compete with the corporate farmers using the new chemical methods of producing crops. Thirty million people left these abandoned farms and the rural areas and went into the towns and cities, millions of them to get on relief. In 1970, the last year for which I have reliable figures, two thousand farms a year were going out of production. These are the farms on which we brought up our grandparents, the people who won the civil war, indeed, the people who fought in the First World War, and, in many cases, even in the Second War. Will the tractors be able to fight the next war when there are no farm boys to fight? (Of course, whether there are farm boys or not, they won't want to fight.)

In a similar way, by urban renewal and other things, we are destroying communities in the cities. Much of the legislation of the last forty years in this country has been aimed at the destruction of families, ghettos, parishes and any other communities.

All these processes create frustrations on every level of human experience and result in the instability and disorder we see around every day.

Now I come to a topic of delicacy: the United States constitutional crisis. The three branches of government set up in 1789 do not contain the eight aspects of sovereignty. The Constitution completely ignores, for example, the administrative power. The result is that the three branches of government have been struggling ever since to decide which of them will control the administrative power. The growth of political parties was necessary to establish relationships among the three branches. I used to tell my students that the important thing in any election is the nomination. And when you come to the election itself, it doesn't matter who votes, what's important is who didn't vote. Elections in the United States are increasingly decided by people who didn't vote because they're turned off for various reasons.

As a result of the way the three branches were set up, each has tried to go outside the sphere in which it should be restrained. For example, walking over here with Dean Krogh and Professor Brown, I spoke briefly about the Boston Latin School I attended. It is the oldest school in the United States, founded in 1635 as a preparatory school. Harvard was created the next year as a place for Latin School boys to go to college, and in my day, 1929-1930, it was the largest single source of supply for Harvard, although Harvard was doing all it could to cut down on the number of Latin School boys. The chief method they used to keep us out was to raise the entrance requirements, but we could handle that. Today that school is controlled by a Boston judge who has taken it upon himself to tell the school who will be admitted. And he has said they must have so many girls, they must have such-and-such a percentage of blacks, they cannot have entrance exams, and if people fail they can't throw them out. And what was once an absolutely incredible preparatory school is now being destroyed. It had many drawbacks—it was murderous. But it could get students through any competitive system of entrance exams in the country.

Another aspect of our constitutional crisis can be summed up in what young Schlesinger—that's Arthur Schlesinger, Jr.—called the Imperial Presidency. When I look at the President of the United States, what I see is Caesar Augustus. He is commander-in-chief; that's what Imperator, Emperor, means. He's the head of the executive branch. He's the head of state, which means he is the representative of the United States government in all foreign affairs and all ambassadors are accredited to him. Fourthly, he's the head of his political party. Fifth, he's head of the administrative system, which is increasingly making all the decisions as to what will be spent and who will spend it. Do you know who is making the decisions in our Bureau of Management and Budget as to who will get how much? And the president is also the symbol of national unity, the focus of our emotional feeling regarding our country. This is why it is so difficult to get rid of an incumbent President, either by election or impeachment.

We have today a general paralysis of government in the United States, especially in the administrative power, by the very thing we praise most: the so-called rule of law, which should rather be called the rule of lawyers. Let me give you one example. It is perfectly clear in the Constitution that a President can be impeached by a vote of Congress: indictment by the House, conviction by the Senate. This does not require common law procedures; it does not require judicial process. It is not a judicial action at all. It is a simple political action. If you have the votes, he can be removed, simply by counting them. The horrible thing about the whole Nixon business is that impeachment will never again be used in the history of the United States, because every member of the judiciary Committee has to be a lawyer, and the Judiciary committee has to recommend impeachment. And they require all kinds of procedures you would use in a court of law if you were accused of holding up a bank. The result is that never again will anyone try to impeach a President. It would take years and be indecisive, when you could simply have taken a vote and have the whole thing done in one morning.

There are a lot of other things in the Constitution which are perfectly obvious, but you can't get any constitutional lawyer to agree with one of them. It's perfectly obvious, for example, that if the three branches of government cannot agree to do something, it shouldn't be done. That was the theory behind the Constitution. Now we have someone supreme: the court will make the ultimate decision.

I'll just touch on something else: secrecy in government. Secrecy in government exists for only one reason: to prevent the American people from knowing what's going on. It is nonsense to believe that anything our government does is not known to the Russians at about the same moment it happens.

To me, the most ominous flaw in our constitutional set-up is the fact that the federal government does not have control over of money and credit and does not have control of corporations. It is therefore not really sovereign. And it is not really responsible, because it is now controlled by these two groups, corporations, and those who control the flows of money. The new public financing of the Presidential elections is arranged so that they can spend as much as they want: voluntary contributions, not authorized by the candidate, are legal.

The administrative system and elections are dominated today by the private power of money flows and corporation activities. I want to read you a summary from James Willard Hurst's "The Legitimacy of the Business Corporation in the Law of the United States from 1780 to 1970". He points out that there was powerful anti-corporation feeling in the United States in the 1820's. Therefore, it was established by the states that corporations could not exist by prescription: they had to have charters. They had to have a limited term of life and not be immortal. Corporations today are immortal: if they get charters, they can live forever and bury us all. They had to have a limited purpose. Who is giving us this bread made of sawdust? ITT: International Telephone and Telegraph, the same corporation that drove Ivar Kreuger to suicide in Paris in April 1931, when it actually was an international telegraph corporation, controlled by J P. Morgan.

I won't take time to read all these things, but certain thin regulations were established in the United States regarding corporations: restricted purpose and activities especially by banks and insurance companies; prohibition on one corporation's holding the stock of another without specific statutory grant; limits on the span of the life of the corporation, requiring recurrent legislative scrutiny;

limits on total assets; limits on new issues of capital, so that the proportion of control of existing stockholders could be maintained; limits on the votes allowed to any stockholder, regardless of the size of his holding; and so forth.

By 1890 all of these had been destroyed by judicial interpretation which extended to corporations—fictitious persons—those constitutional rights guaranteed, especially by the Fifteenth Amendment, to living persons. This interpretation was made possible by Roscoe Conklin, known as "Turkey Strut Conklin," who told the Supreme Court that there were no records kept by the committee of the Senate that had drawn up the Fifteenth Amendment. But he had kept private notes which showed they had the intended the word "person" to include corporations. It was most convenient. The corporation that was hiring him to do this suitably rewarded him.

Now I come to my last statement. I regret ending on what is, I suppose, such a pessimistic note—I'm not personally pessimistic. The final result will be that the American people will ultimately prefer communities. They will cop out or opt out of the system. Today everything is a bureaucratic structure, and brainwashed people who are not personalities are trained to fit into this bureaucratic structure and say it is a great life—although I would assume that many on their death beds must feel otherwise. The process of coping out will take a long time, but notice: we are already coping out of military service on a wholesale basis; we are already copping out of voting on a large scale basis. I heard an estimate tonight that, for the fourth time in sixteen years the President will probably be chosen by but forty percent of the people eligible to vote. People are also copping out by refusing to pay any attention to newspapers or to what's going on in the world, and by increasing their emphasis on the growth of localism, i.e., what is happening in their own neighborhoods.

In this pathetic election, I am simply amazed that neither of the candidates has thought about any of the important issues, such as localism, the rights of areas to make their own decisions about those things affecting them. Now I realize that if there's a sulphur mine or a sulphur factory a few miles away, localism isn't much help. But I think you will find one extraordinary thing in this election: a considerable number of people will go to the polls and vote for the local candidates, but they will not vote for the President. That is a reverse of the situation fifty years ago.

Now I want to say good night. Do not be pessimistic. Life goes on; life is fun. And if a civilization crashes, it deserves to. When Rome fell, the Christian answer was, "Create our own communities."

Thank you, Ladies and Gentlemen.

COLLECTED WRITINGS

DR. QUIGLEY EXPLAINS HOW NAZI GERMANY SEIZED A STRONGER CZECHOSLOVAKIA FACULTY CORNER

The Courier, December 12, 1952

For the Faculty Corner this week, the Courier has been fortunate in obtaining permission to print an exchange of correspondence between Mr. Jay Burke, a student in the Georgetown College of Arts and Sciences, and Dr. Carroll Quigley of the School of Foreign Service. We are indebted to both parties for this permission.

Dr. Carroll Quigley
Department of History, School of Foreign Service

My dear Dr. Quigley:

My name is Jay Burke and I am a student at Georgetown University. I am writing in regard to a discussion I have had with a student of yours, James Dowling. It is his assertion that prior to the outbreak of hostilities in 1939, at the time Germany took over Czechoslovakia, Germany had only 36 incomplete divisions while Czechoslovakia had 35 complete and well trained divisions. In Dowling's own words, "The Czech troops were ordered out of the trenches," shortly before the treacherous invasion of the Germans.
    Obviously the Czech army was more potent than the German army. If this is so, why was Germany able to conquer Czechoslovakia so easily, and why didn't the Czechs resist?
    It is my contention that Germany had more than 36 incomplete divisions to conquer a country of 35 complete divisions. Mr. Dowling contends that Germany had but 36 divisions plus their reserves.
    Would you please give us the truth of the matter?

Respectfully yours,
Jay Burke
Mr. Jay Burke
Box 113, Georgetown University
Washington 7, D.C.

My dear Mr. Burke,

Mr. Dowling's statement, regarding the size of the German Army at the time of the Munich crisis of September 1938, is quite accurate. In the third week of September Czechoslovakia had a million men and thirty-four first-rate divisions under arms. The Germans, in the course of September, increased their mobilization to thirty-one and ultimately to thirty-six divisions; but this probably represented a smaller force than the Czechs, as many of the nineteen first-line divisions were at two-thirds strength, the other third having been withdrawn to form the nucleus for the reserve divisions. Of the nineteen first-line divisions, three were armored and four were motorized. Only five divisions were left on the French frontier, in order to defeat Czechoslovakia as quickly as possible. France, which did not mobilize completely, had the Maginot Line completely manned on a war basis plus more than twenty infantry divisions. Moreover, France had available ten motorized divisions. Finally, Russia had ninety-seven divisions and, according to a letter from President Benes to Professor L. B. Namier on 20 April, 1944, Russia insisted on a policy of resistance to Germany's demands in September, 1938. (See L.B. Namier, Europe in Decay, London, 1950. p. 284.)

In air power, the Germans had a slight edge in average quality, but in number of planes it was far inferior. Moreover, Britain was just beginning to obtain delivery planes of quality far superior to those of Germany. In September, 1938, Germany had about 1,500 planes, while Czechoslovakia had less than 1,000; France and England together had over 1,000; Russia was reported to have 5,000, mostly of poor quality, but some of high quality. During the crisis, Russia gave thirty-six of its best planes to Czechoslovakia, flying them across Rumania.

In tanks, Germany was far inferior in quality in September, 1938. At that time, Germany's tanks were all below ten tons (Mark II) and were armed with machine guns, except for a handful of eighteen ton tanks (Mark III) armed with a 37 mm. gun. The Czechs had hundreds of thirty-eight ton tanks armed with 75 mm. cannon. When Germany overran Czechoslovakia in March, 1939, it captured 469 of these superior tanks along with 1,500 planes, 43,500 machine guns, over one million rifles, and a magnificent system of fortifications. From every point of view, this was little less than Germany had at Munich, and, at Munich, if the British government had desired it, Germany (with the possible assistance of Poland and Hungary) would have been opposed by Czechoslovakia supported by France, Britain, and Russia.

Before leaving this subject, it might be mentioned that Germany, in 1939, brought into production a Mark IV tank of twenty-three tons armed with a 75 mm. cannon but obtained only a handful of these by the outbreak of war. Up to that date (September, 1939), Germany had obtained delivery of only 300 Mark III and Mark IV tanks together. In addition, it had obtained, by the same date, 2,700 of the inferior Mark I and Mark II tanks which suffered break-downs of as much as twenty-five per cent a week. Even in 1939 Germany's production of tanks was less than Britain's. In the first nine months of 1939, Germany produced only fifty tanks a month; in the last four months of 1939, in wartime, Germany produced 247 "tanks and self-propelled guns" compared to British production of 314 tanks in the same period. From 1936 to the outbreak of war in 1939, German aircraft production was not raised but averaged 425 planes a month of all types (including commercial planes). This gave Germany an air force of 1,000 bombers and 1,050 fighters of varying quality in September, 1939. In contrast with this, the British air program of March, 1934 provided for a first-line R.A.F. of 900 planes. This was later increased, at Chamberlain's urging, and the program at May, 1938 planned for a first line force of 2,370 planes. This was increased again in 1939. Under it, Britain produced almost 3,000 "military" planes in 1938 and about 8,000 in 1939. Because of differences in categories between "planes," "military planes," and "combat planes," it is not possible to make any exact comparison of air strength between Britain and Germany, but it is clear that Britain's planes in 1939 and 1940 were more recent and of superior quality than Germany's. It was this superiority which made it possible for Britain to defeat Germany in the "Battle of Britain" in September, 1940.

The above figures are derived from various sources, mostly official documents. Obviously, the best source for figures on the German Army are in the papers of the German Ministry of War which were captured by the American Army in 1945. At the order of the Secretary of War (Stimson) these archives were studied from this point of view by Major General C.F. Robinson. General Robinson's report, dated 15 October, 1947, is available under the title Foreign Logistical Organizations and Methods (210 pages). At the time I saw this, it was a classified document, and, even now, you may have difficulty obtaining a copy. If so, you will find its contents on this topic summarized in B. Kain's "Germany's Preparation for War," American Economic Review XXXVIII (March 1948), pp. 56-77. These figures on the relative strengths of the German and French armies have recently been supported completely by the French parliamentary investigation into the causes of the 1940 defeat. That the British government was familiar with the situation clear from the recently published papers of the Foreign Office of Great Britain, E.L. Woodward, ed., Documents on British Foreign Policy, 1919-1939, third series, 5 volumes so far published covering 1937-1939. Nevertheless, at that time and since, prominent British political personages such as Lord Halifax, Churchill, and J. Wheeler-Bennett have tried to convey the impression that Germany had overwhelming military force in 1937-1940. This impression has, unfortunately, been generally accepted in America. From the published British documents we can see that the British military attachés in Paris and in Prague protested at the time against this misrepresentation. The most influential element in this campaign of misrepresentation was a statement from Charles A. Lindbergh, issued in Paris at the height of the Czechoslovak crisis, that Germany had 8,000 military planes and could build 1,500 a month. We now know that Germany at that time had 1,500 planes, had built 280 a month in 1938, and had abandoned all plans to bomb London even in a full-scale war because of lack of planes and distance from the target. Lindbergh repeated his talk of woe in London, and the British Government drove its own people to the verge of hysteria by frantically distributing gas-masks, digging worthless slit-trenches in London parks, and releasing rumors of a grave lack of aircraft defenses. Although Lord Halifax, Churchill, and others were informed, about 5 September, 1938, by representatives of the German General Staff and of the German Foreign Office that Hitler would be assassinated by them as soon as he gave the order to attack Czechoslovakia, the British yielded to Hitler and sent ultimatums to Czechoslovakia, to do the the same (See Documents, II, Appendix, and H. Rothfels, The German Opposition to Hitler, Hinsdale, Illinois, 1948, pp. 58-63 and elsewhere). The assassination plot, accordingly, was cancelled at noon on 28 September, 1938. Winston Churchill has continually misrepresented the degree of German armaments and was challenged on this issue by Hanson Baldwin, military critic of The New York Times in that paper on 9 May, 1938. J.W. Wheeler-Bennett in his book, Munich (New York, 1948), says, "By the close of 1937 Germany's preparedness for war was complete... Her rearmament had reached its apogée and could hold that peak level for a certain time... "etc., etc. Mr. Wheeler-Bennett, Britain's outstanding authority on international documentation, was a high official in the Intelligence Department of the Foreign Office during the War, and was, when he wrote his book, the British editor of the captured archives of the German Foreign Ministry. His statements, so far as I know, have never been publicly challenged, and his book is widely accepted as a standard work today. Its interpretation is not supported by the documents which have been published since he wrote, including those published by his organization under the title Documents on German Foreign Policy, 1918-1945, from the Archives of the German Foreign Ministry. Volume II, Germany and Czechoslovakia, 1937-1938, (Washington, 1950).

The Czechs did not resist in September 1938, as a consequence of a series of ultimatums from London and Paris which stated that if they did not yield they would fight alone. Benes was apparently afraid that if he resisted, he would be supported by Russia; would be attacked simultaneously by Germany, Hungary, and Poland; would be denounced as "a spear-head of Bolshevism in Central Europe" (as he was even after he yielded); and that Britain and France would send aid to Germany to order to drive Germany into a war with the Soviet Union. Since Britain and France did try to attack Russia in January-February, 1940 (at a time when they were technically at war with Germany) and were prevented only by Swedish resistance, there may have been some validity in Benes' fears. On this last point see the documents published by the Swedish Foreign Ministry Forspelet till det tyska angreppet pa Danmark ich Norge den 9 April 1940 (Stockholm, 1947) pp. 153 and 235-236. My own opinion is that if Benes had resisted Germany in 1938 and Germany had attacked, either Hitler would have been removed by his generals or public opinion in France and England would have forced these governments to declare war on Germany. However, none of us knows what might have happened. I assure you it is difficult enough, in the face of propaganda from all sides, to determine what did happen.

Sincerely,
Carroll Quigley

POLITICS

By CARROLL QUIGLEY, Ph.D.
Appeared in the 1957 edition of the SFS yearbook Protocol.

We cannot compare the domestic politics of 1957 with the political situation of 1932 for the simple reason that they are not comparable. In 1932 we were in the depths of the world depression, while in 1957 we are still near the peak of a boom. If any comparison is to be made, it must be between 1929 and 1957. In these two years we find a business boom still climbing, the hectic social atmosphere which goes along with spending beyond our means and keeping up with the Jones', in the White House a Republican administration symbolized by a great man (in the earlier period a "Great Engineer" who was also a "Great Humanitarian," today a "Great General" who is also a "Great Pacifier"). And in both years, while Wall Street poured out securities, Detroit poured out automobiles and, over it all, the Federal Reserve Board, in hesitant and indecisive fashion, made motions toward restraining the inflation by nudging up the discount rate. Yes, at first glance 1957 looks much like 1929.

But really things are not the same. The superficial appearance may be similar, but the whole tone and above all the minds of the people are different. The difference arises from two things: in 1957 we have lived through the world depression and World War II. And as a consequence the gaiety and heady optimism of 1929 are replaced by the secret worries and fears beneath today's surface appearance. This change is reflected in the fact that the graduate of June 1929 was eager to get out into the prosperity rat-race, while the graduate of June 1957 is hesitant to leave the relative quiet of academic life. The goal of the new alumnus has shifted from riches to security.

The great change in American domestic life goes back to the New Deal. The Republican Administration of 1929 was an alliance of Wall Street and heavy industry lording it over unorganized labor, disorganized farmers, resentful commercial interests, and sheep-like consumers. The selfishness of its policies combined with its totally unrealistic economic and (above all) financial ideas to lead America to economic collapse. The Republican Administration of 1957 is again an alliance of Wall Street and heavy industry but, with one exception, the rest of the picture is different. Consumers remain ignorant, unorganized, sheep-like, and exploited; but labor is organized, alert, and powerful; commercial interests are much better informed, more independent from financial controls; and, in most circles, economic and financial ideas are so much better than the dangers of economic collapse are remote. The big changes are to be found in the relative shift in power of financial groups and farmers. In 1929, the bankers were at the top of the heap, guiding and exhorting on the basis of completely erroneous theories; today, bankers have been reduced from master of all to servant of the rest and have much more adequate ideas of their own role and functions.

The greatest Structural change is to be found in the position of the farmer. In 1929 the typical American farmers were tenants who had lived less than two years on the same land, had neither electricity nor plumbing, and were largely ignorant of the influences which trapped them between high industrial prices, low farm prices, high interest rates, and an exploitative distributive system for farm commodities. Resentful of their fate, they were politically helpless because the memory of the Civil War divided them between Southern farmers, who would vote only Democratic, and Western farmers, who would vote Republican or for a third-party but would never vote Democratic. In 1957, as a consequence of the New Deal, the farmer owns his own land, has electricity, plumbing and at least one car, can get reasonable interest rates, is fully aware of the parity ratio between farm prices and industrial prices, and is only moderately exploited by high cost of distribution of farm produce. The events of the last quarter century have pushed the memory of the Civil War far enough away so that farmers are able to unite their voting impact on either parry. No longer is the Southern farmer a social outcast if he votes Republican, and even less resentment is directed at the Western farmer who votes Democratic. The chief consequence of all this is that the Republicans control the White House, but not the Congress, in 1957, and the Farm Bloc independents and third-parry movements of the 1920's are no more.

The diminishing bitterness of Civil War sectionalism which allowed the two great farming areas to come together to support the New Deal in the 1930's and to support Eisenhower in the 1950's is reflected in a number of other trends. A quarter of a century ago most negroes automatically voted Republican and most Catholics voted Democratic. In spite of this fact, as the election of 1928 clearly showed, the Democratic South would not support a Catholic for President.

Today these old antipathies have greatly weakened. On a class, sectional, racial, or religious basis our country is much more homogeneous, the lesser political parties and lunatic fringes have become insignificant, the two major parties are very much more alike and both are closer to the middle of the road. And underneath all of this, the older social and economic system which was exploitative and class-orientated has been replaced, as a New Deal heritage, by a pluralist and cooperative system functioning as a balance among heavy industry, finance, consumers industry, commercial groups, organized labor, organized farmers, and, unfortunately, disorganized consumers. As an economic, social, and political system it has much to recommend it. It is prosperous; it is powerful; it has refuted all the Liberal Cassandras, Marxist revolutionaries, and motley prophets of doom of twenty-five or mote years ago. The chief things that it needs is some salt in the stew—a seasoning of idealism and heightened spiritual awareness which the Class of 1957 might well seek to provide.

FATHER WALSH AS I KNEW HIM

by Carroll Quigley, Ph.D.
The 1959 Protocol, the yearbook of the
School of Foreign Service,
School of Business Administration,
and Institute of Languages and Linguistics
of Georgetown University.

It would be presumptuous for any of us who were his juniors to write of Father Walsh except in the limited sense indicated in the title of this essay. He was far too broad, too versatile, and too subtle for us to attempt a full portrait. For that reason we must speak in a limited and subjective fashion of how he appeared to us.

One of the first impressions which Father Walsh made on his faculty was one of great energy and drive. When he became interested in a subject he threw himself into it, day and night, week after week, until he had got from it what he wanted. In this process he never spared himself, and spared his co-workers only because of his unfailing personal courtesy. Just when these co-workers began to flag in zeal, he would return to the task with a new burst of enthusiasm, having, as likely as not, obtained his new energy from a solitary night-long vigil over the problem. In this way Father Walsh lived through a series of lives associated with the Foreign Service School: the Russian Revolution, geopolitics, Washington "society," Washington real-estate, maps, speech, The Institute of World Polity, the Nuremberg trials, and the Institute of Languages and Linguistics. I am sure that there were other enthusiasms of which I am ignorant.

Father Walsh's habit of approaching anything which attracted his interest with unremitting enthusiasm had both advantages and disadvantages. On the one hand, his drive and concentration on each enthusiasm while it held the center of his attention resulted in almost unbelievable achievement in that matter, but, on the other hand, once a new enthusiasm attracted his attention, the previous one became relatively neglected. Having obtained from each enthusiasm the stimulation and knowledge he needed, he left it pretty much to its own resources as he turned to something new.

It would be a grave error to infer from what I have said that Father Walsh was fickle. Nothing would be more untrue. One of his most impressive qualities was loyalty—loyalty to his intellectual beliefs and spiritual values, to his associates and faculty, and to his own past. Whenever he turned the focus of his attention to something new, this did not imply in any way a rejection of the old. His attention, like a searchlight shining on a dark, complex, and fascinating world, moved slowly from one object to another, illuminating each with a blinding concentration of energy, but as it moved on, left each as a firm and undeniable part of reality.

Father Walsh's loyalty was no narrow or restricted quality. In fact, narrowness in any sense was absolutely foreign to his outlook. He had an essential bigness about him which reminded me of some of the clerical figures of the Renaissance of the Sixteenth Century, a versatility, largeness of outlook, and diversity of interests which fell just short of being extravagant or flamboyant. And with all this went a self-assurance which was not egotism but simply a firm knowledge of where he stood.

The loyalty to which I refer included a profoundly convinced allegiance to his own country, to his Church, to his Irishness, to his family, and to mankind. When Bernard Shaw made deprecating remarks about the Irish, Father Walsh did not hesitate to challenge him in newspaper controversy. Yet above all he was cosmopolitan, at home with all kinds of people and intensely interested in them. He had lived, for extended periods, in Italy, Germany, Iraq, Mexico, Japan, and Russia and, except perhaps for the last, felt quite at home in all of them. Close friends from all parts of the world, speaking a wonderful variety of accents, streamed into his office almost every day he was here on the campus.

I have emphasized this quality of loyalty in Father Walsh because I have come to value it increasingly as the years pass. From personal knowledge I can say that his loyalty to his faculty, a loyalty which remained undiminished through months of absence and apparent neglect, was one of the things which made teaching at the Foreign Service School worthwhile. In time of personal, professional, or financial difficulty any member of the faculty could appeal to Father Walsh and receive instant help. Because of his extraordinary broadness and flexibility, such an appeal could be made at any time, day or night, on any subject and receive the same sympathetic reception.

A favorite pastime of Father Walsh was his pet Doberman, Prince. in 1943

In 1943, when I had been in Washington two years, the rented house in which I lived with my family was suddenly put up for sale. Lacking sufficient cash for a down payment on any house and unable to find another one in war-crowded Washington, I was puzzling over what to do. I mentioned my problem to Father Walsh one day, in a rather incidental way because I felt that it was my problem, not his. He asked, "How much money do you need?" I answered, "With what I have, $1500 would do." He at once picked up a checkbook from his desk, wrote out a check for the amount I had named, and, as he gave it to me, said, "I'll take this back from your paycheck, $500 a year, for the next three years."

Perhaps the most typical part of this story occurred a couple of months later when Father Walsh stopped me one day and said, "No one else knows about that $1500 so if I were to die suddenly there would be no record of it. Won't you write me a letter stating the arrangement as we agreed it, and I'll leave it among my papers for my successor?"

Father Walsh did many kindnesses like that, often to people he knew only in a distant way. To those whom he knew even better he was always available. His loyalty to his associates never wavered, even when it was not reciprocated. In many cases he must have known that people deeply indebted to him were not supporting him or his projects, but I never saw it influence his attitude toward them. This attitude he held because it seemed the proper one, not because it depended on any quid pro quo relationship. And just as quietly, when it seemed proper, Father Walsh struck back like lightning, so quickly that the victim hardly knew what hit him, but there was never any personal animosity in these reactions. I remember one occasion when Father Walsh discharged a full professor who had been on the faculty for many years. I do not know the details; I doubt if anyone does; but I am sure there were good reasons. The point is that the case occurred in the middle of the semester, with courses meeting daily. It came to a head one afternoon; the professor was fired that night; and the same evening Father Walsh called up a friend and placed the discharged professor in another job at a substantial increase in salary.

A well-traveled personality, Father Walsh poses with Vatican Guards.

The motives for this last act were largely rooted in loyalty, but there was also another factor. No priest was more fully aware than Father Walsh of the problems of living in the secular world. This is something which men in Holy Orders may easily lose. Father Walsh never did. In this matter his awareness continued to grow until his last illness. It was really much more than awareness, our late Regent was a very sophisticated man, fully at home in very diverse social conditions and completely master of almost any situation. He was like some legendary Old World prelate, tolerant, wise, and self-assured.

This was a part of his personality which was widely misunderstood and sometimes resented. Father Walsh enjoyed sophisticated social life. He was on a basis of personal friendship with some of the most influential persons in this country and abroad. I have heard him criticized on the grounds that his association with the wealthy and the influential was a kind of snobbery or even of social climbing. It was nothing of the sort.

Father Walsh enjoyed brilliant social affairs, elaborate parties, even what might be called "high-level intrigue," but he never ceased to be fully objective about it. It always remained to him enjoyable without becoming important. He was fascinated by people, but he was just as happy working alone all night in his study.

This leads to another aspect of this complex personality. Father Walsh had that child-like quality which seems to be universal with all very great men. This quality made it possible for him to approach everything with a freshness of outlook as if he had never seen it before, even when he had lived through the same experience many times. This quality appeared equally readily when he went to one of Mrs. McLean's parties as when he went poking about in a Georgetown slum—and he did both frequently.

This childlike quality was the basis for his enthusiasm for so many diverse things and the key to why so many persons who barely knew him loved him. I remember one day five or six of us, including Professor Leahigh, the Regent's assistant, my wife and myself, were standing in his office. My wife and Father Walsh got into an animated discussion about children's games and why they had been so quickly forgotten during the last ten years after having survived with only slight changes for centuries. We were all standing in a circle when suddenly Father Walsh went down on his hands and knees, demonstrating the various ways that marbles were played in different regions and the relative advantages of two different methods of "shooting" a marble. That wonderful ability to forget himself and his company was the key to his enthusiasm and one of the chief reasons for his success.

Some of these enthusiasms such as the Russian Revolution, the Foreign Service School, geopolitics, or the Institute of Languages and Linguistics are well known and need not be mentioned. But there were others. At one time Father Walsh was filled with enthusiasm for local real estate. Each day he clipped from the morning papers the advertisements concerned with real estate sales in the area bounded by Rock Creek, Chain Bridge Road, and Massachusetts Avenue. Each clipping was glued to the top of a sheet of 8"x 11" paper. Below was jotted down all the information obtainable on the property and his reactions to it. If he was not personally familiar with the property, he telephoned to the agent for information and often went to inspect it. As a consequence, Father Walsh acquired an amazing knowledge of houses and real-estate values in the area mentioned. This could be matched by few persons. I have myself heard Father

Walsh ask someone to give his address and then he would proceed to tell the amazed individual all about the house and its neighbors: where the stairway was, how the kitchen was situated, the number of closets, the relationship between bedrooms and baths upstairs; or the age of the heating plant downstairs. And as he did this, Father Walsh's face would sparkle with mischievous enjoyment at his listener's amazement. Once I foolishly asked why he made this detailed study, and he explained to me with an appropriate mixture of mischief and gravity that his brother, who lived in Boston and was blind, owned a house in the area, and it was necessary to protect that investment by keeping up with real estate developments around it!

Father Walsh was an enthusiastic builder and renovator. When the two temporary annex buildings outside the main gate were erected, the Regent spent a good part of every day among the workers, asking questions, giving instructions, and planning decorations. Later, when the Institute of Languages and Linguistics was installed on Massachusetts Avenue, he spent much of each day, and night, on the task of supervising the work. He personally mixed paint to get the colors he wanted and designed decorations for the interior. Twenty years ago much of the area between Thirty-fifth street and the University's main gate was slum, inhabited, to a considerable extent by Negroes. Directly opposite the main gate, on the south-east corner of Thirty seventh street and O street, a colored family with many children lived in a decrepit building which lacked foundations, plumbing, electricity, and probably heat. It was an offense to the nose as much as to the eye. This area has now been largely rebuilt, a process which still continues.

Frankfurt, 1946. Father Walsh is photographed with the German Minister of the Interior, Hans Venedey, Major Wessels of the U.S. Army, and Professor W. Hallstein, Rector of Frankfurt University.

It was by no means unusual, while renovation was going on in such a building, for a passer-by to glance into its destroyed interior and see Father Walsh in animated conversation with some carpenter or electrician, surrounded by piles of broken laths, plaster, discarded boards, or obsolete plumbing. A strange place, one might think, for such a fastidious man, and, yet, on such occasions he sometimes seemed to be happiest. He was a great builder and was, indeed, most content when he was building either people or edifices.

The Founder of the School of Foreign Service was a regular attendant at auctions. Sometimes he bought what no one else wanted or things for which he could see no use himself at the time. But when the time came to decorate a renovated building, Father Walsh would recall his earlier purchases and find a place for them. Even today we use many heavy old tables, book cases, clocks, filing cases, and other objects which were obtained in this way. When the annexes were equipped much of the interior had such an origin, including most of the decorations of the main lounge, where students reclined on the old steamer chairs of the transatlantic liner Normandie quite unaware of their history. One product of Father Walsh's auction exploits are the two stone pillars at the foot of the stairs leading to the medical school path near the northwest corner of White-Gravenor Building. I pass between those pillars many times on my walk home and invariably think of Father Walsh bidding them in at that auction so many years ago. Another of Father Walsh's enthusiasms which is now rarely remembered was maps. He dearly loved maps and could hardly ever resist a map or a map salesman. Father Walsh once told me, again only partly seriously, that he lectured every winter to the ladies of Washington on the Russian Revolution in order to get money to buy maps. The wonderful relief maps in Room 9 Healy or the excellent German map of Central Europe opposite Hirst Reading Room are remains of this interest. The German map is in two parts; ordered before the war, one part came immediately, while the other arrived after the war was finished. At one time Father Walsh used his lecture fees to engage a man to make hundreds of hand drawn and colored maps of small portions of the earth on glass slides for a projector. I first heard of these when the Regent took me into his inner office, tenderly unwrapped them from their boxes and with loving care held several dozen of them up, one by one, to the window's light so that I could admire them.

The most persistent and most pervasive of Father Walsh's enthusiasms was his interest in communication. By this I do not mean technical matters of electronics, but the old and far from simple problem of how a feeling or idea possessed by one person can be communicated to another person. This concern resulted in a constant interest in speech, in words, in connotations and in all the emotional overtones in conveyance of thoughts and feelings. His awareness of the meaning, the implications, and the usage of words was very highly developed. He went over his own writings again and again, pondering shades of meaning or the niceties of word order. In some ways, the basis of this interest was poetical rather than prosaic, for he frequently sought ambiguity or multiplicity of meaning rather than simplicity or clarity, seeking to heighten the effect of the sentence or to include a larger area of appeal to its readers. Father Walsh frequently suggested changes of words in the writings of others, or jotted comments of this kind in the margins of printed books which he was reading. There can be little doubt that he could have been a highly successful editor, as he had been an outstanding teacher of English Composition in his early career.

Japanese students listen attentively as Father Walsh teaches in a Tokyo high school.

He would have been an even greater success as an actor. For Father Walsh's interest in the spoken word surpassed his interest in the written one. This interest went much further than the word itself as a vehicle of expression and included all aspects of speech — tone, cadence, bodily pose, lighting, background, and everything else associated with the impression to be made on the audience. His own speeches were carefully written out before delivery and were read and re-read, both silently and aloud, by himself and by others. At each reading, changes were made and notes digested to guide delivery. All the old oratorical or rhetorical devices which he had learned in the study of the Classics were used, manipulated, considered, or rejected. The whole environment was carefully considered—the light radiating his silvery hair, the gestures with his delicate hands, the hang and sway of his clerical cloak. The result was a performance rather than a speech, but the result was also, very frequently, a sensational success. He gave lectures on the Russian Revolution, year after year, in Washington, to enthusiastic audiences of paying customers and, also, year after year, to the Army Command School at Fort Leavenworth. It would be a mistake to imagine that these lectures were weaker in content because of the speaker's concern with the manner of presentation; in each case the content was as carefully prepared as the manner, always being geared to the level of the audience and achieving, in most cases, exactly the effect which had been planned. I have been told by Army officers who attended his lectures at Leavenworth that they were highly valued parts of the course there, and were received with such great enthusiasm that the question period following the lecture would sometimes run for an hour or more beyond the time allowed.

As a consultant, Father Walsh served his country throughout the Second World War.

At one time Father Walsh's concern with speech led him to establish a "Speech Institute" whose remains can still be seen in Room 21 of Old North. There he set up a stage with curtain and footlights, control booths on each side, a huge clock to guide the speaker on the rear wall, and elaborate recording equipment backstage to preserve the speaker's efforts for instructional analysis later. Few students who now marvel at or suffer with the tape recordings of the present Language Laboratories realize that the remote seed of that elaborate organization rests in Room 21.

Father Walsh was a devoted student of the United States Constitution. He was constantly reading and re-reading it, usually in the Government Printing Office's large annotated edition, which constantly lay on his cluttered writing table. This devotion to the Constitution was combined with his enthusiasm for renovation in the so-called "Constitution Room" (Healy 8), another remainder of his personal enthusiasms. While Father Walsh had a profound recognition of the more significant merits of the Constitution, I have no doubt that part of his admiration rested on the fact that a document, apparently so brief and so clear, could have such varied meaning in its words as has been revealed in 170 years of history. When he wrote university regulations, catalogues, or brochures he tended to seek a similar mode of expression: words brief and clear which could change their meaning if conditions ever required it.

This tendency to feel that words written to-day must never become barriers to activity to-morrow rested, I believe, on the fact that Father Walsh was a man of action rather than a scholar. I do not mean that he was not a thinker, for he was constantly thinking, planning, and organizing with a remarkably quick and able mind. But I do mean that he was never satisfied merely with thought or merely with words. He felt that thought must lead to decision and decision to action. Thus he was a man of action and, as such, a leader. In any group, he became, almost at once, the center of attention and of decision. As a man of action and of convictions, as a leader and an actor, it was as natural for Father Walsh to take the direction of a situation as it was to breathe. And it was always done with such consummate skill and such elegant courtesy that it was a joy to watch. Nothing that he did of this kind was ever done in any brash, vulgar, or offensive way, but always with grace, consideration, and good humor.

In this, as in other things, there was always an aristocratic element about his actions, his tastes, and even his foibles. When I think of him today, I often recall the injunction of the fifth General of the Society of Jesus. "Tenacity in purpose, suavity in manner."That, at least, is how he appeared to us who worked for him in his later years.

CONSTANTINE MCGUIRE: MAN OF MYSTERY

by Carroll Quigley
Courier, December 1965, pp. 16-20

CONSTANTINE E. McGUIRE, PH.D.,
FOUNDER OF THE SCHOOL OF FOREIGN SERVICE,
AND MAN OF MYSTERY,
DIED IN NEW YORK ON 22 OCTOBER 1965,
AT THE AGE OF 75.

Constantine E. McGuire was a man of mystery. Although he was member of the American Historical Association for more than fifty years and was treasurer of that association for six years, at his death the available records showed little beyond the date he had joined the association, and did not indicate even where he had been educated, nor in what university or field of study he had worked. The situation was no different at the American Catholic Historical Association, of which he had been president in 1933. Although he resided in Washington for 38 years, his closest associates did not know where he lived, but simply knew that he could be reached by writing to him at Box 1, the Cosmos Club. This was his address for 48 years and continued to be used until his death, although he had moved from Washington to Geneva, New York, at the end of 1952. In that town also he had no published address, but received communications at Post Office Box 447.

In some ways, the Cosmos Club was the center about which McGuire's public life revolved. For decades he could be found there, almost every day, in its lounge rooms, library, or dining room. Most of his acquaintances assumed that he lived at the club, but an associate who saw him almost daily for years told me that McGuire had a house at Chevy Chase, cared for by an ancient housekeeper. This ministrator may have been a relative, for, when McGuire was himself already in his sixties, he told various people that he was the economic support of seven very old persons, of whom three were in ill health.

I wrote above that McGuire could be found at the Club "almost every day", but in fact he vanished from Washington for weeks or even months, every year, on business trips abroad, chiefly to Latin America. Many who knew him casually at the club were puzzled as to what he did, and tended to assume, from his obvious great learning, that he must be some kind of a professor. Indeed, as we shall see, that is what he planned to be and probably should have been, but, in fact, for more than forty-five years, his chief living came from his work as a private and very confidential consulting expert in international economic affairs, especially in matters of international finance and foreign commercial law. When still in his twenties, he drafted numerous treaties and other international agreements in commercial affairs for our State Department and was, for years, economic adviser and financial adviser to various foreign governments. It was rumored among McGuire's friends that he was one of the most influential Catholic laymen in the United States, had been adviser to the papacy on American financial matters, and, in the summer of 1929, just before the stock market crash, had advised the Vatican to transfer its security holdings here into gold in anticipation of a panic.

While we are concerned with rumors, it might be mentioned that a character in Somerset Maugham's novel, The Razor's Edge (a part played by Clifton Webb in the film version) was reputed to have been inspired by McGuire.

Whatever truth there may be in such rumors, it is a fact that at the age of thirty-two (in February, 1923), McGuire was made a Knight of St. Gregory the Great by Pope Pius XI, and included among his associates and friends many influential scholars and officials of the cosmopolitan world in which he lived. None of these, however, was allowed to have any overall view of his activities, so that it is no easy task today to give an adequate account of his life.

Constantine E. McGuire Ph.D.

Constantine McGuire was born in Boston on 4 April 1890 and, like many ambitious Boston-Irish, penetrated the precincts of Yankeedom by attending the Boston Latin School and Harvard University. At both places, he was a contemporary of Joseph P. Kennedy. McGuire took three Harvard degrees: a bachelor's degree, magna cum laude, in political science in 1911. a master's degree in history the following year, and a doctorate, also in history, in 1915. His chief interest lay in the history of public law and institutions of the Middle Ages, so that much of his study was with Charles Homer Haskins and Roscoe Pound. With the latter he studied Roman law and comparative law. In 1913-1914 he went to Europe on a Harvard Travelling Fellowship, chiefly to Madrid and to Paris, where he studied law. He also attended classes or courses at Leiden, Bonn, and Salamanca. In Paris he attended the École des Langues Orientales Vivantes, and began to dream of seeing a similar institution in the United States.

On his return to Harvard in 1914, McGuire became an instructor in history and wrote his doctoral dissertation on the history of immunities from royal jurisdiction. He took his Ph.D. in 1915 and looked forward to becoming a Harvard professor, but, in the course of that year, it was made clear to him that, as he expressed it, "Harvard had an unwritten rule which barred any Roman Catholic from teaching medieval history".

Bitterly disappointed at this blow, from which he never really recovered, McGuire left Harvard and gave up all aim of a teaching career. He took a position as research assistant in the office of the Secretary-General of the Inter-American High Commission in Washington, and within a few months, was made Assistant Secretary-General. At that time, the High Commission had much prestige, since its ten members consisted of John Bassett Moore, Samuel Untermyer, Paul M. Warburg, John H. Fahey, Duncan U. Fletcher, David F. Houston as chairman, Guillermo A. Sherwell, Leo S. Rowe, and ex-Mayor Andrew J. Peters of Boston. The Commission had twenty-nine national sections, made up of experts and civil servants of the different countries, each presided over by each nation's Minister of Finance. It was by these connections that McGuire established the contacts through which he later exercised his influence and made his living. Within a few years, in a manner which is unknown, he established those contacts with the Vatican which he later transferred, to some extent, to Father Walsh.

The High Commission worked to facilitate international economic relations between states, seeking to stabilize monetary exchanges, remove conflicts of laws, smooth all international transactions, and, if possible, unify or coordinate regulations on business organizations, including corporation laws and bankruptcy. In these efforts, McGuire worked closely with the State Department, drafting international agreements, and became the chief figure in these activities when Leo Rowe, the Secretary-General of the High Commission, became Assistant Secretary of the Treasury in 1917. It might be pointed out that Rowe in 1919 became Chief of the Latin American Division of the State Department for about a year and then, for twenty-six years, until his tragic death in an automobile mishap in 1946, was both Director-General of the Pan-American Union and, at McGuire's behest, Lecturer in Latin American History at the Foreign Service School.

McGuire left the High Commission in 1922 to join the staff of the Brookings Institution as an economist. He stayed there seven years during which he wrote numerous economic reports and collaborated with Harold G. Moulton on a large volume, Germany's Capacity to Pay; A Study of the Reparations Problem(McGraw-Hill, 1923). In 1923 McGuire edited a study of American Catholicism entitled Catholic Builders of the Nation (5 volumes, Continental Press, Boston, 1923). He made numerous trips abroad and in 1928-29, lectured in Berlin and Milan.

In 1929 McGuire resigned from Brookings and devoted full time to his activities as a private economic consultant. He served for many years as economic adviser to Venezuela and engaged in a similar role with Argentina, Paraguay, Colombia, Nicaragua, and other countries, as well as for private concerns and individuals.

As we have mentioned, McGuire was treasurer of the American Historical Association in 1930-36 and was president of the American Catholic Historical Association in 1933. In World War II he acted as civilian adviser to many high military and naval officers, including Major-General George Strong, then head of U.S. Military Intelligence.

From his arrival in Washington in 1915 to his death, McGuire avoided all publicity and covered his activities with a cloak of secrecy which is almost impenetrable. He refused to appear in Who's Who in America, in the American Catholic Who's Who, rejected offers of honorary degrees and, it is believed, of foreign decorations. He did, however, accept, in addition to his Papal title, the Venezuelan Order of the Liberator, and a nomination as a trustee of Notre Dame University. In 1922, when Father Walsh published a volume called The History and Nature of International Relations, which consisted of public lectures by ten outstanding authorities given in the auditorium of the Smithsonian Institution in 1922-1921 (a series instigated and arranged by McGuire), the book appeared with a dedication to McGuire. The latter wrote at once to the University, acknowledged the compliment, and expressed his regret that his name had appeared in public. Two years before, he had written to Father Walsh to insist that his name be removed from the School catalogue. At that time the catalogue also listed the names of an "Advisory Committee"; McGuire wrote to Father Walsh in the same letter, "I also recommend that the phantom 'committee' be notified of its existence and then discharged."

To the Georgetown community, McGuire's chief interest must rest in the very great role which he played in the founding of the School of Foreign Service in 1919, the founding of the Institute of World Polity in 1944, in Father Walsh's whole career, and, more remotely, in the establishment of the Institute of Languages and Linguistics in 1949. Much of this should be expressed in McGuire's own words.

In a letter dared 29 April 1953 to Father William F. Maloney, S J., then Provincial of the Maryland Province, McGuire wrote, "The plan for the school was drawn up by me in 1916-1917 and discussed by me with Father Thomas I. Gasson, S.J. [then Dean of the Georgetown University Graduate School] and Father John B. Creedon, SJ., [then President of Georgetown University]. Father Creedon could not see his way clear to take it on. I then tried to interest Bishop Thomas J. Shahan, of the Catholic University, who likewise felt it beyond his resources. At this stage, one day in the summer of 1918, I recounted the story to Father Richard H. Tierney, S.J., on one of his visits to Washington....He took the school plan with him that afternoon to Georgetown. The next day he told me that Father Creedon would receive me the following Sunday so as to discuss it once more. It was then accepted in principle; and when the armistice came, the plan was given effect. Father Walsh had reported back from the Student Army Training Corps work and was assigned to take on this task.... Very few persons have any knowledge whatever that I had something to do with the origin of the school; in fact, few persons, in or out of the Society, are now living who know that I had. Probably Dr. J. de S. Coutinho is the only man at Georgetown University other than Father Walsh, who knows it...."

For about three years, 1919-1922, McGuire acted unofficially as executive secretary of the school. He assumed the task of finding and hiring the faculty, obtained the first substantial financial contribution ($20,000 from James A. Farrell, President of the U.S. Steel Corporation), and made constant suggestions, often about very minor matters, regarding the operation of the School. For example, he sent Father Walsh numerous "memoranda" in which he suggested, among other things, that monitors be appointed in each class to take attendance and exclude unauthorized persons, that the language classes were getting too large and should be divided into sections of no more than thirty students, that specific numbers of text books be ordered and that a designated number of these be placed on reserve in the library, that some courses were larger than had been anticipated and that, accordingly, assistants must be appointed to correct papers and that the salaries of the teachers concerned should also be increased. In addition, McGuire sent Father Walsh drafts of public speeches, including that given by the Regent in the Smithsonian on 14 January as one of the first series of public lectures mentioned above.

In finding a faculty, McGuire showed an unusual talent for discovering men of ability and scholarship, who were then almost unknown but subsequently became famous. At that time McGuire was definitely "persona grata" with the Russian Ambassador. Through him in 1919, he discovered three recently arrived refugees: Michael I. Rostovtseff, Michael Karpovich, and Baron Korff. All three were unknown at the time in the United States, yet Rostovtseff, who became a professor at Yale in 1925, was regarded as the greatest scholar in ancient history working in the United States; Karpovich, who taught Russian history at Harvard from 1927 to 1957 is still remembered with affection and respect by all who knew him; Baron Korff unlike the other two, accepted a teaching position at the Foreign Service School and stayed there until his death. In a similar way, in 1919, McGuire sent Sherwell from the High Commission to be Professor of Spanish. At the same time, he hired a 26-year old State Department official, Dana Gardner Monroe, to teach Latin American history. Monroe was with the State Department until 1932, when he went to Princeton as a professor of history and became Director of Princeton's Wilson School of Public and International Affairs until 1958. When he was transferred to Chile in 1920, McGuire replaced him with his own former boss, Leo S. Rowe, who taught at the School until his death twenty-four years later. Others whom McGuire engaged in those early years were Ernest L. Bogart, W. F Willoughby, James Brown Scott, John L. Latané, and Stephen P. Duggan, all of whom were outstanding authorities in their areas of competence.

Within two years (that is by 1921), McGuire was becoming disillusioned with the School, partly because he hated all pretense or any facade of publicity, but chiefly because he had, despite his expertise, little grasp of the financial needs of such a school. Basically, he did not want any undergraduate study or any strictly vocational training, but wanted a high-level research institute concerned with the broadest principles and the fundamental realities of international affairs, to be used as a foundation for policy decision-making. What he had in mind was much more like Chatham House (the Royal Institute of International Affairs), or All Souls College at Oxford, or the American copy of All Souls, the Institute For Advanced Study in Princeton. The separation of McGuire from the School after 1923 rested on a difference with Father Walsh on priorities: McGuire felt that expensive projects could well begin before the necessary money was in hand (in the faith that God, or perhaps McGuire himself, would provide); Father Walsh, on the other hand, with a better grasp of household economia, if not of international economics, could not commit the University to expenditures before the money was available. Certainly he felt that no grandiose projects could be undertaken without endowment, and that until such funds were provided, the School had to have undergraduate students to provide the tuition needed for survival. On this score the Regent's position seems to have been more realistic.

That McGuire's dreams were grandiose is evident from his letter of 1953, already quoted; he said there: "What I had had in mind was the intensive study of those factors which determine the course of foreign policy, combined with special auxiliary training in languages. I had myself attended the great École Des Langues Orientales Vivantes of the French Government in Paris before the war of 1914-1918, and I knew that nowhere in the United States better than in Washington could that admirable establishment be used as a model.... The range of studies should be carefully focused on the policy-making and long-ranged aspects of international relations." Even in 1953 McGuire was still suggesting that the school be turned in that direction. The elementary, undergraduate instruction should be left to other institutions, especially to other Jesuit colleges, under Georgetown's guidance, with the advanced work provided at the School of Foreign Service. He wrote:" The coordination of training in the elementary courses might well have local variations to meet specific situations, but it would mean the bringing into line all the work throughout the country under authoritative and experienced guidance, and it would furnish a substantial number of men suited for foreign trade and related activities in their communities or elsewhere. The 'switch board' of all this would be in Washington at Georgetown ... In the field of research itself, at Washington, seminars with but limited numbers of men could turn out, in the course of a few years, an impressive volume of performance of high average quality; and in less than one generation, the Western Hemisphere's most authoritative center of the interpretation of the economico-social, psychological, and other factors which affect the conduct of international policy would be recognized as established at Georgetown."

As a result of McGuire's disillusionment with the development of the School of Foreign Service as an undergraduate institution, he became rather remote from it and from Father Walsh for almost twenty years, 1923-1943. But the Second World War re-affirmed his conviction of the need, in a Catholic context, of a research institute concerned with policy making. Accordingly, he persuaded Father Walsh, for whom he always had a deep personal respect, to establish, as an appendage of the School, an Institute of World Polity to consist of fifty highly qualified experts in various aspects of international affairs, with a small paid staff of research workers. The latter were to carry on research and prepare reports on such research (reports pointing toward policy decisions) under the guidance of the fifty experts. Such guidance as to be exercised by individual suggestions, by critiques for revision of the preliminary reports, and by joint dinner discussions of the problems involved. This plan and technique was very similar to that practiced by the English Round Table Group (which had been established by Lord Milner in 1910, was financed by Rhodes Trust and other moneys, and had founded the Royal Institute of International Affairs in 1919), which played a very significant role in British foreign policy in 1910-1940.

The Institute of World Polity as planned by McGuire was established in 1944, with a Research Director named by him and a membership of fifty almost all chosen by him. The Director was Dr. Ernst H. Feilchenfeld, a recognized expert in McGuire's own area of international economic law and an extraordinary teacher. This Institute still functions under the direction of Professor William V. O'Brien. Typically, having set up the Institute, McGuire concerned himself very little with its functioning and, in most cases. did not even attend its plenary conferences. Equally typical was his remark in 1953: "I thought its name gratuitously pretentious."

To some extent McGuire's neglect of the Institute of World Polity, when he finally got it, resulted from his personal unhappiness at the condition of the world; he looked with growing horror at the rise of the authority of the state and the decline of religion, a combination which, he felt, could lead to nothing but disaster.

Despite his alienation from the Foreign Service School after 1923, McGuire's influence still continued to be exercised because of the extraordinary effect he had on Father Walsh's outlook and associations. It seems likely that the links between Father Walsh and the Vatican outside the regular channels both of the Society of Jesus and of the ecclesiastical hierarchy resulted from McGuire's influence. It probably was McGuire who suggested that Father Walsh lead the Papal Relief Mission to Russia in 1922, an event which opened the door to the Regent's subsequent missions to Mexico, the Near East, Germany and Japan. It is not, for example, generally known that Father Walsh, when occasion arose, had direct access to the Pope, and, by his private nocturnal conferences with Pius XI, roused the ire of the then Papal Secretary of State.

Moreover, it is quite certain that it was McGuire who first directed the Regent's attention to the importance of Russia. In 1920, fifteen months before the surprising appointment of Father Walsh to the Russian mission, McGuire was urging on him the supreme importance of establishing an integrated Institute or Department of Slavic studies at Georgetown. On 5 November 1920, he wrote to Father Walsh about this: "Five or ten years from now the demand for men who know Russian well will relatively far exceed the demand for men who know other languages; and those who are acquainted with Russian life and the conditions under which it is carried on, with Russian literature and history, will find themselves in very great demand. I think the time is ripe to organize a distinct Slavic movement under the aegis of the Foreign Service School (incidentally promoting the best foreign policy of this government, demonstrating the foresight of the school authorities, and taking the wind out of the sails of any mere Pan-American Institution), which would aim to teach comprehensively the language, ethnography, economics, social conditions, history, and international position of Slavic peoples." He suggested that the program begin with a speech by the Russian ambassador and consist at the beginning of a course on the history of Russia given by Karpovich and a course on the economic conditions given by Baron Korff. Once this is started it should be followed by a course on Hungary and the Hungarian language given by Dr. McEachern of the Catholic University. The passage ended with a rhetorical questions as to where the money for such projects is to come from. To this McGuire answered, "I will guarantee (as a sort of moral obligation, in the words of President Wilson, rather than a legal obligation), that the money will be found for this Slavic division and for as many other 'ethnic' undertakings as you can set on foot."

It seems very likely that these urgings and the call to Russia in 1922, had a good deal to do with the direction of Father Walsh's interests for the next fifteen or more years, until he became interested in geopolitics at the end of the 1930's. In this way, and through his duties in managing the Foreign Service School, the Regent found his life drastically modified by Constantine McGuire, even in the lengthy period in which they met only infrequently.

Note: From McGuire's secrecy the task of compiling a biographical sketch such as this is very difficult and could hardly be achieved without assistance from other persons. For much of what appears above, I am indebted to the late Ernst Feilchenfeld. Most of the documentary support for this came from the Georgetown University archives, where I found Father Belwoar most helpful. Other information was provided by the Papal Legation, by Dr. Neusse of The Catholic Encyclopedia, by J. R. Trainor, former secretary of the School, by Professor Sherbowitz-Wetzor, from the Cosmos Club, and from others. I wish to thank all of these for their assistance.

BETTER TRAINING FOR FOREIGN SERVICE OFFICERS

An article by Carroll Quigley in The HOYA (November 16, 1967) pp. xx.

"Quigley Probes Possibilities for Foreign Service Curriculum Reform"
Congressional Quarterly Senate

Hon. Birch E. Bayh of Indiana
In The Senate of The United States
Wednesday, April 24, 1968

MR. BAYH. Mr. President, next October begins the 50th anniversary year of the School of Foreign Service, Georgetown University. The school is now in the process of revising its curriculum in the hope of making it even more effective in preparing young men and women for serving their country abroad. As the Nation's oldest institution for the training of personnel for careers in both diplomacy and trade, the School of foreign service has produced in its half century an impressive number of graduates.

Dr. Carroll Quigley, a professor of history at the School of Foreign Service for 28 years, has written an informative and interesting article about the changes now underway in this leading institution. He argues persuasively that when the founder and regent of the school, Rev. Dr. Edmund A. Walsh, S.J., revised the curriculum in 1951, shortly before his death, he envisioned a course of education that would provide the student with a broad, interrelated background in government, economics, history, languages, and philosophy. This, rather than any specialized or narrow training, would best prepare men to grapple with the problems of international relations and foreign trade. Because of the significance of this development, not only to other colleges and universities but also to those who are intending to prepare themselves for service abroad, I ask unanimous consent that the article, which appeared in the November 16 issue of *The HOYA*, be printed in the Record.

There being no objection, the article was ordered to be printed in the Record, as follows:

QUIGLEY PROBES POSSIBILITIES FOR FOREIGN SERVICE CURRICULUM REFORM

(By Carroll Quigley. Ph.D.)

Those who ignore history are condemned to repeat it.
Ends should determine means.

These two rules should be the guide posts to any reform of the curriculum of the Foreign Service School, as to most other things. That means that anyone talking or planning on this subject must be aware of what the aim of the Foreign Service School is and of what has been done in the past for achieving that aim.

In the last few years, there has been a fair amount of talk about SFS curriculum reform, but most of it has been very badly informed in respect to these two indispensable foundations. This article will seek to sketch these as I have come to know them in my 26 years in this School.

The goal of the SFS never was to prepare students for careers in the Foreign Service of the United States, since the latter was not established until the School was five years old. The similarity of name is thus only coincidental. The School was established in 1919 in recognition of the fact that the United States had just become a World Power with obligations in private as well as public areas. There was a new need for trained personnel for many international agencies besides those of our own government. The fact that the League of Nations was founded in the same year as the Foreign Service School is much more significant than the fact that the Diplomatic Corps and the Consular Service of the United States were combined into a single agency called "the Foreign Service of the United States "in 1924, five years after the School was established. Moreover, it was always expected that more graduates would go into private activities overseas than would go to work for public agencies. For this reason, the curriculum included study of accounting and commercial law as required courses until fairly recently.

The wisdom of this early and persistent view of the goals of the School will be evident to anyone who examines the areas in which Foreign Service graduates have worked successfully. In the years after World War II, when the largest classes were graduated, not over 3 or 4% even took the State Department Foreign Service examinations. On the other hand, many graduates went into a great variety of overseas work, in airlines and shipping, in education and journalism in foreign areas, as well as all kinds of overseas business. For these positions they needed a broad and integrated preparation in all aspects of international work.

In time this broad and integrated program came to provide one of the best undergraduate programs in general social sciences available in the United States, and it thus became, without anyone intending it, one of the best preparations available for law school or for graduate work in one of the social science specialties such as history, political science, or economics. For graduate school the SFS curriculum was better preparation than an undergraduate major in the same field, either here or anywhere else, because it meant that a SFS alumnus at graduate school in one of these fields had a solid grounding in the other two, something which is absolutely essential, but is rarely obtained from an ordinary undergraduate major, since most colleges do not require this and many advise against it. Yet anyone who examines what is done in graduate schools and by their graduates can see that a history major, for example, needs some knowledge of both economics and government, just as concentrators in the latter two fields need some knowledge of the other as well as of history. Moreover, knowledge of these fields used to be obtained in the SFS in an atmosphere where the emphasis was on teaching and understanding these subjects, and on explaining their mutual interrelationships in the actual experience of human life, and, above all, on the understanding of this nexus as a basis for decision-making in active life, and not taught, as they usually are in university-colleges today, as preparation for specialized work, especially research, on the graduate level. This last point is fundamental: it was at the basis of the thinking of Constantine McGuire and Father Walsh when they founded the School (Sec my article, "Constantine McGuire, Man of Mystery," in Courier, December 1965).

WARTIME EFFORTS

The curriculum of the SF's was directed to these ends, as judged best by Father Walsh and his advisers, from 1919 until the School was mobilized for the war effort in June 1943. During that time, there were no departments and no faculty ranks (all the faculty were called "lecturers"). For much of that time, most of the faculty and many of the students were part-time, and all courses were offered in the evening, although by 1930, most courses were repeated in the day-time. Each course was two credit hours, and a student often took eight or more courses at a time. In time, as new courses were added, the integration among them came to be less than desired. By 1940 or so, curriculum reform was very necessary, but the outbreak of war put such demands on the School, and above all on Father Walsh, that the task could not be tackled until 1950.

The SFS made a major effort in the war, turning almost entirely to training of men in uniform in June 1943 and being swamped with returning veterans as soon as the fighting stopped. In 1947 the School had about 2300 students (more than twice its present enrollment). In those first postwar years, Father Walsh was very busy with missions to Germany and Japan, with writing two major books, and with the establishment of the Institute of Languages and Linguistics. As a result, the long needed reform of the Foreign Service curriculum was not undertaken until the spring of 1950.

Perhaps because this task had been so long delayed, it was done very thoroughly. Members of the faculty and administration met about a dozen times, under the chairmanship of Father Walsh and with Walter I. Giles as secretary, in Room 8 Healy, the "Constitution Room." Most of these assemblies lasted several hours, some of them for a good part of Saturday mornings. The whole group was divided up into smaller committees which met elsewhere to work on parts of the problem before reporting back to the plenary sessions. The general ground rules were set by Father Walsh, after discussion with many others.

REVISED CURRICULUM

These general rules were as follows: (1) The number of courses taken at any one time must be reduced, and the courses themselves strengthened so that they should leave the student with a real familiarity with the subject concerned; (2) the courses should be made more general, with the numerous specialized courses which had grown up over the years either eliminated or made electives; (3) a balance must be maintained between the various academic disciplines so that a graduate would be familiar in some depth with all the tools he might need in his post-graduate experience; and (4) the School must ensure that these various disciplines and courses are integrated in the students mind, and not simply memorized as discrete academic subjects.

Two difficulties, from opposite directions, arose in the general discussions. On one side, those who had been teaching specialized courses, such as "Staple Commodities in World Trade," or "Exporting Practice," or commercial law, accounting, and shipping, objected to their subjects being reduced in time or made electives. On the other hand, a group of the political scientists insisted that international affairs was merely one part of the general subject of political science and should be treated as such, with the main core of the curriculum built on a political science department expanded to include additional courses, especially a new course in "International Relations." Father Walsh was most emphatic in rejecting this last suggestion, insisting that the whole program of study of the School was on International Relations, and that this subject was not simply a matter of political science but was equally concerned with economic, psychological, intellectual, and other issues. He emphasized, against the efforts of this group to cut down the time devoted to economics, that even in the Foreign Service of the United States 80 percent of the time of personnel on the lower levels was devoted to economic issues not to political ones.

In this reform, most courses which were retained as required courses were increased from two to three hours a week, and, at the same time, the number of courses taken each year was reduced, with freshmen and sophomores taking only five courses. Father Walsh insisted that this adoption of the standard three-credit course must not lead students to look at the achievement of the degree as simply the accumulation of a number of discrete and separate courses. To avoid this danger, it was decided to introduce an oral comprehensive examination for all seniors to force them to review the work of the first three years and to look at the assemblage of courses as a single comprehensive body of knowledge. To assist in this end, each professor was to prepare and submit for mimeograph publication a syllabus of the content of his course so that all might know what was in each course and how it fitted in with the others.

This curriculum reform of 1950 took months of work and established the outlines of the program still found at the School of Foreign Service. However, it has been so much subjected to tinkering and manipulation that much of its original value has been lost. These changes arose from two directions. On the one hand, new administrators who knew nothing about the original reasons for the courses as they were established made or allowed changes which weakened the whole effect. On the other hand, the establishment of university-wide departments, which did not exist in 1950, led to changes in the content, sequence, and perspective of both faculty and courses so that they fitted together less effectively for the SFS curriculum.

As set up in 1950, there were four years of history and political science, three of economics, and two each of English, philosophy, and language. The two years of required religion for Catholics were non-credit courses. In the early 1950's, the religion courses were given credit to force students to take them more seriously. A few years later, a new Regent could not see why Catholics had to take 12 credit hours more than non-Catholics to get the same degree, so the latter were forced to take 12 hours more of history of political theory as a substitute for religion. These 12 hours have since been juggled in various ways. About the same time, a University official felt that freshmen were not able to handle generalities, so used his influence to have the SFS required freshman course in "Principles of Political Science" abolished, with the result that most of them now never get much of the material which was in that course.

The greatest changes in the curriculum, however, were not ones which could be seen in the catalogue, but were simply the result of the establishment of University-wide departments since 1950. During Father Walsh's regime, the SFS was a completely separate entity whose only connection with the University was that it gave its degrees under then University charter and rented room-space from the University. It had a separate library, bank account, admissions policy, administration, and faculty. In fact, about that time the College issued a ruling that no one who taught in then> College could also teach in the SFS. As a result of this order, William Flaherty, one of the greatest teachers in the history of the School, resigned from both and left to become, in a short while, chief statistician of Chrysler Corporation.

The creation of University departments meant that the course syllabi were forgotten, the content of the courses changed even when names remained the same, and the whole context of the School's educational process changed, with the substitution of departmental courses aiming toward preparation for graduate work in that departmental discipline replacing foreign service courses aiming at the establishment of an integrated understanding of international affairs as an area of decision-making and action. At the same time, the new University faculty, possessed by the unique value of their own subject, or even of their narrow specialty within that subject, were increasingly unable to ask or to judge comprehensive questions on the oral comprehensive examinations. In fact one of the amusing evidences of this process has been the growing reluctance of the examiners to judge the candidates in all three fields as the rules of the examination have always required them to do.

CRUCIAL PROBLEMS

There is no need to explain in detail what has gone wrong with the SPS curriculum in recent years. It should be sufficient to say that many of the courses no longer contain what they should contain or even what their titles would lead one to expect, because their teachers are often off riding hobby-horses instead of teaching what the SFS curriculum requires them to teach. Thus students often have had no logic, even when their transcript lists a course called "Logic," their courses in English now often consist of impressionistic studies of literature rather than the training in verbal communication skills which the curriculum requires; they may well graduate with all kinds of specialized knowledge in government, but are unable to define such basic concepts as "state," "nationalism," or "democracy," in a similar way they often miss fundamental movements in the historical past depending on which section they happened to be in the required history courses; and, most astounding of all, they take a degree in "Foreign Service" without ever having studied geography, simply because the teacher of that subject refused to teach the course described in the syllabus. And, finally as a culmination of all these erosions of a once excellent program, the fitting together and integration of the courses have become disjointed, the years of study have become unbalanced (so that the freshman year is now too easy and the sophomore year too difficult), and the better students in the last few years are constantly being drained away from the SFS curriculum to fill up special electives and proseminar courses so that teachers whose primary interest is in some special subject on the graduate level may have as sufficiently large group of good students to make his efforts satisfactory to himself.

Additional Notes: This and a similar article by Prof Giles (put into the record by another Senator) ignited the 1968-69 commotion that resulted in the SFS getting budgetary autonomy, a new Dean, and its own faculty.

IS GEORGETOWN UNIVERSITY COMMITTING "SUICIDE"?

History Professor Relates School's Difficulties To
Lack Of Direction, Loss Of Christian Foundations

by Carroll Quigley, Ph.D.
Professor of History
(The Hoya, Friday, April 28, 1967)

Long study of the history of many social organizations has convinced me of one thing: When any such organization dies—be it family, business, nation, religion, civilization, or university, the cause of death is generally "suicide." Or, if we must be more specific, "suicide by self-deception."

Like most truths, this one has nothing very new about it. The Hebrews and the Greeks, who are our cultural parents, and our own western civilization descended from these two, have always agreed that the only sin, or at least the greatest sin, is pride, a particularly aggressive type of self-deception. And anyone who is concerned with the health of individuals knows well that neuroses and psychoses are basically simply forms of self-deception, combined with an obstinate refusal to face the facts of the situation.

This kind of illness is prevalent in all American higher education and in all the sub-divisions of it, existing, indeed, in a more obsessive and virulent form in the aspirant "Great Universities" than in the so-called "Great Universities" themselves. It is to be found in its acute form in Catholic education, in Jesuit education, and at Georgetown.

Of course, that is not what we are being told. Today, in education, as in government and in everything else, the propagandists flood us daily with rosy reports on how well things are going. Larger and larger expenditures of manpower, money and facilities (such as floor-space) are devoted to telling the world about the wonderful job being done in every organization worthy of the name from the Johnson Administration down (or up) to Georgetown University. Fewer and fewer people are convinced, or even listening, but in the process the money and facilities (if not the manpower) which could have been used on the goals of the organization are wasted on propaganda about what a wonderful job is being done, when any sensible person with half an eye can see that, every year, a poorer job is being done in the midst of self-deceptive clouds of expensive propaganda.

But beneath these clouds, ominous cracklings can be heard, even at Georgetown. If they come from within the University, they are drowned out with another flood of words, denials, excited pointings to a more hopeful, if remote, future, or by the creation of some new organizational gimmick, a committee or a new "Assistant Something-or-Other," to deal with the problem.

If, on the other hand, these criticisms come from outside the University, they are ignored or attributed to jealousy, sour grapes, or to some other unflattering personal motivation of the critic. When these criticisms come, as they often do, from some departing member of the faculty, they are greeted by reflections on his personal competence or emotional stability, both of which had been highly esteemed as long as he remained here. As a result, most departing faculty, to avoid such personal denigration, depart quietly, but they depart. Their reasons for leaving are then attributed to the higher pay to be obtained elsewhere, an explanation which fits in well with the Big Lie at GU, that all its problems would be solved if the University only had more money. Anyone who knows anything about the situation knows perfectly well three things: that Georgetown's problems would not be solved by more money and have not been, but, on the contrary, have grown steadily worse as the supply of money has increased; that resigning faculty have been leaving because they were discontented; and that the chief cause of that discontent has not been inadequate pay, but the generally chaotic and misguided Administration of the University. In the last two years, the Mathematics and Classics Departments, as well as the Law School, have seen their faculty depart in droves, but the kind of administration from which they were fleeing continues, even in the hands of different administrators.

The judgment on what is wrong at Georgetown should not rest on verbiage from either defenders or denigrators; it can be based on facts. No university which wastes as much money, time and effort on non-educational matters as Georgetown does could possibly be doing a good job in educational matters. And it is no defense to say that every other university is doing the same. By non-educational matters I mean such things as building, parking, food-service, public-relations, planning, campus police, committees, paper-shuffling, traveling by University officials, and constant verbalizing on non-educational matters.

I'll admit that things are just as bad, and may be worse, at other universities. But this very fact makes it easier for Georgetown to become a better university. All it has to do is decide what an education is and do it, instead of driving hell-bent, as it now is, to become exactly like all other universities of the country. For those other universities are going, at high speed, in the wrong direction, as must be clear to any observer who has any idea what education should he and compares that idea with what is actually going on. Or, even if the observer has no idea what education should be, he can grasp, merely by looking and listening, that education is not healthy anywhere.

A few months ago, *Newsweek* asked, "Why is there no first-rate university in the nation's capital?" This assay created a minor ripple locally but did not divert the rulers of Georgetown an iota from their mad rush in the wrong directions. Their chief reaction to the *Newsweek* question was resentment. But any honest and observant person examining the local scene in higher education could have only one reaction: surprise that anyone should be either surprised or resentful at *Newsweek*'s article. A judicious assessment by anyone who has any regard for real education would conclude that *Newsweek* had been too kind to us, for Georgetown, the best of the five local universities, is third-rate and deteriorating, and it does not help to see that our neighbor, the George Washington University, is fourth-rate and is deteriorating even more rapidly. What does hurt is to realize that Georgetown has, for years, had a golden opportunity, such as GW never could have, to make a great contribution to American education, but has, again and again, muffed that opportunity because of the increasingly frantic pursuit of strange, alien gods by the rulers of Georgetown.

CONANT-DODDS INFLUENCE

Georgetown has had this opportunity for one simply stated but complexly true reason: because it was Catholic. But, instead of being Catholic, or even Jesuit, Georgetown has rudely turned its back on its one chance of making any contribution to American education and has instead almost totally destroyed its opportunity for becoming an excellent Catholic university and a good American university, in its frantic drive to become a fifth-rate Harvard. Those who vaguely feel this error, including the rulers of the University itself, correctly attribute it to "lack of leadership" on the part of those rulers. But again, in another rejection of their own traditions—the traditions of the Christian West—they neglect to define what they mean by leadership and, at the back of their minds, use a purely operational definition, that educational leadership is what poor misguided men like James Conant and Harold Dodds have done, or advocate doing. Any observer who has even a glimmering of an idea what education and leadership really imply and, in addition, knows what Conant and Dodds did to Harvard and Princeton, can only hope that Georgetown can be spared the Conant-Dodds influence and, instead, finds the way to real education and real leadership by getting back to our Christian heritage (not as indoctrination but as a technique for responsible cooperative activity in terms of real goals with real values).

The rulers of Georgetown University have never stopped to ask themselves: What is real education? What should we be trying to do? What can we do best, or better than anyone else around? What can our own traditions contribute to the improvement of American education? From the answers to these questions Georgetown could achieve the best undergraduate education in America and do it with less money than is now being wasted on the misguided, mis-emphasized, present drive to follow the so-called "great universities" down the slope after Harvard, Princeton, and Berkeley.

Georgetown cannot copy these institutions, even if they have been on the correct road (which they have not), because they are rich and G. U. will never be rich. A rich university, like Harvard with an endowment of over a billion dollars, can, perhaps, afford to make mistakes, and can, perhaps, afford to indulge in that faddism which is the chief bane of education in America, but G.U. cannot afford these things. Moreover, the effort to copy Harvard or Princeton is bound to fail when the men who make the decisions at G.U. do not really know what happened, or is happening, at Harvard or Princeton. They do not know that the innovations in education which began at Harvard and Princeton like the free elective system, the "case method", the tutorial and preceptorial systems, narrowly specialized departments with overly specialized undergraduate training, the College Board system of admissions, "General Education," "Advanced Standing," and many other innovations have contributed little to the improvement of American education and are coming to be recognized increasingly as expensive and temporary fads. But they have swept the country, except for those things like tutorial instruction or residential colleges which have proved too expensive to be copied by most universities.

Twenty years ago, in recognition of the injury being inflicted on undergraduate education by over-specialization, Harvard spent about $46,000 on a faculty committee which came up with the famous "Harvard Report on General Education." On the basis of that report, courses were set up at Harvard on "general education." Today, the undergraduate can take his choice from 94 courses in "General Education," the most recent of which is on computer programming. This is the kind of educational nonsense which goes on when an American university has hundreds of millions of dollars to spend. And this is the kind of nonsense which a growing Georgetown budget is bringing to G.U. This kind of nonsense will spread and continue to spread as long as there is money available to finance it and as long as university decision-makers refuse to define what they mean by education in analytical terms and continue instead to emphasize activity over thought and accept, without questioning, a purely operational definition which believes that "education is what goes on in universities especially at Harvard." Such a definition may be fine for administrative careerists, but it is death to real education, although the university administrators will not recognize their demise until students, rather than faculty, depart in droves from universities, a movement which will come when students decide that they want a real education rather than a diploma and will reconcile themselves to the fact that lack of a diploma may exclude them from entrance into the great bureaucratic structures of business, government, education and the professions, but will not prevent them from living a better life than is possible in such bureaucratic structures.

THE CHRISTIAN WEST

Education, correctly defined, means training toward growth and maturity to prepare a person to deal, in a flexible and successful way, with the problems of life and of eternity. It does not mean, as it increasingly is taken to mean by the educational operationalists who now control our educational bureaucracy, obtaining a ticket of admission to some other bureaucratic structure, however large and rich that may be.

Education in operational terms has no meaning (as all operational definitions have no meaning) because it has no reference outside itself, and all meaning must be based on reference to something outside the object being defined. Until recent centuries, meaning was defined in terms of purpose and goals, but, as teleology fell into disrepute, meaning came to mean context as a whole (a belief which has always been held in most Asiatic countries). Today, over-specialization and the great speed of change have destroyed, or almost destroyed, the context of everything, and we are reduced to purely operational definitions and meanings. But, since all operational definitions are solipsist, and everything in the world today has become isolated and subjective, any meaning in either teleological or contextual or even functional terms has become impossible and we are faced with the total triumph of the Meaningless and The Absurd. American education has followed this process and is now speeding toward ruination of all education in terms of individual maturity and ability to cope with any whole human experience or meaning.

We might ask: Why is it necessary for Catholic education or for Jesuit education to follow that road to ruin? The reason they do so is clear enough.

For more than a century, from 1830 to after 1940, Catholics in America lived in a ghetto. When American Catholics decided to leave their ghetto (right after the Jews and just before the Italians and Negroes), they did what any people fleeing a ghetto do: they uncritically embraced the outside world, without seeing that that world was moving rapidly toward increased chaos, corruption and absurdity. They abandoned completely a basic principle of the Christian West: that salvation is to be found, either for the individual or for the community, only in slow growth in terms of one's own traditions and background. If Catholic education had been willing to do that, it could have made a great contribution to American education and to American life, because the only thing which can save America or our world is to get back to the abandoned traditions of the Christian West and to resume the process of growth and development of our society on the basis of those traditions. By aping the un-Christianized, de-Westernized world of American life and American education outside the old Catholic ghetto, the Jesuits have betrayed Christianity, and the West, to a degree even greater than has occurred at Harvard or at Princeton. And now young people all over the country are trying desperately to get back to some kind of real, if primitive, Christianity, with little real guidance from their so-called teachers and clergy. What is even more ironical is that they, and the more progressive of their teachers, in their efforts to get back to the mainstream of Western Christian growth are trying to work out, by painful application, all those things (like multi-valued logic, or the role of daily good-works in Christian life) which were worked out within the Christian West long ago, but are now forgotten, and now have to be re-discovered as something new.

If Catholic education, and especially Jesuit education at G.U., had reformed itself in the true sense, by getting back to its own traditions and growing from that base, great contributions could have been made to an American educational system and an American life which are thirsting for them but falsely believe that they can be found only by blundering forward into an unexplored future (as in existentialist philosophy or in the contemporary flood of writings on theology) or by copying the age-old errors of Asia.

CATHOLIC SCHOLARSHIP

Moreover, on the basis of the Catholic Christian tradition of the West, enormous opportunities are offered for research and writing. The secular world's versions of economic theory or of the history of political theory, are biased, naive and mistaken. Many of their errors rest directly on their rejection of the Christian tradition. In my own field of history, the versions of the middle ages, of the renaissance, of the rise of science, of economic and constitutional history are still based on the anti-Catholic biases of the nineteenth century. The history of ideas in Western civilization cannot be understood by anyone who is not familiar with Western religion, and the Catholic version of it, from the inside. Yet all the widely read "authorities" on this subject are non-Catholic, generally non-Christian, and often anti-Catholic. As a result, they cannot understand what has happened or even organize the subject (except on a biographical basis). The history of these subjects has been distorted for years by anti-Catholic bias, but the task of straightening out these errors has been left to places like Harvard, instead of being done, as could have been more easily done, by Catholic campuses. Fifty years ago, the Protestant version of the rise of modern science as a reaction against medieval obscurantism was being corrected by a remarkable group of Catholic historians of science like Duhem and Tannery. Their work was never finished, because it was abandoned by Catholic scholars, until it had to be taken up by non-Catholics like Marshal Clagett, who had been trained at Harvard by George Sarton. The whole Whig interpretation of British history has to be re-written along lines which were sketched out, in a very unscholarly way, by Catholics like Christopher Hollis. But instead of doing these urgent tasks, Catholic universities are trying to adopt the kind of pedantic, secularized micro-research of the prevailing "great universities" and will leave these great tasks undone, until someone there, rather than here, does it, and has to do it, in all probability, by an almost superhuman effort of re-discovering, on his own, the necessary Christian Catholic tradition which will have vanished completely from the Catholic universities under the stresses of their efforts to become secularized fifth-rate Harvards. What a great lost opportunity! And what a pity!

Much of the process of deterioration of the West lies in the fragmentation and excessive specialization of life and of education. In the latter, this was reflected in the division of universities into exclusive departments, of departments into courses, of courses into preparation for successive examinations, the whole reflected in a purely arithmetic accumulation of credit hours (at so many dollars per credit hour), which mechanically entitle the student to a degree when some designated total is reached. It should be noted that this monstrous and destructive violation of all real educational process was never fully accepted at Harvard or Princeton, although it is now solidly entrenched at Jesuit universities.

Another example of the fragmentation process can be seen in the way in which the purely operational idea of education has blurred and destroyed the successive levels of the educational process. Today the activities of graduate schools have come to dominate and destroy the work of colleges, the work of colleges has come to distort and destroy the work of secondary schools, and the secondary schools have come to eclipse and eliminate the tasks of the elementary schools. As a result, each level is trying to do the work of the next higher level and refusing to do the work of its own level, all educational emphasis is on "advanced" preparation, "advanced standing," and "advanced placement", and students are everywhere being taught to fly before they can walk or even crawl. Today, first and second grade teachers are too concerned with how to shift a number system from base 10 to base 2 to find time to teach reading; high school teachers are so involved in the historiographical problems of the American Civil War that they never find time to train students in how to analyze or to outline, while, on the same level, biology students are so involved in the problems of the genetic code and molecular biology that they never learn the basic hygiene and physiology of their own bodies. And on the college level, all the emphasis is on seminars and research to the detriment of any training in understanding the world, or even in getting acquainted with the subject. Naturally, nowhere along the line does anyone find time to train students to read, to digest, to organize, to think, to correlate, with the result that every educational institution at all levels must now surround itself with remedial, counseling, and psychotherapeutic offices to do what the whole educational system should have done years before but which they all resolutely refused to do because they insisted on doing, not their own jobs, but the job of the next higher level of the educational system. One of the latest examples of this fad is Cornell's acceptance of "qualified" freshmen for their new 6-year Ph.D. program.

As a consequence of this process, it is today impossible for a decent undergraduate college to exist on the same campus as a burgeoning graduate school. This was the reason behind the student revolt at Berkeley; it was a revolt of undergraduates at the shabby treatment, neglect and exploitation they get from the fact that the undergraduate college there is drowning in that morass of undergraduate irrelevancies summed up in Clark Kerr's idea that the Berkeley campus was a "multiversity." But, of course, like everything today, this simple truth was buried in mountains of irrelevancies in all the discussions about the Berkeley fiasco, a consequence which is inevitable when Berkeley, and all the other American universities, are pouring out graduates who are untrained in either analysis or critical thinking, but instead have been trained in a narrow specialization whose verbiage is irrelevant outside its own field, except to the degree that it has diffused to other specialists as clichés and slogans.

A DIFFERENCE OF GOALS

The reasons that a graduate school eclipses and strangles an undergraduate college are two: (1) because the faculty come to be chosen for what are regarded as qualifications for graduate instruction, instead of for the quite different qualifications needed for undergraduate teaching; and (2) the difference between the aims of the two levels become confused, so that undergraduate aims become submerged and lost and are replaced by departmental emphasis, in its own undergraduate teaching, on preparation for graduate school, despite the fact that only a minority, or even a very few, of its students are ever going to graduate school in that subject.

The consequences of this double process are fully evident in the recent history of many undergraduate institutions and perhaps most clearly in the School of Foreign Service. Twenty years ago the School of Foreign Service was completely autonomous; there were no departments, and there was no faculty rank and tenure. The faculty were concerned with teaching, and the courses were supposed to prepare graduates to understand international problems and to operate in the field of such problems. Neither the faculty nor the courses were aimed at preparing students for graduate schools. But, surprisingly, the School was, in fact, outstandingly good in preparing for work on the graduate level in any of the social science departments, such as history, economics, or political science, and was, indeed, perhaps the best preparation available for going to law school (this despite the fact that Father Walsh tried to exclude from the School all students who intended to go to law school). And, at the same time, the SFS did an excellent job preparing people for international work.

For years, I asked all returning alumni of the Foreign Service School if they were, on the basis of their post-graduation experiences, satisfied with their undergraduate education at the SFS. The overwhelming majority were very satisfied. Many said something to this effect: "In the years since I graduated from the School of Foreign Service, I have been in direct contact, and often in competition with, outstanding graduates from Harvard, Princeton, or other big name universities, and have consistently had the feeling that I had a better grasp of the problems we were dealing with than they did."

TRAHISON DES CLERCS

The reasons for this last statement have always seemed clear to me. Our students were trained to understand, and trained on a non-specialized basis, which included philosophy, religion, languages, and all three of the basic social sciences, while the Ivy League graduates, as often as not, had been trained on a far more specialized basis and trained as preparation for "research," not for dealing with foreign problems as ecological wholes. In fact, the need for the latter, which is increasingly recognized in foreign problems, in economic development, in adaptation of political institutions, or in community development, had to come into overspecialized departments of political science and economics from other disciplines which use such an ecological approach, such as undergraduate anthropology, non-experimental psychology and biological ecology.

Over the past twenty years, as Georgetown has tried to become "a Great University" (meaning a fifth-rate Harvard), University-wide departments have been established, the faculty for these departments have been recruited on quite a different basis, and the courses have been subtly changed from explanations of the subject to preparation for graduate work in that subject.

The most obvious change has been in standards of faculty recruitment—or, as it is miscalled everywhere, "raising faculty standards." Undergraduates should be taught by men who have a broad understanding of the subject, who are themselves of broadly cultured background and who are, above all, good teachers. They should be men who understand students, the world, and the relationship of their subject to both of these, and they should be men who seek to impart understanding and do not confuse understanding with either knowledge or pedantry.

No "Great University" uses, or will use, standards such as these in hiring faculty. Instead, every aspirant "Great University" emphasizes earned degrees, the place where these were earned, research reputation, and the number of publications (regardless if these works are ever read by anyone). The disastrous consequence of faculty chosen and promoted on this basis on the aims and quality of undergraduate education must be obvious, especially in combination with the previously mentioned shift in course content from explanation and understanding of the subject to preparation for graduate work in that subject.

When these changes take place in a university in which other changes (already mentioned) are taking place, such as the passing of university control into the hands of careerist administrators and the loss of all conception of the meaning and value of education by university decision-makers who adopt purely operational ideas of educational purpose and educational activities, it is clear that the aspirant "Great University" rapidly becomes an educational sewer.

Real education requires a teleological or contextual (biological) understanding of educational purpose and meaning. It requires, beyond that, only three things: books, students, and faculty—in that order, with the faculty less significant than good books and motivated students. In fact, a motivated student today can get a better real education (but no diploma) in any large urban public library than he can from the harassed and disconcerted faculty of the most highly touted multiversity.

Moreover, no solution of the present crisis of our society, of the personal problems and quandaries of the individual members of our society, nor of our multifarious educational problems, is possible or conceivable unless it is firmly rooted in our Western Christian heritage. This does not mean going back to anything we had before, but it does mean going back to our roots in the past, and growing onward from those roots, which must be found in a period in our past before the alien gods of material affluence, of power-thirsting, of sex-obsession, of egotism and existential self-indulgence, became the chief aims of life, eagerly embraced, as they now are, by our contemporary "trahison des clercs".

OBSOLETE ACADEMIC DISCIPLINES

The HOYA (1967 or 68)
by Carroll Quigley, Ph.D. Professor of History

No education is worth much which does not help those who receive it to understand the world in which they live and to feel more at home and more confident in the world. For many years, the experience of Americans in their academic institutions has not been helping, but rather has hindered, that process. That experience has tended to be a kind of brainwashing, seeking, in most cases, to establish a bourgeois or (in recent years) a petty bourgeois outlook. On the higher levels of the system, this has been supplemented by a steadily narrowing of training for a place in the bureaucratic structures which now dominate American life, in business, in government, in education itself, in religion, t he law, medicine, and the defense forces. This is reflected in earlier, and in more and more narrow, specialization and i n the increasing pedantic nature of so much of the work done in all fields.

On one side, this leaves so-called educated people incapable of understanding the rapidly changing society in which w e live and, as the opposite side of the same situation, leaves us facing gigantic problems to whose understanding and solution the existing educational structure has little to contribute (that is why they became gigantic). This can be seen most clearly by asking ourselves the simple question: " In which of our academic disciplines do these problems fall? " Or more concretely, " From which of the existing academic disciplines would we recruit someone to enlighten us on each of these problems ? " However we word these questions, there is no answer, for the simple reason that the great problems of our day do not fall into any one academic discipline, and, indeed, cannot be dealt with by committees made up of persons from different academic specialties.

TODAY'S PROBLEMS

The problems are obvious:
war and peace;
1. urban problems;
2. environmental pollution and destruction of our natural basis for living;

3. the rising tide of mental ill-health, emotional instability, and personality disorders;
4. racial problems;
5. growing social disintegration and violence;
6. the problems of under-developed countries.

Not one of these falls into one of the academic departments into which our educational establishment is divided. These disciplines were separated toward the end or the Nineteenth Century, when it was possible to believe that politics was separated from economics, and that neither of these was closely related to psychology, literature, history, technology, mathematics, or the natural sciences. But today anyone who does not recognize that all of these are closely interrelated and that all of them are intermingled in all the major problems facing us is disqualified, by that belief, from having any authority in any of them. None of these problems which we must solve if we are not to perish falls cleanly, or even mainly, into any existing academic discipline. That is precisely why we are so helpless in dealing with them.

ON THE BORDERS

Take the last of the problems listed above, that of the underdeveloped areas. On this we have spent untold billions of dollars in the last 20 years, with almost no constructive results. We were told it was an economic problem, capable of solution with technical training and inflows of capital. We poured money into backward countries, corrupting them, and making millions of native peoples discontented, only to discover that the real obstacles were in the minds of those peoples, in the way they looked at human experience, and in their value systems, which were largely incomprehensible to us. The only real help we got from the academic community, and that chiefly as an explanation of why we were failing, came from anthropology, which did have a glimmering of the truth because it was almost the only academic field which tried to study societies different from ourselves as functioning wholes.

Today, even in the natural sciences, the only real advances are being made, not within subjects, but on the borders of the older academic fields where subjects are mixed (as in space). The only great scientific discovery since the war, molecular biology, is of this type.

Today no great advances can be made, nor can the problems facing us be understood, by anyone who stays within the borders of one of the present academic disciplines. In each, the workers are smothered in overspecialization and pedantry. Yet in each the majority of members are very busy congratulating each other on the wonderful work they are all doing. That is self-deception, for the regular academic disciplines are now bankrupt, incapable of providing their explanations or solutions to problems.

The chief group of discontented are, of course, the students, who grow increasingly restless, discontented, and alienated because of their recognition of the large-scale irrelevance of so much of what they have to learn. Within these fields, some teachers realize, more or less unconsciously, that much is wrong. Yet they feel that they must go on, and do so, rationalizing that they have to make a living somehow, and this is the only way they are equipped to earn what is needed, and, secondly they assure themselves and their students that the latter must have a college education. This latter belief is correct only if the student is determined to make his living by finding a place in the great and ever-growing bureaucracies which envelop our world and now overshadow it. But all of these bureaucracies do their work inefficiently and badly. They look good only if we accept their own fraudulent bookkeeping. If a student wants to spend his life en-capsulated in the interstices of one of these monstrous structures, I suppose he does need a college education, not because college prepares him to do their work but simply because these structures increasingly demand a college degree as a ticket of admission to their employ. They demand that only because it indicates that the, holder of that ticket has submitted to years of brainwashing in irrelevancies and will put up with the myths of the bureaucracy he joins.

SELF-EDUCATION

If a young man today simply wants to make a very good living associated with freedom and variety, he can do it much better without a college education. Of course he must be educated, but real education today can he obtained much m ore easily (although it is never easy) in constant attendance at a good public library than at the so-called "best" universities (which are frequently the worst ones). Today, as almost never before, the way lies open to any enterprising young man to find something to do which is now being done badly or not done at all by our bureaucratized society. To do this the first task of the young man must be to dismiss as the myth it is what passes for truth in existing universities. There is a truth and it can be found; it has been found, to some degree, by men in the past, and by men in other societies. The task of finding it is lifelong, and probably continues after bodily death, and the greatest joy of living is the search for it. That is why we are here, but to find it in the accepted wisdom of the existing academic structure is to put oneself in an intellectual prison, which does not help.

Of course, if someone can go to college and not become a prisoner of its myths and can continue free from the bureaucratic structure toward which the average college seeks to direct students, he can also live a good life and, like a non-college man, get rewards greater, even in material things, than the average college-bureaucracy-tied person. And in addition, like Ralph Nader, he will be able to keep his freedom and self-respect, which is worth something.

NEEDED: A REVOLUTION IN THINKING

An article by Carroll Quigley in *Today's Education*, March-April 1975, originally published in the *National Education Association Journal* 57 (May 1968), pp. 8-10:

SPECIAL SECTION ON THINKING AND LEARNING

By Carroll Quigley Professor of History, Georgetown University, Washington, DC. (Originally published in 1968)

Every event, every human experience, is unique. It occurs at a certain place, at a certain moment, to persons at a specific age and condition and in an arrangement of all these which will never be repeated. Never again will that event happen at that place, at that time, to those people, under those conditions.

People can deal with such unique events by action. The baseball player at the plate faces that unique and never-to-be repeated pitch and by making a never-to-be-repeated swing at it may be able to hit the ball over the fence for a home run. This is an example of how individuals, by action, can deal successfully with the unique events that make up the living experience of humankind.

But people also try to deal with the continuous stream of unique events which make up their lives by other methods besides action. They try to think about them and to communicate with others about them. To do this, they classify unique events into general classes or categories and they attach names or labels to such categories.

This process of classification and labeling ignores the qualities which make events unique and considers only those qualities which events are believed to share or to have in common. In this process, each society (and each person in that society) classifies its experiences and events into categories and then gives labels to these categories and puts a relative value on them — regarding some of them as good or desirable and others as less good and less desirable.

Each society has such a system of categories and of valuations of categories. This is known as the society's "cognitive system." It is the most important thing we can know about any society and the most difficult to learn. When individuals speak of the "inscrutable Chinese" or the "mysterious East," they are really saying these remote peoples have cognitive systems that are different from theirs and are therefore more or less incomprehensible to them.

Getting to know the cognitive system of any people (or even of other persons in our own society, since no two persons have exactly the same cognitive system) is difficult because it is not easy even to take the first step to recognize that we ourselves have a cognitive system, a distinctive way of looking at the world that is not the way the world actually is but is simply the way our group conventionally looks at our world.

The best way to recognize that one's own group has a distinctive way of looking at things and that our own way is not the way things necessarily are is to deal with groups who have cognitive systems different from ours and who are just as certain that their way of seeing things is the way things actually are.

Such an experience, called "cultural shock," may lead to cognitive sophistication — the recognition that all cognitive systems are subjective; that each is misleading to those who have it; and that although each enables those who have it to function within their own group, it handicaps them in dealing with persons from other groups. Moreover, even within a single society or group, cognitive sophistication is necessary whenever the experiences of that society are changing so rapidly that the old ways of looking at actuality handicap rather than help in dealing with the society's problems.

When people or groups with different cognitive systems interact, frictions and clashes occur, in many cases, without anyone's being able to see why. This happens even where there may be a maximum of goodwill on both sides. The difficulty occurs because individuals are unaware that they have a cognitive system of their own and, while seeing fully what other people do that irritates them, they cannot see why anything they are doing should irritate anyone else.

Cognitive sophistication makes it possible to know both one's own cognitive system and that of the different group with which one works so that one may be able to translate both talk and actions from one such system into the other, while recognizing the conventional and arbitrary nature of both.

Cognitive sophistication is so rare and so difficult to acquire that interaction across cultural barriers is a frequent cause of conflict. This applies to all relationships across cultural barriers — not only to those with other nations and major cultures but also to those within a culture, such as relationships between suburbanites and slum dwellers or between races or social classes.

The cause of such cognitive conflicts may arise in large part from the different ways in which peoples look at time. Time is undivided duration, but in order to think or talk about it, each culture must divide it.

Our culture divides time into two parts, the past and the future, which meet at the present moment — an instant without duration. This is reflected in European languages, which have tenses in the past, present, and future. But some peoples, such as the Bantu of Africa, do not have time classes of this sort in their language or social outlook. Many Bantu tongues divide verbs into those concerned with completed and uncompleted actions. They have no future tense because they categorize the future and the present together into a single form concerned with unfinished actions. (Similarly, in English we sometimes say, "I am going to school tomorrow," using the present tense for a future action.)

In the usual Bantu cognitive system, time is quite different from what it is to middle-class Americans, since it consists of a present of long duration and great importance; a past of less importance and moderate duration, such as can be held in personal memory; and almost no future distinguishable from the present.

Among some of these people, the future is not conceivable beyond the next few days and certainly has no meaning in terms of years. These people live in and value the present with all its problems, pleasures, and human relationships. Such people, even if they are given birth-control devices, are unlikely to use them, simply because they have no training in subjecting present relations to a hypothetical event nine months in the future.

Such cognitive differences are of great significance, especially when value systems are different. The African values the present, whereas many middle-class Americans put all emphasis on the importance of the future and are ready to make almost any sacrifice in the present for the sake of some hypothetical future benefit. In contrast to both, the aristocrat of today, like the ancient Greek, usually puts highest valuation on the past.

In our society, the latter viewpoint is now generally ignored, but the conflict between the "future preference" of the American middle-class suburbanite and the "present preference" of the lower-class slum dweller leads the former to regard the latter as shiftless, irresponsible, and lacking in self-discipline, while slum dwellers may regard the suburbanites' constant present sacrifice for future benefit as making them dehumanized and inhibited. In my opinion, the collapse, over the past two decades, of middle-class efforts to export our "self-enterprise" economic system to "underdeveloped countries" or to abolish ignorance and poverty in our own cities has been caused primarily by the existence of cognitive barriers—specially the one associated with time.

But there is much more to the problem than this. People can deal with their experiences consciously only if they have a cognitive system. This is why individuals cannot remember the events of the first year or two of their own lives, before they had acquired a cognitive system by learning to talk and rationalize. The events of that period of "infantile amnesia" are incorporated in people's neurological and metabolic systems, as can be shown by getting individuals to relive an early experience under hypnosis, but they cannot consciously recall and verbalize the experience until they have categorized it, something they could not do when it occurred.

The cognitive system of any people is of major importance because it includes all those unconscious classifications, judgments, and values which trigger most of an adult's initial responses to events. Every culture, including our own, has a cognitive system at its very foundation, and this is what really keeps it functioning, because it enables large numbers of people to live in the same society without constant clashes and conflicts. A few examples will serve to show this.

We divide the whole range of colors, as found in the rainbow, into six colors: red, orange, yellow, green, blue, violet. With our European background, we think a view is beautiful if it consists of alternating horizontal bands of green and blue, as in a landscape consisting of a foreground strip of green shore, a blue lake beyond, a farther shore of green trees and hills, and a blue sky beyond that.

But to a Bantu of dry Africa, such a view is a rather boring panorama of a single color, for many natives of that language group place green and blue in a single category with one name, although they divide the lower red-orange-yellow portion of the spectrum into a larger number of basic colors with different names. That is why what impresses us as a beautiful view of shore, lake, and sky strikes them as a rather monotonous field of one color, whereas, conversely, an African landscape, which to us seems to be a dull expanse of semi-parched soil with dry grasses, may seem to them to be an exciting scene of many different colors.

(As Americans of European background have become familiar with the African-like views of Arizona and New Mexico, many have come to feel that these semi-desert views are preferable to the more "conventional beauties" of New England, Wisconsin, or upper Michigan. And the Navaho or other natives of our Southwest show their preference for the red-orange-yellow portion of the spectrum by their extensive use of these colors and their scanty use of green, blue, or violet in their arts.)

A somewhat similar example exists in respect to distinguishing and naming the various states of H_2O. In our culture, we divide that range into no more than five or six categories, such as ice, snow, slush, water, and steam. But some Eskimo groups who are vitally concerned with how a dogsled moves on snow divide snow alone into 50 or more different categories, each with a distinct name. Today, in our own culture, as the sport of skiing grows more popular, we are developing numerous names for snow conditions on ski slopes to describe different skiing conditions.

Another significant example of any culture's cognitive view of experience may be seen in the way it divides the life span, especially the preference it places on these divisions.

Many native societies of Africa, for example, are formally divided into six or seven rigid stages, and the transitions from one to another are marked by formal, often painful, "crisis ceremonies." Frequently, there is little contact between different age classes. Thus, youths of seven to 11 years may live together in bands with almost no contact with parents, while the age group 18 to 28 may be almost totally devoted to war or hunting and forbidden to marry until they move, as a group, into the next age range, say from 28 to 45.

By contrast, in the medieval period, Christian Europe divided a person's life into only two stages, childhood and adulthood, separated at about age seven by First Communion. There was a slight tendency, arising from the Jewish Bar Mitzvah, to make another division at about age 13, marked by the sacrament of Confirmation, but generally, anyone over seven was spoken to and treated as an adult.

Over the last five centuries or more, however, our Western culture has changed its cognitive view of this matter to become more like the African, until today we have at least six or more age classifications: infants, children, teens or adolescents, the college crowd, the young marrieds, middle-aged people, and retired persons. There is increasing segregation of these—in education, in living quarters, in reading and entertainment, and in commercial markets (as in a department store).

The generation gap has become a familiar problem, and communication across age-group barriers has become a major issue. Moreover, female preference for the adolescent period has given us hordes of 40-year-old women trying to look like adolescents. The influence of such cognitive changes on all aspects of life is evident.

The power and affluence of Western civilization do not result from our technology, our political structure, or even our economic organization but from our cognitive system, on which they are based. That system began to develop before 500 B.C. with the introduction of the idea, in Palestine and Persia, of one God—omnipotent, omniscient, and perfect—and with the growth of two-valued logic in Persia and Greece.

Although our cognitive system has made our civilization the richest and mightiest in the world, its continued use without cognitive sophistication is leading us to disaster. Lynn White, Jr., pointed this out in his article, "The Historical Roots of Our Ecologic Crisis," in Science for March 10, 1967.

Professor White's thesis is that when the Judeo-Christian faith established the view that there is no spirit in nature other than the human, the world was reduced to a created object to be exploited by humans, and the way was thus opened to the destruction of nature and to the total pollution of the world — a consequence that may have become inevitable with the rejection, in the latter thirteenth century, of the message of St. Francis to treat all nature as sacred.

The cognitive techniques derived from our underlying outlook have included (a) using analysis rather than synthesis in seeking answers to problems; (b) isolating problems and studying them in a vacuum instead of using an ecological approach; (c) using techniques based on quantification rather than on qualification study done in a contextual situation; (d) proceeding on the assumption of single-factor causation rather than pluralistic, ecological causation; and (e) basing decisions and actions on needs of the individual rather than needs of the group.

In our society, if we want to know how something functions, we take it apart, cut it up, isolate it from its context; we analyze its factors and assume that only one is an independent variable. We then quantify the changes this independent variable makes in all the other variables that are assumed to be dependent on it. Then we make the independent variable one link in a chain of such independent variables, each surrounded by its system of dependent variables, the whole forming a chain going back to some original cause in the past or extending forward in a similar chain to some ultimate goal in the future.

From such reasoning, given to us from the Greeks through Aristotle, we got the "final" causes (or goals) and the "Unmoved Mover" (that which is the first cause of all movement and does not itself move) of Aristotelian metaphysics, and, today, we still use this way of thinking, even though we no longer believe in Aristotle's metaphysics.

The now obsolescent mode of thought and cognition just described might be contrasted with a newer method which is, incidentally, closer to the thinking processes of southern and eastern Asia, which were never much influenced by transcendental Hebrew monotheism or by Greek two-valued logic.

This newer (or older) way of looking at experience tries to find how anything functions by seeing its relationships to a larger system and, ultimately, to the whole cosmos. To do so, it uses an ecological and qualitative approach, seeking to grasp the whole contextual situation of innumerable factors, all of which are changing at once, not only by quantitative changes within a fixed identity (such as Western logic can handle) but with constant shifts of identity and quality.

This more intuitive and less logical point of view is now sweeping the West as is evidenced by the fact that our traditional Western categories and cognitive assumptions were rejected not only by youthful hippies but also by those hardheaded, analytical people on whom the survival of the West depends.

The stumbling block, of course, is that our whole institutional setup is based on the old method of thought. For example, our educational system is based on the methods of categorization, specialization, and quantification, which must be replaced. This old method of thought is seen on the lower levels, where objective tests assume such things as two-valued logic (True, False), the principle of contradiction (Yes, No), and the principle of retained identity, just as, on the highest levels, the great increase in the use of computers assumes the possibility of objective analysis and quantification of life experiences.

It is difficult to reform our old methods of thinking no matter how bankrupt they may be. Standing in the way of change are the pressures exerted by institutionalized establishments, the profits of powerful groups producing equipment based on old ways of thinking, and the need which the large bureaucratized organizations have for persons with narrow technical training in the older cognitive patterns.

On the other hand, if we do not make such reforms, we may well be destroyed by problems that cannot be handled by the established methods of specialization, isolation, and quantification. These problems are already swallowing us up in the crises of environmental destruction, urban blight, social and racial tensions, poor mental health, and international conflicts that threaten to lead to nuclear annihilation.

THE PARTISAN SIDE OF QUIGLEY

Background: GU Philosophy Department chairman Tom McTighe had been an early supporter of Sen. Eugene McCarthy in his campaign to win in 1968 the presidential nomination of the Democratic Party in opposition to the expected effort of then President Lyndon Johnson's to run again.

Many Democrats that year had urged Sen. Robert Kennedy to lead the resisters to anti-Viet Nam war in opposing a Johnson re-nomination, but Kennedy chose to hold back and only McCarthy made the effort.

Then, when McCarthy came very close to beating Johnson in the early New Hampshire primary, Kennedy re-considered and decided to enter the race- taking much of the wind out of the sails of McCarthy's movement.

McTighe wrote an article in The HOYA urging anti-war Dems to stick with McCarthy and said some negative things about Kennedy's last minute decision to run.

Quigley, ever a strong Kennedy family man, responded with this letter:

Thursday, May 2, 1968 THE HOYA

Letters to the Editor...

RASH JUDGMENT

To the Editor:

In a democracy every citizen has the right to have and to express his political opinions. It is, however, incumbent upon teachers, and, especially upon those who call themselves philosophers, to practice self-restraint in the exercising of these rights. By that I mean no professor, especially when he is advising students, and above all when he is a philosopher, should allow himself to appear in print when he is in a state of purely emotional reaction on a subject which he is obviously ignorant. Professor McTighe's article in THE HOYA of 4 April, was written, he says, while he was boiling with anger (for a week!). His personal remarks on Senator Kennedy are both non-philosophical and ignorant. The Senator's personality is nothing like what Professor McTighe seems to believe. The professor may know nothing about the Senator's personality. If so, he should recognize that fact and keep quiet on a subject on which he is ignorant. The professor also knows nothing about the Senator's views on the issues and says, "About all he has come up with are tired generalities and absurd accusations blaming Johnson for all the ills of society."

Professor McTighe should be told that no person mentioned today for the presidency has given his views on more issues and in more detail over the past five years that Senator Kennedy. If Professor McTighe ignored these statements, that is his right, but, when he made the decision to ignore them, he should also have made the decision to refrain from public statements on matters on which he had decided to be ignorant. The worthy professor asks, "Has Senator Kennedy anything solid to offer on the agonizing problem of Viet Nam?" I am astonished. Does he not know that the Senator has offered detailed plans on this? As one who has read millions of words on this subject, I am prepared to say that the chapter on Vietnam in Senator Kennedy's book, To Seek a Newer World, published last year, is the best brief statement (in 30 pages) on what went wrong in that area and what should be done about it. On this and other matters, the Senator's knowledge of specific detail and his willingness to express frank opinions on his views are matched by few public figures in this country. It is a shame that Professor McTighe has not been paying attention and does not know this.

Carroll Quigley
Professor of History

MEXICAN NATIONAL CHARACTER AND CIRCUM-MEDITERRANEAN PERSONALITY STRUCTURE

An article by Carroll Quigley in the American Anthropologist, Volume 75, Number 1, February 1973, pp. 319-322:

Martin Needler's article on "Politics and National Character: the Case of Mexico" (1971) is perfectly correct as far as it goes, but it must be pointed out that the personality traits which he identifies as Mexican are products of a considerably wider and much older cultural entity. Mexico is a peripheral and very distinctive example of the Latin American cultural area which is itself a peripheral and somewhat distinctive example of the Mediterranean cultural area. Some time ago I identified the whole cultural area and the personality structure it tended to produce as aspects of "the Pakistani-Peruvian Axis" (1966:1112-1122, reprinted as 1968:452-463). If I am correct in this, Needler is parochial in attributing "Mexican national character" to a combination of "the Indian's fatalism and the proud self-assertion of the Spaniard" (Needler 1971:757).

A broader view of this subject would show that Mexico is a peripheral example of the "Pakistani-Peruvian cultural area" and that Mexican national character is merely a local variant of the personality structure of this larger area. That is why Silverman's picture of south Italian personality is so similar to Needler's idea of Mexican character (Silverman 1968).

This Mediterranean personality type is marked by various traits mentioned by Needler: low self-esteem, fatalism, defeatism, distrust of all persons outside a narrow kin group, pessimism, preoccupation with death, self-assertion, and machismo. These traits, however, should be associated in clusters and correlated with other cultural manifestations such as: (1) low respect for manual work, especially for agricultural work; (2) higher esteem for urban residence than for rural living, associated with neglect of the countryside, damage to natural vegetation, and much cruelty to animals, especially to domestic animals; (3) emphasis on honor, both personal and family, as a chief aim of life; (4) dietary customs which mix protein and vegetables within a nest or container of starch, on the same plate and in the same mouthful, unlike the core of Western civilization, which tends to segregate these three kinds of food, on the same plate or even into separate dishes. The personality traits of this larger area tend to cluster about two points: (1) The restriction of personal trust and loyalty within the kinship group (usually the extended or nuclear family) with a consequent inability to offer loyalty, trust, or personal identification to residential groups (villages, neighborhoods, parishes), voluntary associations, religious beliefs, or the secular state, resulting in large-scale lack of "public spirit," combined with "corruption," and paralysis of these other kinds of associations. (2) The combination of powerful patriarchal social tendencies with female inferiority (except as a mechanism for producing sons) leads to many psychological ambiguities: strong emphasis on female premarital virginity (both as a symbol of family honor and as an economic good), segregation of the sexes in social life, fear of women as a threat men's virility (witches and belief in "the evil eye"), the need to demonstrate male virility by social "touchiness" and other behavior, including fantasies of demonstrations of male dominance over bulls, other men, and unattached women.

In the last generation or two, we have had numerous local studies of the culture-and-personality type dealing with portions of this wide area (Pitt-Rivers and Kenny on Spain; Banfield, Moss, Cancian, Silverman, and others on Italy; Campbell, Kavadias, Kanelli and others on Greece; and numerous studies of the Near East or North Africa). Many of these consider the personality types they observe as consequences of local conditions of economic, national, religious, or historic origin. A few have seen the wider range of what they observe. Thus Balikci (1966:164) wrote, "Behind obvious cultural differences, many Mediterranean societies share certain basic cultural patterns... [with] basic cross-cultural similarities in regard to sex behavior, certain family roles, the position of the family in society, and the dichotomy of kinsmen and strangers." Opler (1970:866) recognizes both the areal spread and the deep historical roots of these traits when he writes, "The Southern Italian family is in great measure understood if one considers it as a peasant society, as a circum-Mediterranean type, as one influenced by Roman history or even by the earlier pagan Classic Greek, or later Hellenistic traditions."

What I wish to emphasize is that this personality structure is geographically wider than the Mediterranean, since it extends to Latin America, and is the consequence of historical experience going back even earlier than the ancient Greeks. There are works (Peristiany 1966) which see some of the geographic range, but from both points of view, the most suggestive work is Raphael Patai's *Golden River to Golden Road* (1962), whose original title (now abandoned in a 1971 edition) shows that his attention extends from Rio de Oro to Samarkand.

The Pakistani-Peruvian axis does not now demark the area of a functioning society or civilization. This is one of the chief keys to its personality types. It is now largely an area of debris of traits and peoples surviving from the wreckage of deceased civilizations. The existing traits have historical origins covering thousands of years. For example, the diet, sexual symbolism of bull and "eye," architecture, and other traits come from the archaic cultures before 600 B.C., including Minoan Crete; the urbanism and low esteem for manual labor derive from Classical Mediterranean society; while the emphasis on honor, female inferiority, and kinship groups flow from pastoral invaders, both from the northern grasslands (Indo-European) and the southern grasslands (Semites).

Other traits, such as fatalism, distrust of strangers, cynicism toward the state or the local community, come from the difficulties of farming in the Mediterranean environment or from Mediterranean history. Historically the Mediterranean has passed through three distinct experiences: (1) as a frontier area of cultural diffusion from Western Asia during the Archaic period (4500-600 B.C.); (2) as the central backbone of Mediterranean civilization in the Classical period (600 B.C.-A.D. 600), and (3) as a boundary conflict area between the three post-Classical civilizations (Byzantine, Western, and Islamic) since A.D. 600. T he shift from the second to the third of these was so disruptive of community life in the area from the Golden River to the Golden Road that its problems have not been solved since, especially in view of the social and ethical failures of the two post-Classical religions, Christianity and Islam, on either side of the line from Tangier to Batum. These failures of religion, whose consequences were clearly seen by Christ and Mohomet, made it impossible to create any religious, territorial, or social community, and forced living patterns back toward the "amoral familism" of the extended family. In extreme cases this broke down further to amoral nuclear familism or even to amoral individualism. This basic outlook and personality type was given a distinctive twist in the Iberian peninsula, from Saracen and anti-lslamic influences. The export of this distinctive type to America and the changes made in it by the shattering of American Indian cultures gives us the distinctive Latin American personality patterns which Needler (1971) sees as "Mexican national character."These patterns have been modified in various circumstances by the "culture of poverty,"by modem industrialism and nationalism, by various nineteenth century ideologies such as Marxism, and by other influences, but the basic Pakistani-Peruvian outlook is still identifiable. What is distinctly Mexican, and potentially revolutionary, is the new political ideology which Needler reports thus: "the cynicism and alienation of Mexican respondents... did not extend to two elements of the political system: the president himself and the idea of the Mexican Revolution" (1971:760). Any discussion of Mexican national character should recognize the revolutionary implications of these exceptions and the remote sources of the other aspects of Mexican personality.

Silverman, who has a good appreciation of this Pakistani-Peruvian cultural area, has also glimpsed the nature of its northern boundary. This boundary, which roughly follows the lines of the Highland Zone of the Old World, is marked by the southern limits of the archaic peasant cultures, in which rural life was valued higher than urbanism, the land was loved (as a female entity), pride in skillful tillage was evident, fertility was prized over virility, and the cow was more valuable than the bull (whose usefulness was increased by castration). In this peasant culture the southern concept of honor was non-existent, female virginity or chastity were considered unnatural, pre-marital sexual relations were practiced (often condoned by a betrothal ceremony), and marriage often followed pregnancy, rather than preceding coition as in the south. This peasant culture accepted a female centered house-hold and tended to revere local, semi-pagan, female saints (or Mary seen as a Mother rather than as a Virgin) instead of the rather war-like male saints popular farther south. Above all, in the north the basic social units were territorial (villages or parishes), not kinship groups, and functioned as communities.

Studies of these distinctions are frustrated today by academic specialization, both areal and chronological, so that students attribute cause to whatever social feature strikes them as significant. This includes ethos (Banfield 1958), agricultural organization (Silverman 1968), transhumance pastoralism (Campbell 1964), Bedouin Arabism (Carmichael 1967), urbanism (Pitkin 1963:123.129), social hopelessness (Cancian 1961), and many others. A comparison of the similarities of values and personality between a rural pastoral people like the Saracatsan (Campbell 1964) and a modern, professional, urban Greek family (Kanelli 1963) will show the need to seek explanation on a wider and deeper areal and historical foundation.

This foundation must be a historical-cultural framework similar to that used in historical geology, so that local outcroppings of earlier cultural strata can be identified and coordinated. I gave a brief outline of such a framework for the Old World in 1961, but other historians have rather scorned any efforts at establishing a matrix of macro-history. Feeble efforts are now being made to remedy this lack in other disciplines, including anthropology and sociology, but these attempts will find almost insurmountable difficulties so long as historians do not do their part of the task.

REFERENCES CITED

- Balikci, Asen; 1966 Review of Honour and Shame: The Values of Mediterranean Society; J. G. Peristiany, Ed. Science 153:164.
- Banfield, Edward C.; 1958 The Moral Basis of a Backward Society; Chicago: Free Press.
- Campbell, John K.; 1964 Honour, Family, and Patronage. A Study of Institutions and Moral Values in a Greek Mountain Community; London: Oxford University Press.
- Gancian, Frank; 1961 The South Italian Peasant: World View and Political Behavior; Anthropological Quarterly 34:1-18.
- Carmichael, Joel; 1967 The Shaping of the Arabs; a Study in Ethnic Identity; New York: Macmillan.
- Kanelli, Sheelagb; 1965 Earth and Water: A Marriage into Greece; New York: Coward-McCann.
- Kavadias, Georges B.; 1965 Pasteur-nomades mediterranees: Les Saracatsans de Grece; Paris: Gauthier-Villars.
- Kenny, Michael; 1960 Patterns of Patronage in Spain; Anthropological Quarterly 33:14-22.
- Moss, Leonard W.; 1960 Patterns of Kinship, Comparaggio, and Community in a Southern Italian Village; Anthropological Quarterly 33:24-32.
- Needler, Martin C.; 1971 Politics and National Character-The Case of Mexico; American Anthropologist 73:757-761.
- Opler, Marvin K.; 1970 Review of Belief, Magic, and Anomie: Essays in Psychosocial Anthropology,; by Anne Parsons; American Anthropologist 72:865-867.
- Patai, Raphael; 1962 Golden River to Golden Road: Society, Culture, and Change in the Middle East; Philadelphia: University of Pennsylvania Press. 1971 Society, Culture, and Change in the Middle East. Revised edition; Philadelphia: University of Pennsylvania Press;
- Peristiany, Jean G., Ed.; 1966 Honour and Shame: The Values of Mediterranean Society; Chicago: University of Chicago Press.
- Pitkin, Donald S.; 1963 Mediterranean Europe; Anthropological Quarterly 36:120.129.
- Pitt. Rivers, Julian; 1971 The People of the Sierra. Revised edition; Chicago: University of Chicago Press. (First published in 1954.)
- Quigley, Carroll; 1961 The Evolution of Civilizations; New York: Macmillan; 1966 Tragedy and Hope: A History of the World in Our Time; New York: Macmillan.; 1968 The World Since 1939: A History; New York:

Collier Books.
- Silverman, Sydel F.; 1968 Agricultural Organization, Social Structure, and Values in Italy:; Amoral Familism Reconsidered; American Anthropologist 70:1.20.

THE '74 INTERVIEW

1974 INTERVIEW WITH RUDY MAXA OF THE WASHINGTON POST

QUIGLEY: ...the year, which would be to the end of '44, and by that time we were ready to take over and move them in and so forth.
Now, in that group there were fifty-five who already had Ph.D.s.
You see.

INTERVIEWER: ... Huh.

QUIGLEY: So it was a very good group.
The only one I had any trouble with had been a district attorney in Indiana and a Republican politician.

INTERVIEWER: Ha, ha, ha.

QUIGLEY: And I had trouble with him over certain things.
For example, the civil war in Spain.
I gave him the truth of the civil war in Spain.
I mean, this was not a Communist revolt against the Catholic Church or something like this, you see.
And that was what this guy was.
So... this is the substance of the book 'Tragedy and Hope'.
Do you see?

INTERVIEWER: Did you know while you were working on this that [it was going to be a book]?

QUIGLEY: No, no. I was just trying... you know.

INTERVIEWER: Keep up.

QUIGLEY: Keep a day to day basis.

INTERVIEWER: You realized that at the end of the accumulation, of research and...?

QUIGLEY: Well, yes, I knew... I knew a hell of a lot more about most of this than most people.
Now, I then spent 20 years writing it—from '45 to '65.
And put it in, you see, in '65. In the meantime, I had written a shorter book which fifteen publishers had rejected. And I had set it aside.
I had, wrote it the first time in the only summer I had off, which was 1942.
In that whole period, I went twenty years without any time off.
No sabbaticals, no anything. From '42 to... '60, '61, when I took off and went to England and did research.
And then I got another sabbatical in '71, when I again went to England on a sabbatical.
And I only... So... The only sabbatical time.
Whether I get it or not, I have asked for a one semester sabbatical before I retire, that is assuming I get full pay for one semester, you see, instead of half pay, or whatever it is. I don't know what it is.
And I can't even look it... I don't have time, time to look it up.
But in any case, I... worked out all of these things.
And, my first book had been rejected by fifteen publishers.
I had written it first in the summer of '34; I then spent the summer of '42 in Princeton, in Donald Stauffer's [office]—and he died as Eastman Professor of Literature at Oxford, after climbing the Pyranees, running up and down the Pyranees—and... I re-wrote it in '42. Then, I set that aside and wrote it a third time—just dashed it off—and that is the book 'The Evolution of Civilizations'—it's only 279 pages, but it's still the best thing, and there are a number of books that quoted it as the best thing on why civilizations rise and fall, and how they do, and so forth.
So it's a big thing.
Now this... 'The World Since 1914' covers seventy years, from 1895 to 1965, and it's in that way, but it covers the whole world, so again it's a pretty big thing, because it goes into science and technology, as you will discover, if you start reading the paperback, and... economics, and as you see, I can do more with economics than economists can.

INTERVIEWER: One thing that intrigues me, more on just that (last night my wife and I were talking about you), was the title of the book: 'Tragedy and Hope'.

QUIGLEY: ... "And Hope". Yes. Because I...

INTERVIEWER: Such a large title.

QUIGLEY: Yes. Now what it means is this: I think it is absolutely tragic, it is shameful, it is sinful that Western Civilization is going to go down the drain. When I wrote that book, which was less than ten years ago, I had hoped that we could save Western Civilization.
I am extremely skeptical now that it can be saved.
I think we're just about finished.
And I just threw a few things out here this morning in the class.
You know, if we are going to allow a coal strike and if we are going to overthrow the Portuguese government.
Because as soon as... all these military dictatorships are not going to last.
So we get rid of a democracy because it wants to be a little liberal, and we put in a military dictatorship which then collapses and what happens? The Communists come in.
This is what happened in Portugal. Salazar was there since 1927. You see?
All right, now they suddenly try to establish some kind of a non-military dictatorship—he wasn't military, he was a college professor, but he was supported by... the reactionary groups.
And now they want to do something about that.
And the same thing could happen in Greece.
They're now going to, probably, in Greece try these generals who established the military dictatorship because we got them to do it. You see.
And, this gives the Communists—and it could well be—now this is what's worrying Kissinger, he thinks the whole Mediterranean now is going to go Communist. So we're going to go to war to prevent this?
Oh, I mean, it's sick.

INTERVIEWER: Now, let me go back.

QUIGLEY: Yeah. Now...

INTERVIEWER: When did you find a publisher for your book?

QUIGLEY: I found a publisher instantly, because the first book—I'm in 'Current History', an editor, and I wrote, used to write, a good deal for them. (And that's who called me up on Monday and wants me to write about Spain

to-day. What's going to happen in Spain and I said, I, it would take too much time, I don't want to do it).
So the people at 'Current History' said to me, in 1960.
I... just mentioned that I had this book.
(I have many books, I have a whole lot of books, half written and almost totally written, you see).
And they said, "Have you ever given... asked Peter Ritner?" And I said, "I never heard of him. Who is he?
They said, "Call him up, at Macmillan". So I went right to the "phone — I was at the American Historical Association in New York, the meeting of 1960 — and I went to the phone and called Macmillan and asked for Peter Ritner and he came on, and I said 'I have a book and I have somebody here who's the editor of 'Current History' who says that you would like it.' And so forth.
He says 'Send it to me.' A week later I got a letter from him: 'It's a marvelous book'.

INTERVIEWER: How many pages did you send him?

QUIGLEY: I sent him the whole thing.

INTERVIEWER: Which was?

QUIGLEY: And, well...

INTERVIEWER: In fact.

QUIGLEY: Yeah. Just about...

INTERVIEWER: In fact!

QUIGLEY: It came out as a book of 279 pages. He accepted it within a week.

INTERVIEWER: Which book is this now?

QUIGLEY: This is the first book.

INTERVIEWER: The first book. O.K.

QUIGLEY: Right.

INTERVIEWER: Right.

QUIGLEY: This is in 1961. You'll find all of this in "Who's Who?" You see. The dates.

INTERVIEWER: All right.

QUIGLEY: That is how I got my first book published.
Now when I signed the contract for that, 1961.

INTERVIEWER: Uh... Huh.

QUIGLEY: They... made me agree I would give them my next book.

INTERVIEWER: Sure.

QUIGLEY: You see. So in a couple of years I said to Peter Ritner that I want the next book to be 'The World Since 1914' and he said 'O.K., let's sign a contact'.

INTERVIEWER: Did he say anything like 'That's a rather large subject'?

QUIGLEY: ... Peter Ritner thinks I am the greatest writer ever around.

INTERVIEWER: O.K. Is he an editor?

QUIGLEY: He's a scholar. That's who... You see.
Now here's what happened.
And I don't know whether you want to get this on tape or not.
But I'll put it on tape. But look... you've gotta be discrete.

INTERVIEWER: Sure.

QUIGLEY: You know, you have to protect my future.

INTERVIEWER: Sure.

QUIGLEY: As well as your own.

INTERVIEWER: Sure.

QUIGLEY: All right. Ah, when 'Tragedy and Hope' was signed, the contract and rights, up to the last minute, which would be the spring and summer of '66, they were planning to bring it out in two volumes, boxed, for $17.50.

INTERVIEWER: Uh... Huh.

QUIGLEY: Macmillan had been bought by, from Harold Macmillan, at Macmillan Company of England.

INTERVIEWER: Uh... Huh.

QUIGLEY: for $5 million. Because he needed the cash. In the summer of '66, a holding company, Collier Books, which originally was Morgan... and they published Collier's Magazine. Remember Collier's Weekly?
And stuff like? All right. Collier's Books. Now, I don't know who controls it now. And, it's one of these holding companies.

INTERVIEWER: Uh... Huh.

QUIGLEY: Came in... they bought up the Free Press, you know, in Illinois. They bought up Brentano Book Stores. They bought up Macmillan.
They came in and they looked at what they'd bought and they said 'You're spending money wildly and we're not taking in money. You got to stop it'.

INTERVIEWER: The accountants did that?

QUIGLEY: Yeah. So they said 'No advertising on any books that are published for the next six months. You spent too much on advertising'.
And, the editors like Peter Ritner screamed and said 'We're not going to stay if this is how you're going to do things'.
So they said 'All right. One ad for each book'.
All right, I got one ad for 'Tragedy and Hope', and it was a quarter page in The New York Times Book Review, I believe.
That's all.

INTERVIEWER: How do you spell Ritner's name?

QUIGLEY: R-I-T-N-E-R, Peter Ritner. He, I imagine he's in "Who's Who?"... he should be. Anyway, he has since left them. I do not know what he is doing.

He still lives in the same place that I visited him in Riverside Drive, up near the George Washington Bridge.
But he works for some World Book... thing. Or something.

INTERVIEWER: Third World Publishers?

QUIGLEY: Eh, Something else. And what he does I don't know, because he's never got in touch with me since he left.

INTERVIEWER: And they also did not come out with the two volumes.

QUIGLEY: No. And then, when they saw it, they said "Oh, this is going to cost too much. Cut it to one volume and cut the price five bucks".
So they, that made it $12.50.
But they never sold it at $12.50. They made it $12.95.
So this is what it was sold.
Now, it went out of print, that was '66, it went out of print in '68.
But in '68 Collier Books got in touch with me, I do not know how or why, and said... "We'll bring out the last half of this as a paperback", and that's what I gave you. That came out in '68.

INTERVIEWER: Right.

QUIGLEY: And that, I think, is still in print.
But I can't get an answer. I can't get a straight answer to any question, from them. For example: They never told me until 1974, when I was trying to fight the pirate who reprinted 'Tragedy and Hope'.

INTERVIEWER: Right.

QUIGLEY: That it had been out of print. They'd told me it's out of stock and we will re-publish when we get two thousand [orders].
But they never could get two thousand (I have told you this, haven't I?).

INTERVIEWER: Right.

QUIGLEY: Because they were telling everyone who wrote in that it is out of print.

INTERVIEWER: Now.

QUIGLEY: They lied to me.

INTERVIEWER: Now, when did you realize there was a pirate edition? How did you find out?

QUIGLEY: I found out... telling everyone who wrote in that it is out of print.

INTERVIEWER: Now.

QUIGLEY: Which they denied to me.

INTERVIEWER: Now, when did you realize there was a pirate edition? How did you find out?

QUIGLEY: I found out when somebody got a plain envelope with a slip of paper in it: 'Available again, in short supply.'

INTERVIEWER: 'Tragedy and Hope', the whole book?

QUIGLEY: The whole book. And they...

INTERVIEWER: They came to you and said...?

QUIGLEY: No, they called me up and said, eh 'Did you know that your book is re-printed?'
I said 'Which book?' (Because they're both out of print, you see.)
And they said 'Tragedy and Hope'. I said 'No, it isn't.'

INTERVIEWER: You don't know who this person was?

QUIGLEY: No, no. Because it's exact copy. Exact.
The dust jacket, everything, the binding is the same.

INTERVIEWER: Did they re-set the type? Or is it photo-reproduced?

QUIGLEY: Photo... photo-reproduction. Exactly the same. Now, I can tell instantly that it's different. Because they didn't notice that the original had a gold, had yellow top on the pages. Here...

INTERVIEWER: All right.

QUIGLEY: You see, the original. The new one is white.

INTERVIEWER: So you, I would imagine, would call Macmillan and say 'Hey, you must be upset that they're re-printed?' That would be a logical reaction...

QUIGLEY: They didn't give a damn, and I'll tell you why.

INTERVIEWER: Well did you call...? How much is? Well, we'll talk when we're done with it. And I'll ask you how much it is you're comfortable with, in light of your losses, etc., etc.

QUIGLEY: Yeah. Well.

INTERVIEWER: O.K.?

QUIGLEY: I don't, I don't know.

INTERVIEWER: We can talk about that.

QUIGLEY: And I don't know why Macmillan acted like this. Now, immediately...

INTERVIEWER: But my logical reaction would be to call Macmillan and say, 'Gee, you must really be upset'?

QUIGLEY: No, I didn't. I, not right away, I didn't. Because they had lied to me so many times on so many [occasions].

INTERVIEWER: You already knew...

QUIGLEY: That there's something funny. They lied and lied and lied and lied to me, you see. On, on everything. And... I have letters to prove that, because I had from Ritner letters apologizing for information previously given to him. Because, they had lied to him when he called up to ask...

INTERVIEWER: Right.

QUIGLEY: ...if they're out of print or not, you see. And they said 'no', and so forth.
Now, oh, oh, the big thing is. My contract, both, had in it that, if it went out of print, I had the right to recover the plates.

INTERVIEWER: Right.

QUIGLEY: They never got in touch with me offering the plates. I learned in March of this year that they destroyed the plates, of 'Tragedy and Hope'. I learned in the summer, 1971, because my wife got mad and called Macmillan on the phone, every week, while I was in England, and finally got from them a letter in which they said the plates had been destroyed. They said 'inadvertently destroyed.'
The plates of the first book, 'Evolution of Civilizations.' You see?

INTERVIEWER: Umm, hmm. O.K. So you find, so a guy calls you, an anonymous caller...

QUIGLEY: Yeah, well, he identified himself, you know, to me, but he, he... No. And he gave me his name and so forth. And he had got this, and...
Do you want to shut that off? One second?

INTERVIEWER: Sure.

QUIGLEY: And the way I found out was: I sent an order. I let somebody else send an order.
Now this was my assistant, who sent a check... sent an order.
And nothing came. And then we discovered they'd only pay if you sent them cash ahead of time, you see.

INTERVIEWER: A check wouldn't do?

QUIGLEY: Well, I guess I did sent a check.

INTERVIEWER: But not enough?

QUIGLEY: No, I sent the check. The whole thing.
But they, for example, will not send to book stores unless they send cash.
And they're all suspicious. Because if you ordered ten copies and that would

be $120, because he was asking $12.
... eh, you, he could vanish, because there was no way to find out who it is.

INTERVIEWER: Sure.

QUIGLEY: You have no name. You have a box number, out in California, and so forth.
And anyway, I... I couldn't find out anything.
I gave... got it back. And I was shocked, because it was identical, you see, or almost identical. So then I got [word] other companies were offering it.

INTERVIEWER: When is this now?

QUIGLEY: This was in... this year.

INTERVIEWER: This year?

QUIGLEY: Yes, January.

INTERVIEWER: January this year?

QUIGLEY: in 1974.

INTERVIEWER: O.K.

QUIGLEY: This year. By March somebody came to me and had one of the pirated copies.
I said 'Where'd you get it?' And then he said 'Sidney Kramer.'
I said 'Does he have it?' and he said 'Sure. He has four or five of them there.'
So I called up Sidney Kramer and asked if he had it, and he said 'Yes'.
And I went down there. And... ah, he is very hard to get information out of.
But finally I found out that he sent an order in and they... sent back... 'Send me a check and I'll send 'em.' You see?
And he sold them and repeated the order and repeated the order, and so forth.
So then I told our bookstore.

INTERVIEWER: Using the same address you have.

QUIGLEY: ... yes, he was using...

INTERVIEWER: You still do not know who that is. I mean, at that time, you did not know who it is.

QUIGLEY: I still am not certain...

INTERVIEWER: Really?

QUIGLEY: ...who it is, and I will now, and I'll tell you why... one of the places that was offering them for sale and there were about five places that were offering it for sale, and I've got, since, a number of others... They come to me from students or, fate. They don't come right to me directly, ever.— now, no one ever approached me. Oh, one reason I was suspicious of Macmillan was this: The first, the fact that the radical right, the John Birch Society and so forth, was getting all up over this book...

INTERVIEWER: ... Huh.

QUIGLEY: ...goes back to at least '69.

INTERVIEWER: I was going to ask you about that.

QUIGLEY: '69. Yes. And, a book appeared called 'The Naked Capitalist' by Skousens.
Now, of that book, about a fifth of it is direct quote from my book.

INTERVIEWER: ... Huh.

QUIGLEY: Now, he says it's from my book. It's in quotation marks. But nevertheless it's a violation of copyright.

INTERVIEWER: ... Huh.

QUIGLEY: I got in touch with Macmillan. They would not do a thing. They said, I said 'Aren't you going to defend my copyright?' And they said 'No. If you want to do something, we will support you (and... you know) and be a witness, if you want', and so forth. But I... I wasn't going to sue this guy. He's a professor of religion at Brigham Young University, former police chief of Salt Lake City. You know all about him?

INTERVIEWER: About him, yeah.

QUIGLEY: All right.

INTERVIEWER: He's run the gamut, I know.

QUIGLEY: So whether... He has—had been with the F.B.I. for years.

INTERVIEWER: Right.

QUIGLEY: So whether he would have any money...? It wouldn't be worth my while to sue him, you see. Probably. And another state, and so forth. So I decided I'd let that go. But then I discovered they [Macmillan] wouldn't do anything. And, then, Congressman Rarick, who was beaten in the primary just now, put that [Skousen] book into, uh...

INTERVIEWER: The Congressional Record?

QUIGLEY: Yeah, into 'The Congressional Record'. And a lot of things like this. Then this [Allen] book was distributed to every registered voter in New Hampshire.

INTERVIEWER: And no point, they never called you and said, and I have no quotes. I mean.

QUIGLEY: No. Nobody ever.

INTERVIEWER: It's like writing a story without ever talking with you.

QUIGLEY: Yeah. Nobody ever wrote to me.

INTERVIEWER: Do you...?

QUIGLEY: Hmm?

INTERVIEWER: Do you know where they got the picture of you? The PR office here [at Georgetown University]?

QUIGLEY: All right. I think. Let me see which picture it is.

INTERVIEWER: It's up front there.

QUIGLEY: They tried to get pictures from the PR office. And I said 'Don't give anybody a picture if they won't tell you why.'

INTERVIEWER: ... Hmm.

QUIGLEY: Oh, they got this is from the PR office. Now Skousens couldn't get a picture of me.

INTERVIEWER: Hmm.

QUIGLEY: You see, they could have gotten off the back of the... there's a full picture of me on the back of the jacket of the first book. From Bachrach, here in town. But you know, that's the one they have in the public relations office here now, still.
It's the only one there is. And that's where they got that.

INTERVIEWER: It's a good picture.

QUIGLEY: Well, all right. But then they put it on the same page with J. P. Morgan, you know. It's nonsense. To me.

INTERVIEWER: Ha ha ha.

QUIGLEY: You laugh, right to laugh. It's a joke. But it's all so silly, linking me with Morgan, or any of those people. But then they... full of statement.
Anyway, Rarick and other people... filled The Congressional Record with this. Then the John Birch Society started talking about it in their various publications — and then, of course, this [Allen] guy is a John Birch employee.

INTERVIEWER: Sure. Right.

QUIGLEY: And he published, even before this, did he?, the book... 'Nixon: The Man Behind The Mask'. Yeah, that, that's in '69.
And I knew nothing about that until two weeks ago.

INTERVIEWER: Really?

QUIGLEY: 'Nixon: The Man Behind the Mask'.
Yes, That's when one of the priests here met me and said 'I've been looking for you.' I said 'Well, look. It's free. Go right [ahead] and look all you want.' And he said 'No, I want to ask you about… this Gary Allen who wrote a book about Nixon.' And I said 'Well, I know Gary Allen, I didn't know he wrote a book about Nixon.'
(Since I don't keep up with this stuff.) And he said "Well, I have it and the whole third chapter is about you, and your book 'Tragedy and Hope.'"
I said 'Really?' So, he let me have it. And I read it, and it was.
And, now there's others.

INTERVIEWER: You don't know Gary Allen personally? Do you?

QUIGLEY: No. Now, here's what happened. A crisis occurred at Brigham Young.
And I should not go in it in detail, because I don't know anything for sure.

INTERVIEWER: Yeah, I know something.

QUIGLEY: All right. A hell of a… The… The campus was blown apart by a fight between the political science department and Skousens and in which they declared that he was unworthy to be a Mormon professor. And should be fired.

INTERVIEWER: Right.

QUIGLEY: And he defended himself. And what happened I do not know. All I know is this.

INTERVIEWER: He lost it.

QUIGLEY: Who?

INTERVIEWER: He lost it.

QUIGLEY: Oh, Did he?

INTERVIEWER: And he got ousted.

QUIGLEY: Oh, I didn't know that. You see, I never find out. Nobody ever tells me these things.

INTERVIEWER: I'll check. [mumbles while going through his notes] I read...

QUIGLEY: So they did get out... they did get rid of him, eh?

INTERVIEWER: He did. I think he lost that fight within the university. I'll check, I know more...

QUIGLEY: Well the reason... All I know about it is this: I gave three papers at this American Association for the Advancement of Science. And I going to give you one of them.

INTERVIEWER: Yep.

QUIGLEY: And because they liked it so much, they printed thousands of them. Or, you know, processed thousands of them and distributed them through all the press, in the press room.

INTERVIEWER: Right.

QUIGLEY: They liked this one. So, it wasn't the best of them:
'General Crises in Civilization.' You know, which, this is an attractive title.
Now, somebody called me up, and wanted to talk to me, at this.
It wasn't the best of them: 'General Crises in Civilization.' You know, which, this is an attractive title.
Now... somebody called me up and wanted to talk to me, at this. And I think it was at this. And he said his name was Larson and he was a scientist from Brigham Young and he wanted to see and talk to me because of what was going on up there. I said 'What is going on up there?' 'Oh,' he said, 'They're have mass meetings on this', and he says 'It is just an uproar all the time.' And I didn't know.
Now, he made an interview with me, and he wanted to play it on the campus radio, or the local radio, station, and I said 'All right.'

INTERVIEWER: What was the interview about?

QUIGLEY: About, this, this.

INTERVIEWER: This book?

QUIGLEY: Yeah, no, about the Skousens controversy. And I said 'All right. Let me know what happens' But he never wrote to me. I never found out. I never made any effort. So I don't know if it was ever broadcast or not.

INTERVIEWER: Hmmm. What was, what, why, what was your input in that. What did you have to say about the Skousens controversy?

QUIGLEY: Well, I simply told him Skousens wrote this book. He never... talked to me about it.

INTERVIEWER: Never talked with you.

QUIGLEY: He violated my copyright. It's full of lies. There are things that are untrue.
It takes things out of context and misinterprets them. And I gave him the specific things where I disagreed. The group that I'm writing about was originally, in my mind, the group established secretly by Lord Milner in 1908, 1909, called The Round Table Group, which still publishes a quarterly magazine called the 'The Round Table' in London, which is one of the world's best sources of international relations information since 1910. The first editor of it was Lord Lothian, at that time Philip Kerr. K-E-R-R. And... nobody knew this, really, for years. I got to know things. And I investigated that group. You see?

INTERVIEWER: ... Huh.

QUIGLEY: Now, how I found it is very interesting, I noticed that prominent people in English life had 'Fellow of All Souls College'... Lord Halifax, who was the... Secretary of State for Foreign Affairs and then they made him the Ambassador to America. When they take the Secretary of State for Foreign Affairs and makes him Ambassador to Washington, which most people would consider a downward step, it shows how important they considered Washington's support would be in World War II. You see? All right. He's a Fellow of All Souls. The fellow who summoned Neville... Chamberlain, on the 10th of May 1940, and said 'For God's sake, go.' was... Leo Amery. All right. He was a sidekick, the chief lieutenant, political lieutenant of Lord Milner. See? And he was a Fellow of All Souls. And so, I decided I would study All Souls as a purely historical effort. I got the names of all people who had been Fellows of All Souls from

1899 to whenever I was doing it, which would be about 1947. And there were one hundred forty-nine of them. I discovered that most of them were Fellows for only seven years, which was the regular appointment, which is for seven years. But some of them were for fifty-five years Fellows of All Souls. A man named Dougal Malcolm, who was the head of the British South Africa Company, which is what Rhodesia. You see. And he was fifty-five years. I discovered that Lord Brand, who had been with Milner in South Africa, was for years. And he was the head of Lazar Brothers bankers, in London. And, I discovered that Leo Amery was, for years. And so forth. And above all, I discovered a man named Lionel Curtis, who had no right whatever to be a Fellow of All Souls. You get to be a Fellow of All Souls either because you are a very prominent person and, as an honorary thing, you will become a honorary fellow for seven years. Or because you were an outstanding scholar and you get it by competitive examination when you graduate. That's how Lord Halifax got it. His name was... Charles [actually, Edward] Wood. In 1903, when he graduated from... Oxford, he took a competitive examination and got it. But he's kept it. Now I discovered he kept it because he went immediately to South Africa and met the Kindergarten, which was the group of people that were running South Africa for Lord Milner, you see. They were called 'Kindergarten' because they were all young kids.

INTERVIEWER: ... Huh.

QUIGLEY: You see. Now these are the ones who remained forever after 'Fellows of All Souls.' Or in Lional Curtis's case. He's the man who said 'We've got to change the name from 'British Empire' to 'Commonwealth of Nations.' And the reason is they had been students of Alfred Zimmern, who wrote a book in 1909 called 'The Greek Commonwealth' describing ancient Greece. You see? And who was the man who made Arnold Toynbee a great classical scholar, do you see? And brought him into international affairs. Now, I knew none of this.

INTERVIEWER: ... Huh.

QUIGLEY: All I knew is, that here were, here was a fellow, Lionel Curtis, who was such a poor student it took him fifteen years to get his degree. And then he got it [with] about the lowest pass degree or something that you could ever get.

INTERVIEWER: Uhm huh. Here he was.

QUIGLEY: And he.. And nobody knew it; nobody ever heard of him.

INTERVIEWER: Right. But he was...

QUIGLEY: Furthermore.

INTERVIEWER: ...in very good company.

QUIGLEY: Furthermore, he was Lord Halifax's roommate at All Souls for years. And then I discovered this fellow is behind everything that's going on. Lionel Curtis, do you see? Now, I don't think we should talk too much about this.

INTERVIEWER: Well, No, I, you see...

QUIGLEY: All right. All right. But, having discovered that, I met Alfred Zimmern, when he came here to give a speech. And I said 'Isn't this funny that, that All Souls...' He said 'That's the Round Table Group.' I had never heard of them. That shows how little I knew. And they'd been around since 1909 and publishing this magazine from 1910. And this was 1947. And I said 'What is the Round Table Group?' He named them, who they were. And he said 'I was a member of them, for ten years. From 1913. And they added, they brought me in, invited me because I was in their Workers' Educational Alliance.'
This is extension programs. Night courses, summer courses for workers. Workers' Educational Alliance. And he said... 'That's why they brought me in to it. I was for ten years.' And he said 'I resigned in 1923 because they were determined to build up Germany against France.' He said 'I wouldn't stand for it. So I resigned.' Now, when I met Lord Brand later and asked him about this, he [said] he had never seen the letter of resignation.
Now, so I'd better start talking, because you see, this gets into all kinds of things.

INTERVIEWER: O.K.

QUIGLEY: Now, this is. I knew the Round Table group was very influential. I knew that they were the real founders of the Royal Institutes of International Affairs. And I knew that, all the stuff that is in print, that they were they real founders of the Institutes of Pacific Relations. I knew that they were the godfathers of the... Council on Foreign Relations here.

INTERVIEWER: Uh hmm.

QUIGLEY: I knew that, for example, you know the big 'Study of History,' many volumes of... Arnold Toynbee?

INTERVIEWER: ... Huh.

QUIGLEY: All right. I knew the manuscripts of that were stored in Council on Foreign Relations during the War so they wouldn't be destroyed by German bombing, do you see?

INTERVIEWER: ... Huh.

QUIGLEY: And so forth, and so forth.
So I began to put these things together and discovered that this group was working for the following things. They were a secret group. They were working to federate the English-speaking world. They were closely linked to international bankers... they were working to establish a world, what I call a three-power world. And that three-power world was: The Atlantic Bloc (of England and the Commonwealth and the United States), Germany (Hitler's Germany), Soviet Russia. The three power world. They said Germany, we can control because [it's] boxed in (and all of this is in my book), it's boxed in between the Atlantic Bloc and the Russians. The Russians will behave because they're boxed in between the Atlantic Bloc (the American Navy and Singapore, and so forth) and... the Germans. Do you see?

INTERVIEWER: Right.

QUIGLEY: And, therefore... Now, this all described in my book, and this was their idea.
Now notice, it's a balance of power system.

INTERVIEWER: ... Huh.

QUIGLEY: It's essentially what Kissinger, but he doesn't know what he's doing. He's bungling everything.

INTERVIEWER: Hmm.

QUIGLEY: Because he's just a prima donna, you know... emotionally unbalanced... person. He doesn't know what the hell he's doing. But it was a

good idea. And what he should have been doing is described by me, and you really should read this, in 'Current History' for October 1968. Now, if I had a copy, I'd give it to you.
But I don't have it. It is how to construct a multi-bloc world, in which the United States would be secure as the other candidi [sic] and would be independent and have freedom of action. Do you see?

INTERVIEWER: ... Hmm.

QUIGLEY: But he is blowing it. In one way or another. And the whole thing is going to explode in his face, I'm afraid. And I hope to God it doesn't. Because we cannot afford, you know, another mess like this. These incompetents. Now... what is said is here, is: these people are for world domination.

INTERVIEWER: And that you...

QUIGLEY: And the group I am talking about were not.

INTERVIEWER: ... Huh.

QUIGLEY: They were largely, partly financed, for instance, by the... by Rhodes, the Rhodes Trust, and the how ..."
They were largely, partly financed, for instance, by the... by Rhodes, the Rhodes Trust, and the, how Milner got into this was that he was the chief Rhodes trustee.

INTERVIEWER: ... Huh.

QUIGLEY: From 1905, when he came back from Africa, until his death in 1925.

INTERVIEWER: All right.

QUIGLEY: So, this was a... it's an Atlantic Bloc. This, you know Streit, Clarence Streit—S-T-R-E-I- T—'Union Now.' Union now with Great Britain. All right.
He represents what this group wanted. Clarence S-T-R-E-I- T. If he's still alive, he probably lives in Washington. I had his daughter in my class. And, oh, as a visitor, but not as a student of mine. And, he was built up by this people as the only solution. This was in my book; His name and when it happened, and...

INTERVIEWER: By the Round Table people?

QUIGLEY: By the Round Table people. And, it, with, his book 'Union Now,' which came out in 1938, was called, anonymously, in The Round Table magazine by Lionel Curtis 'The Only Way.' It was headed.
It was then reviewed, anonymously, in The Christian Science Monitor by Lord Lothian as 'the solution of our problems.' And what it is essentially a union of the Atlantic Bloc.
Printed pages.

INTERVIEWER: Not about world domination.

QUIGLEY: Not world domination. Of course, this was Rhodes' idea. He wanted the United States in the English... Commonwealth. All right. Secondly, these people are not pro-Communist, as I know them, and certainly the Round Table Group, and the Milner Group, and the people that I'm writing about, and, I notice I follow them up only through 1940, which is the end of the Morgan bank, when they... had to incorporate, because of the inheritance tax, and so forth. They had to incorporate... they were before that... a partnership.

INTERVIEWER: When was the Council on Foreign Relations formed?

QUIGLEY: It was originally established by a group here, about 1919. But they had, in the group that we went, is 'The Inquiry.' 'The Inquiry' was the post-war planning group set up by the Morgan interests in 1917 in the United States, of which the... technical head was... the head of the American Geographical Society.
All of this...

INTERVIEWER: Governor?

QUIGLEY: ...is in my book. No, no.

INTERVIEWER: Oh, yes.

QUIGLEY: National Geographic.

INTERVIEWER: I've got this on my mind.

QUIGLEY: ... Uh.. And, uh. Delahue, was it? No.

INTERVIEWER: Heads up.

QUIGLEY: Well, it doesn't... It's in my book. You see the names are slipping me now.
Anyway, it's called 'The Inquiry'. There's a whole book on it. And it's called 'The Inquiry.' So you can find it by looking up that title. But you can find [it] also if you can look in my book. The unfortunate part is that it's not in the paperback. 'Cause, naturally, it's in the first part, when they were formed. You see? Which is... in the big... version of it. Uh. 'The Inquiry,'... got together in Paris, and agreed to establish an organization, out of which came the Royal Institute of International Affair[s] and that Royal Institute of International Affairs had branches in all the Commonwealth countries: Australia, New Zealand, South Africa, Canada, eventually in India, and they even... I think, had one somewhere else... Pakistan, when it divided, they established one. But in the United States, of course, they didn't have to, 'cause they had the Council on Foreign Relations. But when they came over here... after coming back from Paris, they found that a movement had begun here already to form a Council on Foreign Relations, and so they moved in and took it over. And they could do that because they represented Morgan.

INTERVIEWER: ... Huh.

QUIGLEY: And in that crowd was... Willard Straight, who was a Morgan partner. And he died at the Peace Conference of the influenza. And, of course... the man who was the active... supposed to be, Lamont, Tom Lamont. He was infamous among the extreme right for supposedly being a Communist sympathizer, because his son Corliss was the chief financial sponsor of all kinds of Soviet friendship things, and so forth, and summoned before a Congressional committee, but flatly refused to answer any questions, and took his case to the Supreme Court. And I may be wrong, but I think he won his case. So the right said that these guys are Communist sympathizers, and are for world domination, anti-capitalists. They want to destroy America. And a number of other things. 'Carroll Quigley proved everything', they said. And they constantly misquote me to this effect: that this group financed the Bolsheviks. I can see no evidence that there was any financing of the Bolsheviks by the group I'm talking about. You see, to give you one example of what it in this book. But they'll all say this. People wrote to me. They said 'Do you know about this?' They were mostly students. Once I got a letter from my brother in New Hampshire. He jokingly wrote saying 'I used to be known as Dr. Quigley, chairman of the school committee in my town of Hudson, N.H., but now I'm known as Carroll Quigley's brother.'

I was mad as hell. These people are not only misrepresenting me, but I think they're making me out to be an idiot. 'They're saying' I said 'all kinds of things I didn't say'. It varies. Originally, the John Birch periodical had me as a great guy for revealing this. But then they became absolutely sour, and they're now denouncing me. That I'm a member of The Establishment, and I...

INTERVIEWER: Because you're repudiating it?

QUIGLEY: I don't know.

INTERVIEWER: You don't know why.

QUIGLEY: I don't know. Really. I'm baffled. I'm baffled by the whole thing. I don't know why Macmillan acted the way it did. I don't know why... I can think these guys are just trying to make a living. I think they'd write anything that they got paid for writing. Which is my feeling about it. So... now, I was... angry about this.

Then somebody called, wrote to me from the University of Nevada, I believe it was, in Reno. I think. And he was very angry over what was going on there, over this.

INTERVIEWER: Now this was in... '71?

QUIGLEY: No, this would be '73.

INTERVIEWER: '73. That it came to your attention.

QUIGLEY: Oh, wait a [second]. No, this came in the election of '72.

INTERVIEWER: '72.

QUIGLEY: The spring of '72.

INTERVIEWER: O.K. Fine. So right after it came out.

QUIGLEY: Yeah, I think.

INTERVIEWER: O.K. Then in '73 somebody called you?

QUIGLEY: Then in '73 somebody called me... Now, I can give you the exact dates of this, if I can get to the papers. But I don't have them. Anyway. And he wanted me to do something to stop the influence that this book ['None Dare Call It Conspiracy'] was having in Nevada, particularly as promoting anti-semitism. Because there's a group of people who were using this book—and they're total nuts. I get letters from them all the time. I can show you some of them, if you want—complete nuts, who claim that this is a Jewish conspiracy, that is part of the same thing as 'The Protocols of the Elders of Zion', which we now know was a Tsarist Russian police forgery of 1905. And that this is the same thing as the Illuminati. And the Illuminati were founded in 1776 by a Bavarian named, I think it's, White, Weiskopf.
Or something like that. And the Illuminati are a branch of the Masons and that they took over the Masons, you see. And... the whole thing is a nightmare.

INTERVIEWER: Right.

QUIGLEY: That all secret societies are the same secret society. Now, this was established by nuts. For hundreds of years... there were people who said the Society of the Cincinnati, in the American Revolution, of which George Washington was one of the shining lights, was a branch of the Illuminati. And was a secret society.
And, therefore, that's why the Masons built the monument in Alexandria to Washington. Not because he was the first President of the United States. [but] because he was the Mason and was the head the Illuminati in this country and therefore was the, one of the founders of the Society of the Cincinnati. Do you see what I mean?

INTERVIEWER: ... Huh.

QUIGLEY: And it becomes... You can't believe it.
Now, these same conspirators are the Jacobins who made the French Revolution. A woman named Nesta—N-E-S-T-A—Webster wrote that book.
To refute it, my tutor, who's a Rhodes Scholar, Crane Brinton—B-R-I-N-T-O-N, wrote his doctoral dissertation called 'The Jacobins,' in which he refutes her. You see? Now, I think that, at the end of his life, Brinton probably came

to feel that he was wrong. That there was some secret society involved in the Jacobins. And a student of his named Elizabeth Eisenstein, who is a marvelous researcher (she is now a professor at American University) under Brinton wrote a doctoral dissertation on the founder of the Babeuf Conspiracy. The Babeuf Conspiracy was a conspiracy of the extreme left which burst out in France in 1894 or so, led by a man named Babeuf, who was executed for it. But the man behind it was a descendant of Michelangelo, named Buonarrati. Because Buonarrati's... Michelangelo's family name was Buonarrati. Look, if you can, at Eisenstein['s] book, which is published by Harvard, her doctoral dissertation, which shows that Buonarrati founded many secret societies, do you see?

INTERVIEWER: ... Huh.

QUIGLEY: One of them was the Babeuf people, who are now being praised to the skies by all the neo-Marxists, like Marcusse and others, you see, as the great heroes because they tried to change the... because they tried to change the French Revolution from a middle class, bourgeois, capitalist revolution—constitutional revolution—into a communist revolution. Now Buonarroti is also the founder of the Carbonari, of which Mazzini was the head in the 1840s, which united Italy in the 1860s. Do you see? So, as, if you start with Buonarroti, which as far as I can see is 1893 and 189-, eh, 1793, 1794, I think you can trace a connection down through these various secret societies which culminate in the... Mazzini Carbonari. For example, eh, I'll tell you one thing.

INTERVIEWER: O.K.

QUIGLEY: Italy was able to get free from Austria because, only because France defeated Austria. Why did France do that? Nobody can see why. It wasn't in France's interest. And yet France declared war in 1859 on Austria and at the battle[s] of Magenta and Solferino defeated, and suddenly made a peace treaty with [Austria], without freeing all of Italy. And the reason, we are told, that they suddenly made the peace treaty without... is because the king... the emperor, this is Napoleon III, was so sickened by the sight of the blood. Do you see? Now, why did he do this? He did this because in 1868 [actually, 1858] a Carbonaro threw a bomb at him. This Carbonaro was arrested, executed. But before he was executed, the Emperor went to his cell, as I understand it, and the Carbonaro gave him the secret sign of a fellow Carbonaro, because... the emperor of France in the... who became, was elected president of France in 1848, seized the throne in '51 [actually, he seized power in '51, the throne in '52] and proclaimed a new

Napoleonic Empire, and was overthrown by the Germans in '71, so he was the emperor for ... [in] '70, really... for twenty years. Do you see?

INTERVIEWER: ... Huh.

QUIGLEY: But he had been a refugee from France, because he tried to make a revolt in France, I think it was [in] 1829 [actually, 1836].

INTERVIEWER: ... Huh.

QUIGLEY: And as a refugee, he joined the Carbonari secret society [actually, he had joined many years earlier].

INTERVIEWER: ... Huh.

QUIGLEY: Furthermore, he was a... he was a private policeman in the Chartist march on Parliament in London in 1848, the year he in which he was elected president of France. He's a mysterious figure. Do you see?

INTERVIEWER: ... Huh.

QUIGLEY: So, what I'm summing up is this: I do think there was probably a continuous sequence of secret societies from Buonarroti—[the] 'Baboo, Babeuf conspiracy', which is 1894, or '95 [actually, 1794, or '95]—through the Carbonari unification of Italy, which would be '61, 1861. I cannot see anything since then. It may exist.
I haven't really studied it.

INTERVIEWER: ... Huh.

QUIGLEY: But I cannot see any connection between the Masons and the Illuminati.

INTERVIEWER: ... Huh.

QUIGLEY: Founded in Bavaria in 1776 And I can't see any connection between them and Ba—, and... Buonarroti.

INTERVIEWER: Well, now.

QUIGLEY: Well, now that's what these people are saying is all one.

INTERVIEWER: All right.

QUIGLEY: And some of them say it goes back to Noah building the ark. [chuckles].

INTERVIEWER: Well. One thing that seems to me that... the conspiracy theory of history is appealing because [it's] mono-simple.

QUIGLEY: It's so simple.

INTERVIEWER: It explains everything that's unexplainable. And...

QUIGLEY: That's going wrong.

INTERVIEWER: If you raise one point that doesn't fit, they say 'Ah, see how clever the conspiracy is.'

QUIGLEY: Yes. Now.

INTERVIEWER: They... they.

QUIGLEY: Yes. I want to show you something. This is what they start [with]. They start by showing you a one dollar bill.

INTERVIEWER: ... Huh.

QUIGLEY: And they say 'Why is there a trian—, pyramid, with an eye over it?' Do you see?
This is the symbol of the secret society. Now, if you ask people...

INTERVIEWER: Which secret society? Any secret society?

QUIGLEY: The secret society, because according to them there's only one. You see?

QUIGLEY: According to them.

INTERVIEWER: The secret society that's gone through generations. Through...

QUIGLEY: Yes, yes. Now, if you ask the United States Government why it is there.
They have great difficulty explaining. And they mostly come up with 'It's, eh, it's the Masons, the Masonic symbol.' But then when you say 'Why should the Mason symbol be on the American dollar bill?'.
And they have no explanation. So there is something. If you look at this monument in Alexandria to Washington. It is the pyramid.

INTERVIEWER: ... Huh.

QUIGLEY: You see... you know. Now the eye over it is the light. You see. So... I could go further into this, but won't have to, because this symbol is at least... six thousand years old. And I can give you the history of it [from] four thousand B.C. And it has nothing to do with the Masons.

INTERVIEWER: ... Huh.

QUIGLEY: Now, maybe the Masons adopted it, you see. But it has nothing... But I will not go into that. That's a totally different story.

INTERVIEWER: O.K. So this man from Nevada, this person from Nevada called.

QUIGLEY: Called me up.
And said they were having a hard time with the anti-semites using this book ['None Dare Call It Conspiracy'] as an argument against Wall Street, against bankers, against Jews, against the Communists, and everything else.
And they wanted me to debate, with this fellow who'd gotten in touch with me, who was a professor at the university.

INTERVIEWER: Who believes this?

QUIGLEY: "Eh. Oh, no, he doesn't believe it. He was trying to get rid of it. The same way the fellow who called me from Brigham Young was trying to stop this hysteria which was sweeping that mountain area, apparently.

INTERVIEWER: Right.

QUIGLEY: And so they said 'Would you debate... Gary Allen and Larry Abraham?'
And... I said 'Well, I'd rather not, frankly'. 'But we need you help.'
And I said 'Well, are they both going to be debating me?' They said 'No, there a Dr. So-and-So here, who will... debate with you.' And he is, I think, a medical doctor. I'm not certain of that. But he was Jewish.
And, what he was interested in was the anti-semitism part in this.

INTERVIEWER: He was going to debate on your team, on your side?

QUIGLEY: By my side. And they said 'It's going to be absolutely the strictest thing.'
We'd be on the air for an hour. We'd be hooked up on telephone... through the country. 'I will be the coordinator,' said this fellow, of this. 'And it will be rigorous. You will... must stay on the subject, or I will stop you. There must be no personality attacks, or I will stop you. You can each talk for ten minutes [I think it is, or five minutes it could have been]'.
And 'then, when each of the four has talked (I think it was for ten minutes), then each will have the right to have a five minute rebuttal', or something, you see.

INTERVIEWER: ... Huh.

QUIGLEY: Now, in the course of it, I soon discovered that Gary Allen didn't know up from down. But Larry A...

INTERVIEWER: Who...

QUIGLEY: No. But Larry Abraham was immensely well informed.
He knew all about corporations, finance and bankers, and who were their partners. He know. He's tremendous... I...

INTERVIEWER: How did you find out? From talking with people?

QUIGLEY: I found out from the debate.

INTERVIEWER: Oh, O.K. That's what I was going to ask. You did go to the debate?

QUIGLEY: Yeah. Gary Allen just repeated everything that's in here ['Tragedy and Hope']. When I put in my rebuttal, and said these various things, he [Abraham] then started pulling in this information, I mean, some of it I've never heard of.

Now, I don't know everything. And the new book that's out now, published by the Buckley, I guess it it's the Bill Buckley, press, Arlington House. (I suppose it is Bill Buckley, I'm not sure of that) called 'The Bolsheviks and Wall Street.' Oh, we got to go to lunch. 'The Bolsheviks and Wall Street' has lots of things in there that I don't, didn't know.

INTERVIEWER: ... Huh.

QUIGLEY: Stop this. Now, I... I talked, told you that. Do you want to put [that] down there?
INTERVIEWER: "Yeah.

QUIGLEY: All right. I generally would think that any conspiracy theory of history is nonsense.
For the simple reason that most of the conspiracies that we know about seem to me to be the conspiracies of losers. Of people who have been defeated on the platform; let's say, the historical platform of the public happenings.
The Ku Klux Klan was the, uh... Their arguments and their... point of view had been destroyed, and defeated, in the Civil War. Well, because they're not prepared to accept that, they form a conspiracy, you see, to fight against it in an underground way. And, those people who could fight, up in the open, do so. Those who can't, go underground. It seems to me this is essentially what conspiracy [is]. The Palestinian Liberation Army is a similar thing, you see. Now I think on the whole they're pretty well a group who... has not got really very much. And so, they have to be terrorists. And...

INTERVIEWER: If I could play the Devil's Advocate, I think, you, [with] talking about the 'international banking conspiracy', they have not lost out, they simply don't want any attention. They don't want to...

QUIGLEY: Oh... I... That's...

PROFESSOR QUIGLEY'S QUOTES

QUOTES FROM QUIGLEY'S WORK

THE EVOLUTION OF CIVILIZATIONS (1961) (SECOND EDITION 1979)

• This book is not a history. Rather it is an attempt to establish analytical tools that will assist the understanding of history

— Preface to the First Edition, p. 23

• I came into history from a primary concern with mathematics and science. This has been a tremendous help to me as a person and as a historian, although it must be admitted it has served to make my historical interpretations less conventional than may be acceptable of many of my colleagues in the field.

— Preface to the First Edition, p. 27

• After years of work in both areas of study, I concluded that the social sciences were different, in many important ways, from the natural sciences, but that the same scientific methods were applicable in both areas, and, indeed, that no very useful work could be done in either area except by scientific methods.

— Chapter 1, Scientific Method and the Social Sciences, p. 33

• No scientist ever believes that he has the final answer or the ultimate truth on anything.

— Chapter 1, Scientific Method and the Social Sciences, p. 34

• It is not easy to tear any event out of the context of the universe in which it occurred without detaching from it some factor that influenced it.

— Chapter 1, Scientific Method and the Social Sciences, p. 35

• Even today few scientists and perhaps even fewer nonscientists realize that science is a method and nothing else.

— Chapter 1, Scientific Method and the Social Sciences, p. 40

• Closely related to the erroneous idea that science is a body of knowledge is the equally erroneous idea that scientific theories are true.

— Chapter 1, Scientific Method and the Social Sciences, p. 40

• The range of human potentialities is also the range of human needs because of man's vital drive that impels him to seek to realize his potentialities, this drive is even more mysterious than the potentialities it seeks to realize.

—Chapter 2, Man and Culture, p. 55

• Each individual in a society is a nexus where innumerable relationships of this character intersect.

—Chapter 2, Man and Culture, p. 59

• A fully integrated culture would be like the dinosaurs, which had to perish because they were no longer able to adapt themselves to changes in the external environment.

—Chapter 2, Man and Culture, p. 63

• The social sciences are usually concerned with groups of persons rather than individual persons. The behavior of individuals, being free, is unpredictable.

—Chapter 3, Groups, Societies, and Civilizations, p. 67

• A society is a group whose members have more relationships with one another then they do with outsiders.

—Chapter 3, Groups, Societies, and Civilizations, p. 71

• A civilization is complicated, in the first place, because it is dynamic; that is, it is constantly changing in the passage of time, until it has perished.

—Chapter 4, Historical Analysis, p. 85

• When we approach history, we are dealing with a conglomeration of irrational continua. Those who deal with history by nonrational processes are the ones who make history, the actors in it.

—Chapter 4, Historical Analysis, p. 99

• The backwardness of our religious and social developments is undoubtedly holding back the development of the intellectual and political levels.

—Chapter 4, Historical Analysis, p. 122

• Our political organization, based as it is on an eighteenth-century separation of powers and on a nineteenth-century nationalist state, is generally recognized to be semiobselete.

—Chapter 4, Historical Analysis, p. 123

- It is clear that every civilization undergoes a process of historical change. We can see that a civilization comes into existence, passes through a long experience, and eventually goes out of existence.
  — Chapter 5, Historical Change in Civilizations, p. 127

- Every civilization must be organized in such a way that it has invention, capital accumulation, and investment.
  — Chapter 5, Historical Change in Civilizations, p. 137

- These seven stages we shall name as follows:
  1. Mixture
  2. Gestation
  3. Expansion
  4. Age of Conflict
  5. Universal Empire
  6. Decay
  7. Invasion
  — Chapter 5, Historical Change in Civilizations, p. 146

- The vested interests encourage the growth of imperialist wars and irrationality because both serve to divert the discontent of the masses away from their vested interests (the uninvested surplus).
  — Chapter 5, Historical Change in Civilizations, p. 152

- It is also in theory, conceivable that some universal empire some day might cover the whole globe, leaving no external "barbarians" to serve as invaders.
  — Chapter 5, Historical Change in Civilizations, p. 163

- This priesthood became a closed group, able to control enormous wealth and incomes, and concerned very largely with the study of the solar and astronomical periodicities on which there influence was originally based. With the surplus thus created, the priesthood was able to command human labor in huge amounts and to direct this labor from the simple tillage of the peasant peoples to the diversified and specialized activities that constitute civilized living.
  — Chapter 7, Mesopotamian Civilization, p. 213

- Capitalism might be defined, if we wish to be scientific, as a form of economic organization motivated by the pursuit of profit within a price structure.
  — Chapter 8, Canaanite and Minooan Civilizations, p. 240

- When profits are pursued by geographic interchange of goods, so that commerce for profit becomes the central mechanism of the system, we usually call it "commercial capitalism." In such a system goods are conveyed from ares where they are more common (and therefore cheaper) to areas where they are less common (and therefore less cheap). This process leads to regional specialization and to division of labor, both in agricultural production and in handicrafts.
  — Chapter 8, Canaanite and Minooan Civilizations, p. 241

- The process by which civilization, as an abstract entity distinct from the societies in which it is embodied, dies or is reborn is a very significant one.
  — Chapter 8, Canaanite and Minooan Civilizations, p. 266

- The instrument of expansion of Classical civilization was a social organization, slavery.
  — Chapter 9, Classical Civilization, p. 270

- No slave system has ever been able to continue to function on the slaves provided by its own biological reproduction because the rate of human reproduction is too slow and the expense from infant mortality and years of unproductive upkeep of the young make this prohibitively expensive. This relationship is one of the basic causes of the American Civil War, and was even more significant in destroying ancient Rome.
  — Chapter 9, Classical Civilization, p. 318

- Western civilization presents one of the most difficult tasks for historical analysis, because it is not yet finished, because we are a part of it and lack perspective, and because it presents considerable variation from our pattern of historical change.
  — Chapter 10, Western Civilization, p. 333-334

- No culture has ever exceeded Western civilization in power and extent. Our society now covers more than half of the globe, extending in space from Poland to the east of Australia in the west. In the course of this expansion, most of it during the last five centuries, the power of Western civilization has been so great that it has destroyed, almost without thinking of it, hundreds of other societies, including five or six other civilizations.
  — Chapter 10, Western Civilization, p. 334

- Western ideology believed that the world was good because it was made by

God in six days and that at the end of each day He looked at His work and said that it was good.

— Chapter 10, Western Civilization, p. 337

• The fundamentalist position on biblical interpretation, with its emphasis on the explicit, complete, final, and authoritarian nature of Scripture, is a very late, minority view quite out of step with the Western tradition.

— Chapter 10, Western Civilization, p. 342

• When these extremists argued for "either-or," the Western tradition answered "both!"

— Chapter 10, Western Civilization, p. 345

• One of the chief reasons for the widespread fear of the Huns rested on their ability to travel very long distances in relatively short periods. This ability may well have been based on their use of horseshoes.

— Chapter 10, Western Civilization, p. 349

• In fact, violence as a symbol of our growing irrationality has had an increasing role in activity for its own sake, when no possible justification could be made that the activity was seeking to resolve a problem.

— Chapter 10, Western Civilization, p. 405

• To know is not too demanding: it merely requires memory and time. But to understand is quite a different matter: it requires intellectual ability and training, a self conscious awareness of what one is doing, experience in techniques of analysis and synthesis, and above all, perspective.

— Conclusion, p. 415

• For years I have told my students that I been trying to train executives rather than clerks. The distinction between the two is parallel to the distinction previously made between understanding and knowledge. It is a mighty low executive who cannot hire several people with command of more knowledge than he has himself.

— Conclusion, p. 420

TRAGEDY AND HOPE: A HISTORY OF THE WORLD IN OUR TIME (1966)

• The West believes that man and the universe are both complex and that the apparently discordant parts of each can be put into a reasonably workable arrangement with a little good will, patience, and experimentation.

—p. 1227

• The problem of meaning today is the problem of how the diverse and superficially self-contradictory experiences of men can be put into a consistent picture that will provide contemporary man with a convincing basis from which to live and to act.

—p. 1278

OSCAR IDEN LECTURE SERIES, LECTURE 3: "THE STATE OF INDIVIDUALS" (1976)

• ...a state is not the same thing as a society, although the Greeks and Romans thought it was. A state is an organization of power on a territorial basis.

• The link between a society, whether it be made up of communities or individuals, and a state is this: Power rests on the ability to satisfy human needs.

• ...the levels of culture, the aspects of society: military, political, economic, social, emotional, religious, and intellectual. Those are your basic human needs. ...they are arranged in evolutionary sequence.

• Men have social needs. They have a need for other people; they have a need to love and be loved.

• The basis of social relationships is reciprocity: if you cooperate with others, others will cooperate with you.

• Our society has so cluttered our lives with artifacts [man-made things]... and organizational structures that [our] moment to moment relationships with nature are almost impossible.

• ...human beings have religious needs. They have a need for a feeling of certitude in their minds about things they cannot control and they do not fully understand, and with humility, they admit they do not understand...

When you destroy people's religious expression, they will establish secularized religions like Marxism.

- ...empires and civilizations do not collapse because of deficiencies on the military or the political levels.

- Persons, personalities if you wish, can only be made in communities.

- A community is made up of intimate relationships among diversified types of individuals—a kinship group, a local group, a neighborhood, a village, a large family.

- Without communities, no infant will be sufficiently socialized... and that occurs in the first four or five years of life. ...The first two years are important ...of vital importance. He has to be loved, above all he has to be talked to.

- A state of individuals, such as we now have reached in Western Civilization, will not create persons, and the atomized individuals who make it up will be motivated by desires that do not necessarily reflect needs. Instead of needing other people they need a shot of heroin; instead of some kind of religious conviction, they have to be with the winning team.

- ...we no longer have intellectually satisfying arrangements in our educational system, in our arts, humanities or anything else; instead we have slogans and ideologies. An ideology is a religious or emotional expression; it is not an intellectual expression.

- ...when a society is reaching its end, in the last couple of centuries you have... a misplacement of satisfactions. You find your emotional satisfaction in making a lot of money... or in proving to the poor, half-naked people in Southeast Asia that you can kill them in large numbers.

- ...in the last thousand years. If we go back before [AD] 976... the main core of people's life and experience... was in the religious, emotional and social levels. They had religious beliefs, they had social and emotional relationships with people they saw every day. ...controls and rewards were internalized. ...This is why they could get along without a state in 976: all the significant controls were internalized.

- ...Western Civilization began to expand in 976. ...The economic expansion was achieved chiefly by specialization and exchange... commercialization.

- …today everything is commercialized—politics, religion, education, ideology, belief, the armed services. …Everything has its price.

- [Increasing] politicization means the [economic] expansion is slowing up and you are no longer attempting to achieve increased output per capita, or increased wealth, or increased satisfactions… but you are doing so by mobilizing power. We have seen this going on for almost a century… increased militarization.

- …increasing remoteness of desires from needs …increasing confusion between means and ends. The ends are human needs… Instead they want the means they have been brainwashed to accept… Never was any society in human history as rich and as powerful as Western Civilization and the United States, and it is not a happy society.

- …controls on behavior shift from the intermediate levels of human experience (social, emotional and religious) to the lower (military and political) or to the upper (ideological). They become the externalized controls of a mature society: weapons, bureaucracies, material rewards, or ideology.

- In its final stages the civilization becomes a dualism of almost totalitarian imperial power and an amorphous mass culture of atomized individuals.

- … 1776 is a very significant year, and this is not just because the American Revolution began. Watt's patent of the steam engine… Adam Smith's Wealth of Nations… the failure of the French to reorganize their political system occurred in 1776, and so forth. …The destruction of communities, the destruction of religion and the frustration of emotions were greatly intensified by the Industrial Revolution: railroads, factories, growth of cities, technological revolution in the countryside and in the growing of food and so forth.

- …the nineteenth century Age of Expansion… brought on an acceleration of the main focus of the activities of society… from the areas of internal controls to the areas of external controls. …the increasing role of propaganda… helped create an impression of stability.

- …I offended some of you by saying you had been brainwashed. This is not an insult; it's a simple statement of fact. When any infant is born and socialized in a society, even if he is to become a very mature individual, he has been brainwashed. …given a structure for categorizing his experience and a system of values applied to the structure of categories.

- ...in our society... this has now become a propagandist system in which emphasis is put on the future... the ideology against which the young people of the 1950's and 1960's rebelled. Future preference: plan; study hard; save.

- Another aspect of the nineteenth century propaganda system is the increasing emphasis upon material desires.

- ...we were brainwashed into believing... that the only important thing was individualism. They called it freedom. There is no such thing as freedom. There is something called liberty; it's quite different. ...read [Guido de] Ruggiero's History of European Liberalism... Freedom is freedom from restraints. We're always under restraints.

- The difference between a stable society and an unstable one is that the restraints in an unstable one are external. In a stable society government ultimately becomes unnecessary; the restraints on people's actions are internal, they're self-disciplined...

- ...they have brainwashed us into believing in the last 150 years... that quantitative change is superior to qualitative attributes. If we can turn out more... it doesn't matter if they're half as good. ...We're quantifying everything, and that is why we're trying to put everything on computers. Governments will no longer have to make decisions; computers will do it.

- ...they give us vicarious satisfactions for many of our frustrations. ...People need exercise; they do not need to watch other people exercise... Another vicarious satisfaction is sexy magazines; this is vicarious sex. To anyone rushing to buy one, I'd like to say, "The real thing is better."

- The brainwashing which has been going on for 150 years has also resulted in the replacement of intellectual activities and religion by ideologies and science. ...I have nothing against Marx, except that his theories do not explain what happened.

- The very idea that there is some kind of conflict between science and religion is completely mistaken. Science is a method for investigating experience... Religion is the fundamental, necessary internalization of our system of more permanent values.

• Another thing that they have tried to get us to believe in the last 150 years... is that the nation as the repository of sovereignty can be both a state and a community. ...Why did the English, the French, the Castilians, the Hohenzollerns, and others become the repository of sovereignty as nations... They did so because... weapons made it possible to compel obedience over areas which were approximately the size of these national groups... nationalism is an episode in history, and it fit a certain power structure and a certain configuration in human life in our civilization. Now... They all want autonomy. ...The nation or the state, as we now have it as the structure of power, cannot be a community.

• We have now done what the Romans did when they started to commit suicide. We have shifted from an army of citizens to an army of mercenaries...

• The appearance of stability from 1840 to about 1900 was superficial, temporary and destructive in the long run... because communities and societies must rest upon cooperation and not upon competition. Anyone who says that society can be run on the basis of everyone's trying to maximize his own greed is talking total nonsense. And to teach it in schools, and to go on television and call it the American way of life still doesn't make it true. Competition and envy cannot become the basis of any society or any community.

• The economic and technological achievements of industrialization in this period were fundamentally mistaken. ...based upon plundering the natural capital of the globe that was created over millions of years: the plundering of the soils and their fertility; the plundering of human communities whether they were our own or someone else's.

• The fundamental, all-pervasive cause of world instability is the destruction of communities by the commercialization of all human relationships and the resulting neuroses and psychoses. The technological acceleration of transportation, communication and weapons systems is now creating power areas wider than existing political structures.

• ...another cause of today's instability is that we now have a society in America, Europe and much of the world which is totally dominated by the two elements of sovereignty that are not included in the state structure: control of credit and banking, and the corporation. These are free of political controls and social responsibility and have largely monopolized power in Western Civilization and in American society. They are ruthlessly going forward to eliminate land, labor, entrepreneurial-managerial skills, and everything else the economists once told us were the chief elements of production. The only element of production they are concerned with is the one they can control: capital.

- The final result will be that the American people will ultimately prefer communities. They will cop out or opt out of the system. Today everything is a bureaucratic structure, and brainwashed people who are not personalities are trained to fit into this bureaucratic structure and say it is a great life — although I would assume that many on their death beds must feel otherwise. The process of copping out will take a long time, but notice: we are already copping out of military service on a wholesale basis; we are already copping out of voting on a large scale basis. …People are also copping out by refusing to pay any attention to newspapers or to what's going on in the world, and by increasing emphasis on the growth of localism, what is happening in their own neighborhoods.

- When Rome fell, the Christian answer was, "Create our own communities."

Source: Wikiquote

PHOTO GALLERY

BOSTON LATIN SCHOOL, 1929

HARVARD, 1933

WILLIAM CARROLL QUIGLEY
 Born on November 9, 1910 at Boston, Massachusetts. Prepared at Boston Latin School. Home address: 10 Weld Avenue, Jamaica Plain, Massachusetts. In college four years as undergraduate. Ramblers Football Squad, 1931; Charles Downer Scholarship, 1930-1931; Burr Scholarship. 1932-1933. Field of Concentration: History

1943

CARROL QUIGLEY, Ph.D.
Professor of History

SFS YEARBOOK, 1948

1950

1950

CARROLL QUIGLEY, PH.D.

1951

1951

CARROLL QUIGLEY, M.A., PH.D.

1956

1956

1961

Carroll Quigley

CARROLL QUIGLEY & WIFE LILLIAN, *HISTORY,* **1962**

1963

1963

1966

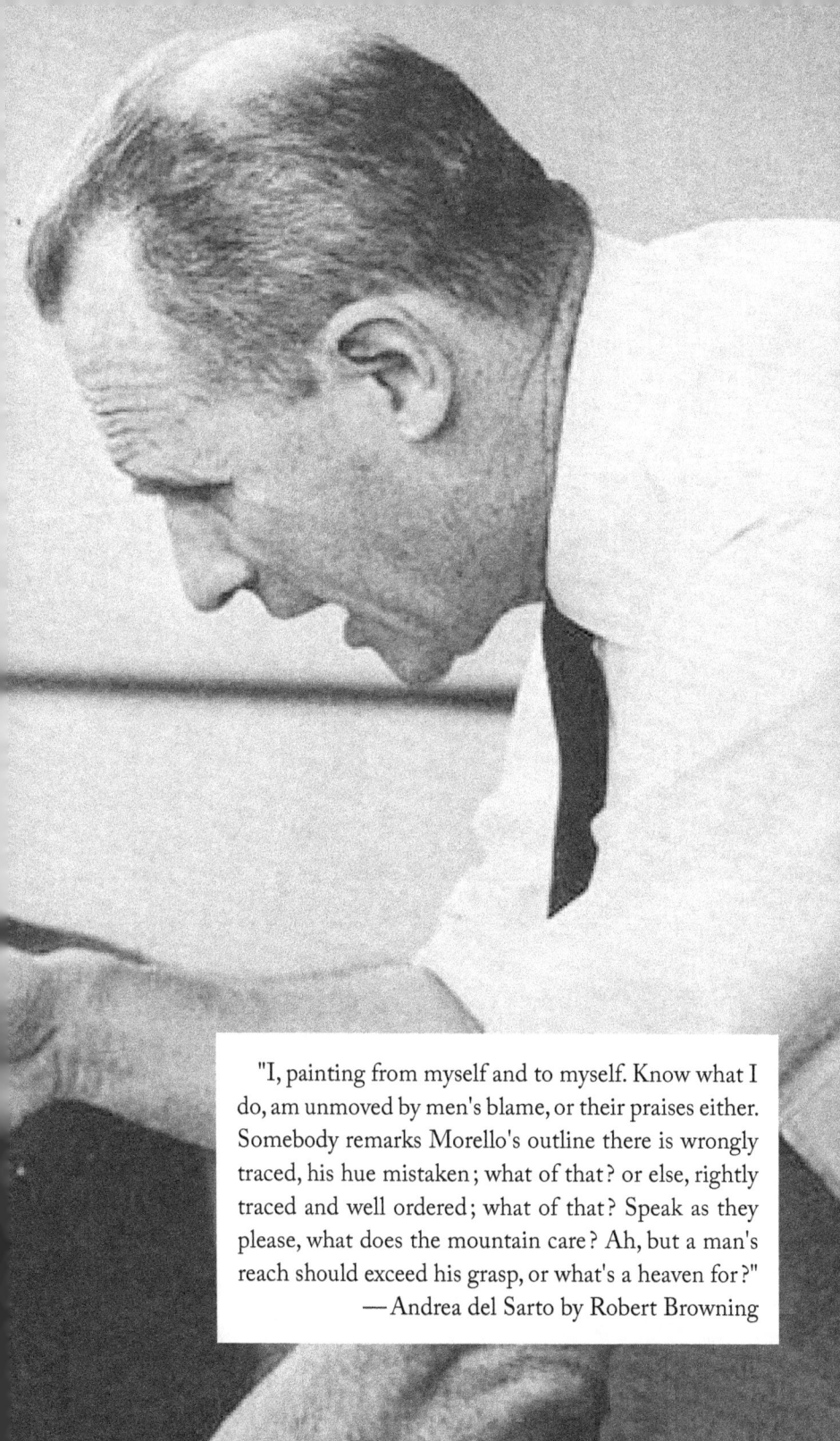

"I, painting from myself and to myself. Know what I do, am unmoved by men's blame, or their praises either. Somebody remarks Morello's outline there is wrongly traced, his hue mistaken; what of that? or else, rightly traced and well ordered; what of that? Speak as they please, what does the mountain care? Ah, but a man's reach should exceed his grasp, or what's a heaven for?"
—Andrea del Sarto by Robert Browning

"I've devoted my life to
Saving Western Civilization."
Hmmph.
"It's easy to make a million dollars."
Hmmmmph.
"There's not a man on God's green earth.
Ah-so...

1966

1967

Carroll Quigley

1969

CARROLL QUIGLEY
Professor of History
  "The two processes—that of predicting the future and that of reconstructing the past—are essentially similar: both are processes of inference and generalization."
  —F. W. Maitland, *Collected Papers*, IV, 285

1970

1970

Carroll Quigley, History
Dorothy M. Brown, History

1971

1973

1976

1976

A Service in Memory of

Professor Carroll Quigley

1910 - 1977

Monday, January 17, 1977

4:00 P.M.

Dahlgren Chapel

Georgetown University

Organ Prelude

Opening Remarks   Dr. Peter Krogh
                                              Dean
                                    School of Foreign Service

Carroll Quigley as Professor   Dr. Dorothy Brown
                                            Chairman
                                     Department of History

First Reading: Psalm 121   Rev. Frank Fadner, S.J.
                                             Regent
                              School of Languages and Linguistics

Meditation

Carroll Quigley as Teacher   Dr. Phil Sharp
                                   U.S. Congressman, SFS'64

Second Reading: "Andrea del   Dr. Michael Foley
  Sarto" by Robert Browning   Associate Professor
                                         of History

Carroll Quigley and Georgetown   Rev. Timothy Healy, S.J.
                                          President
                                     Georgetown University

Benediction   Rev. Joseph Zringi, S.J.
                                      Associate Professor
                                         of Economics

Hymn: "Ode to Joy" by Beethoven
        Worship II No. 151

www.ingramcontent.com/pod-product-compliance
Lightning Source LLC
Chambersburg PA
CBHW022100150426
43195CB00008B/205